LEMONGRASS
&LIME

LEMONGRASS & LIME

SOUTHEAST ASIAN COOKING AT HOME

LEAH COHEN

WITH STEPHANIE BANYAS

AVERY

an imprint of Penguin Random House

New York

AVERY | 🐧

an imprint of Penguin Random House LLC
penguinrandomhouse.com

Copyright © 2020 by Leah Cohen
Photographs by Dylan Kushel

Most Avery books are available at special quantity discounts for bulk
purchase for sales promotions, premiums, fund-raising, and educational
needs. Special books or book excerpts also can be created to fit specific
needs. For details, write SpecialMarkets@penguinrandomhouse.com.

Library of Congress Cataloging-in-Publication Data

Names: Cohen, Leah (Chef), author. | Banyas, Stephanie, author.
Title: Lemongrass and lime / by Leah Cohen with Stephanie Banyas.
Description: [New York] : Avery, an imprint of Penguin Random
    House LLC, [2020] | Includes index.
Identifiers: LCCN 2020001556 (print) | LCCN 2020001557 (ebook) |
    ISBN 9780525534839 (hardcover) | ISBN 9780525534846 (ebook)
Subjects: LCSH: Cooking, Southeast Asian.
Classification: LCC TX724.5.S68 C64 2020 (print) | LCC TX724.5.S68
    (ebook) | DDC 641.5959—dc23
LC record available at https://lccn.loc.gov/2020001556
LC ebook record available at https://lccn.loc.gov/2020001557
p.   cm.

Printed in Canada
10 9 8 7 6 5 4 3 2

Book design by Ashley Tucker

THIS BOOK IS DEDICATED TO MY FATHER,
WILLIAM COHEN. YOUR GENEROSITY AND
KINDNESS HAVE IMPACTED SO MANY
PEOPLE'S LIVES. I WOULD NOT BE THE
PERSON I AM TODAY WITHOUT YOUR
UNCONDITIONAL LOVE AND BELIEF IN ME.

INTRODUCTION

OT TOO WET AND NOT TOO DRY. This was my first lesson in food. If you ask my Filipino mother, it's in relation to rice. If you ask my Jewish father, it's in relation to kugel. Either way, it's all about food and balance.

If I have to make one confession, it's that I actually preferred the kugel. Growing up, I classified Filipino food as weird. I was into a few things—Lumpia (page 67) or Halo-Halo (page 250). Though I guess that makes sense because we're talking about fried spring rolls and an Asian ice cream sundae.

When I was four, we took our first trip to the Philippines. We visited the island my mom grew up on, took the cold showers she was used to, ate the Lumpia Shanghai and the Halo-Halo, avoided a lot of the meat-heavy dishes I didn't yet understand. We would spend time with my family and time on the beach and, as we continued to go back year after year, the food also became a larger part of my experience. Being in the country the food was from made all the difference. I could see it being made, see how much it meant to my mom's family to make it. By the time I was a teenager, the Philippines became my safe space. It's where I could escape my day-to-day in New York and reconnect with my roots.

The funny thing is, I never thought I'd end up in food as a kid. My parents were both dentists and traditionally book smart. I, on the other hand, struggled. I was in classes for students below the expected reading level, disheartened because I wasn't living up to my parents' high standards. I started college and focused on the beer and the pool as much as (realistically, more than) my classes, and I dropped out after only a semester.

Food was actually the place I fell into after that. I needed an escape from home, so I picked up a job as a pizza delivery girl. Not only did I like the extra cash, I enjoyed the job. I got a rush from beating all the boys I worked with—delivering the most pizzas and doing so in half the time it took them. I'd drop into the kitchen here and there, too, focusing mostly on the dough. On weekends or days off, I'd try it out, baking up a storm.

I gave college one more shot, but it quickly became obvious that cooking on the line was where I belonged. When I got into the Culinary

Institute of America (CIA), I proved that to my parents. For the first time, I was good at school—really good. Not only was I good, I was inspired, excited, driven. In culinary school, I excelled, realizing that growing up in a household full of food had conditioned me to care about it in a way I didn't yet understand.

In kitchens, I had to learn to hold my own quickly. My first externship was at Park Avenue Café. At that point, I'd only ever worked in school kitchens. I'd never really cooked on the line before, so when I was thrown in it one night, I just followed the directions yelled at me. I did so the entire dinner service and by the end of the night, I was the new hot apps cook. Working the line was a crazy rush, and I was immediately addicted to that feeling—both the cooking itself and the respect I commanded.

It wasn't immediate, though. One day, the sous-chef came over to taste my butter glaze for the ravioli. He straight up stuck his finger in the dish and tasted it. He then proceeded to toss the dish back at me and asked, "Did you taste this?" Clearly he knew that I hadn't because it was incredibly salty. I lied, knowing that I'd fucked up, and said that I did. He forced me to eat the entire plate of the horribly oversalted ravioli, and then had me prep it all over again. From that day on, I've tasted every dish I've put out and I ask the same of my staff.

The lessons continued in Italy, where I worked at a Michelin-starred restaurant, La Madia. There I learned as much about holding my composure as I did about cooking. That experience absolutely taught me about incredible regional cuisine and ingredients, but it also taught me how to handle myself with men who refused to see women as equals in the kitchen. I had to work my way up, weave my way into the fabric of the kitchen family, and learn to communicate through food rather than language.

When I made my way back to New York, I thought those skills alone would get me a job. Needless to say, I was wrong. I spent months and months hunting down roles, staging in kitchens, and interviewing with different restaurants. After getting to a point of sheer exhaustion, though, I found the right one—at Eleven Madison Park, no less. Until then, I'd worked in good restaurants, but not in great ones, none with tasting menus like EMP or multiple Michelin stars to boot. It was there that I learned nuance, sophistication, and balance. It was also there that I learned that fine dining wasn't for me. I wanted my food to have feelings, wanted the people tasting it to know it was coming from my heart.

So, I took a break. I did something to reconnect with myself, with my past. I went to the Philippines. It was the first time I'd been there alone, and it proved to me that traveling was what I needed next. At that time,

I didn't have the funds to go for an extended period of time, so a bigger trip someday went on the to-do list and I headed back to New York.

I spent six months at Centro Vinoteca, cooking the Italian food that I knew I loved but with a cast of characters that I didn't. When *Top Chef* approached me, it just made sense to go. That story, of course, you may have seen on television, so I won't go into it in detail.

I was in a weird headspace after the show ended, though. I didn't know what my cooking philosophy was, what my food tasted like. I'd always cooked for others, re-created their recipes. I'd grown up in a household of rice and kugel and this whole time, I'd been making pasta. I wasn't cooking the food I'd grown up on, the food that raised me. I wanted to figure out how to change that, so I looked back at that to-do list I'd written before *Top Chef* and took a younger me's advice. That advice was travel.

I'd made traveling a goal as I was leaving the Philippines, so it only made sense for me to go back to Southeast Asia. It had been a place for me growing up where I knew I could find inspiration. Instead of just the Philippines, though, I wanted to branch out.

Although Thailand was at the top of my list, my first stop in Asia was Hong Kong. I had seen an episode of *No Reservations* in which Anthony Bourdain visited a private kitchen in an apartment there. The chef running it was named Alvin Leung, aka the demon chef, and he let me stage there for a month and a half, during which the staff adopted me. They took me to all the best local spots, and we ate and partied hard—a great way to start off my year in Asia. It also helped to have a huge group of eating buddies. So much of Asian food is served family style—I could never have tried so many different dishes if it had been up to me to eat them on my own.

Luckily, I had connections all over. In Bangkok, I had a tentative connection to a certain (and sketchy) "Rob in Bangkok," who casually had an extra flat open to any chef friends who dropped in. Rob's friendship and use of his flat saved me. I lived there on and off for eight months, within walking distance of public transportation, some of my favorite street food stands, all of my favorite markets, and one of the restaurants I staged at here and there.

The flat helped me focus most of my time in Thailand staging in various restaurants, checking out all the local markets, and eating as much street food as I possibly could. I staged at Bo.Lan first, learning Thai cuisine from an Englishman, and then at nahm, a restaurant run by the first chef's old boss. These restaurants taught me the foundation of the Thai food I cook to this day.

I also spent a good amount of time touring the country, hitting up all the different regions in order to explore their unique food. Every time my visa was about to run out, I visited a neighboring country like Vietnam or Cambodia to learn about the food there and stage in restaurants for a few days or even a week at a time.

Singapore proved an entirely different experience. I was working full-time in a Michelin-starred restaurant, but after my shift, I'd go straight to the night markets. The controlled chaos of the kitchen translated into the excitement of the night market. It was an energy that I loved and understood.

I slowed down a bit when I went to Vietnam, booking an entire month to explore the country. The way French technique was incorporated was fascinating to me. I was able to understand so much of how dishes came together because of my background in European kitchens, and that was such a cool discovery. The French influence with the lighter flavors of Vietnam was something that caught my eye because it proved to me that you really could meld those things in Southeast Asian cuisine.

These travels formed my cuisine, taught me the controlled chaos of Asian cooking. They showed me balance and restraint but also the power of certain ingredients. I learned which dishes to add coconut milk to for richness, which ones to add fish sauce to for funk. I learned family recipes for Crispy Pata (page 235), a pork shank cooked in soy sauce and garnished with coriander and Crispy Garlic (see page 43) served with a secret family recipe—sweet and sour liver dipping sauce. I learned how nuanced these cuisines were, how unfamiliar these flavors were in the New York scene. I learned that it was time to introduce them and that I was going to be the one to do it.

In a weird way, this book is my résumé. It starts with the rice that my mom taught me how to cook when I was growing up, builds on that with classic technique from the CIA and my time in Michelin-starred restaurants, and finishes with the flavors I learned while traveling Southeast Asia. I'll teach you to blend these techniques and flavors into something entirely different, something exciting and inspiring, something you never expected to make at home. The ingredients and the names may seem foreign at first, but I'll walk you through where to find them, how to use them, and how, most important, to balance them. These recipes are ones that I've tested a hundred times each—or a hundred and one if that's what it took for my mother's approval.

1

SOUTHEAST ASIAN PANTRY

A well-planned and well-stocked pantry makes whipping up Southeast Asian meals a snap. While overseas, I spent loads of time in outdoor markets. I was exploring not just the ready-made foods but also the spices and herbs that made them possible. I was looking at the most common fish sauce and the way that cooks were chopping garlic. I was investigating where to use fresh herbs and where I could make substitutions.

When I came back to the States, I started looking for the ingredients I'd come to love, ingredients like coconut vinegar, maggi sauce, kaffir lime leaves, and fresh galangal. These were ingredients I couldn't imagine going without but also not ones I knew where to find. After working on these recipes for months, I narrowed down my core ingredients.

In the fridge, I'm never without lemongrass, lime, garlic, ginger, scallions, and shallots. While there are plenty more fresh ingredients I love, those are the basics. The pantry is where I stock up on hard-to-find ingredients. Luckily a lot of the ingredients in Southeast Asian cuisine don't need to be refrigerated. They're chock-full of salt and acid, and so they remain safe at room temperature. It's these ingredients—fish sauce, vinegars, soy sauce—that make Southeast Asian dishes taste the way they should. Fish sauce, for example, is the core of so many dishes. I have plenty of friends who actually call fish sauce the salt of the Southeast. It's made from salt and fermented fish, which may sound gross but adds the most amazing complexity to dishes. It's salty, of course, but also full of funk and umami.

CONDIMENTS/SAUCES

Banana ketchup: Also known as banana sauce, this condiment is used primarily in the Philippines. It's made from mashed bananas, sugar, vinegar, spices, and red food dye. Regular ketchup is an acceptable substitute.

Coconut milk (unsweetened): I use coconut milk in both savory and sweet applications. The two brands that I call for specifically in my recipes are Chaokoh and Chef's Choice. Chaokoh has a creamier, richer flavor that I prefer for desserts, and Chef's Choice is less thick and less sweet, which makes it perfect for curries.

Curry paste: Though it's ideal to make your own (page 83), Maesri is my favorite store-bought replacement for curry paste.

Fish sauce: Fish sauce is a condiment made from fermented fish and salt and a staple in Southeast Asian cuisine. It is one of the most important ingredients used for incorporating umami and salt into dishes. Each country has its own preferred brand of choice, but the two that I prefer are Squid Brand and Red Boat.

In this book, when a recipe calls for fish sauce, I am referring to Squid Brand, which is my go-to all-purpose fish sauce. Red Boat fish sauce, which I specify in certain recipes, is more of a finishing sauce (think of high-end olive oil). You can use Red Boat for all of the recipes in this book (just cut the amount by a quarter when you see a recipe that calls for Squid Brand).

The most important thing to look for on the label of any brand of fish sauce is that it is made with 100 percent anchovies. The recipes in this book have been tested with these two brands of fish sauce only, so please note that if you decide to go with your own brand, you may need to add more or less of yours to the recipe.

Hoisin sauce: Sometimes referred to as Chinese barbecue sauce, this sauce is made from fermented soy, vinegar, and garlic and is great in marinades and grilled Asian dishes.

Maggi sauce: This rich-brown soy sauce–like sauce is an important flavoring agent in Southeast Asian cuisine. The addition of fermented wheat gluten gives its own distinct flavor, which many refer to as an umami bomb. It can't be substituted for anything else, and a little goes a long way.

Nahm prik pao (roasted chili jam): This condiment is used in a lot of Thai cooking. It is made from chilies, garlic, shallots, palm sugar, tamarind paste, fish sauce, and oil. It works well in stir-fries, salad dressings, or just served as a dip. While you can find decent store-bought versions of this condiment, I highly recommend taking the time to make your own (page 51). It has a very long shelf life if stored properly in an airtight container in the refrigerator.

Fermented mustard greens: Fermented mustard greens are one of my favorite condiments of all time. It adds a nice, pungent, pickled flavor to any dish, as well as texture. It can be eaten on its own or used as a garnish or in stir-fries. I highly recommend you make your own (page 41) because the store-bought versions have a muddled flavor.

Shrimp paste: This is a fermented condiment that is primarily made up of crushed shrimp (or krill) and salt and then fermented for weeks. The smell is very pungent and even off-putting, but the flavor adds another layer of umami saltiness that is different from fish sauce or soy sauce. It is essential to dishes such as Shrimp Paste Fried Rice with Sweet Pork, Green Mango, Egg Strips, Long Beans, and Shallots (page 157) and Kare-Kare (page

239). Each country has its own version and therefore it really is necessary to use the paste that is indigenous to the country of origin for the dish you are making. This is why I call for specific brands in recipes that call for this ingredient. Thai and Malaysian versions are interchangeable, so if you want to choose just one, that is totally acceptable.

Thailand—Tra Chang
Malaysia—Belacan
Philippines—Barrio Fiesta Ginisang Bagoong—This paste is already fried in oil and not as thick and dense as Thai. It is completely different and really should only be used in Filipino cooking.

Soy sauce: In Southeast Asia and Asia, soy sauce is the most-used condiment or flavoring agent in dishes. Soy goes back centuries. It adds richness and umami that Asian cuisine is known for. Soy sauce adds salinity to cooking like salt does to the American way of cooking.

Sweet dark soy—Kecap Manis—Malaysian/ Indonesian/Singaporean: The sweet and salty deep flavor and the very thick texture remind me of molasses. Used in sauces or stir-fries, it is also used as a side condiment to dip things in. It's like a soy version of oyster sauce.

Light soy—Kikkoman Less Sodium Soy Sauce: Personally, I use light soy as my all-purpose soy. I like to use light soy when it is the base of a sauce such as adobo because I do not want it to be overpoweringly salty, but I still want the soy flavor. I like to be able to adjust the salt level, and using low-sodium soy sauce is a great way to do that. I also prefer using a Japanese-style soy sauce over a Chinese-style soy sauce as my go-to sauce. Japanese soy sauce

is brewed longer, contains less salt, and never has any coloring added to it.

Premium soy—Lee Kum Kee brand: This soy sauce has a more Chinese flavor to me, and I like using it for dishes that are more Chinese-influenced dishes in Southeast Asia such as Malaysian Butter Prawns (page 213) and Loshu Fun (page 165). I also use it when smaller quantities are called for (such as one tablespoon) for a stir-fry.

Sambal: Any chili sauce or paste from Indonesia or Malayasia. There are literally hundreds of variations of sambal and each consists of ground or pounded chilies and may also include other ingredients such as garlic, citrus juice, and other spices. Most commonly used in Indonesian and Malaysian cooking, this relish is a great way to preserve chilies and is used when fresh chilies are not available. There are two types of sambal: cooked and raw.

Sambal oelek: *Sambal* means sauce. *Oelek* means mortar and pestle. This type of sambal is a raw chili paste often used as a base for making other sambals and other sauces.

Sambal chili garlic: This type of sambal is a cooked version with the same base as sambal oeleck (chili, garlic, sugar, salt, and vinegar) and can occasionally include the addition of shrimp paste, fish sauce, and lime juice.

Sriracha—pronounced (seer-RAH-shah): Sriracha is a hot chili sauce named for the coastal port city of Si Racha in Thailand from which it hails. It is also known as rooster sauce because the California-made Huy Fong brand features a rooster on the bottle. The general recipe for sriracha includes ground chilies, vinegar, garlic, sugar, and salt and was first developed to serve with seafood, but Americans today use it like ketchup and drizzle it over just about everything.

Sriracha (Huy Fong brand): This brand, also known as Rooster because of the rooster on the front of the bottle, is made in the United States. While it is very popular and Americans seem to put it on everything, it is not as complex or balanced as those brands from Thailand and is mainly known for just being a hot sauce.

Sriracha (Shark brand): This brand is milder and made with no preservatives or artificial colors. It is still spicy but more balanced than Rooster brand.

Sweet chili sauce: Sweet chili sauce is a versatile sauce that is predominantly used as a dip for spring rolls or fried chicken. It is easy to make on your own and if you don't have time there are plenty of good store-bought versions. The one that I prefer is Mae Ploy.

DRY GOODS/SPICES

Annatto seeds: This spice is more of a coloring agent than a flavor enhancer. Annatto seeds come from the achiote tree, and the scent is a little sweet and slightly peppery. You can also find annatto in powdered form, which is a good substitute if you can't find the seeds. If you are using annatto seeds in a recipe for oil (Annatto Oil, page 43), use the seeds whole. If using for a spice in cooking, they need to be ground.

Candlenuts: Candlenuts are relatives of macadamia nuts, which are a good substitute. They are used as a thickener and texture enhancer in curry pastes and other dishes. They should not be eaten raw and can go

rancid very quickly, so it's best to store them in the freezer.

Cardamom: Cardamom can be found in either green or black pods. It has a strong, pungent flavor with hints of lemon mint and smoke. Cardamom is usually used whole and then strained and removed from dishes before serving.

Cinnamon sticks: Used in both savory and sweet dishes, cinnamon sticks, or cassia, are usually added in whole and then removed before serving.

Cloves: Cloves are the unopened pink flower buds of the evergreen clove tree that are then dried and turn brown. Cloves have a warm, sweet, and aromatic taste reminiscent of tropical climates. A little goes a long way, so be careful when using them.

Coriander seeds: Coriander seeds come from the cilantro plant. The way coriander seeds are cooked affects the way they taste. When left whole, coriander seeds have a floral, citrusy curry flavor. When the seeds are ground and roasted, they have a nutty flavor. Coriander seeds are used in curry powders and many curry pastes.

Cornstarch: Cornstarch is a white powder starch that derives from corn kernels. It is commonly mixed with cold water and used as a breading and to thicken sauces.

Cumin seeds: Cumin has a very distinct earthy, nutty, spicy flavor with warm undertones. It can be used whole or ground and is commonly found in curry powders and curry pastes.

Dried shrimp: Sun-dried shrimp that have shrunk to the size of a pea pack a ton of umami

ถั่วดำ
จัมโบ้
1 กก. บ.

ถั่วเขียวซีก
1 กก. 80 บ.

บาร์เลย์
1 กก. 45 บ.

ถั่วแดง
เม็ดเล็ก
1 กก. 80 บ.

ถั่วเหลือง
ซีก
1 กก. 40 บ.

ถั่วเหลืองเม็ดเล็ก
ห้าน้ำเต้า
1 กก. 35 บ.

งาดำ
1 กก. บ.

in a unique way. They are used in some curry pastes and relishes, and soaked and fried for garnish in a salad or stir-fries.

Dried chilies

Dried guajillo/árbol chili: These chilies are a good substitute when you can't find the larger whole dried Thai chili for curry pastes. They have a slightly smoky flavor with a subtle amount of heat.

Dried Thai chili flakes: Visit any Thai noodle shop; one of the condiments on your table is ground chili pepper. Ground dried chili pepper is a versatile part of Thai cooking. Whole dried Thai chilies are dry roasted in a pan, stem on, and then pounded in a mortar and pestle and turned into flakes.

Dried red Thai chili: There are several types of dried chili peppers available in Thailand. The size indicates the intensity of the heat; the smaller, the hotter. The chilies are sun-dried. In Thai cooking, the larger dried whole chilies are a key ingredient in curry pastes. The whole chilies are soaked and the seeds are removed to avoid excessive heat. Once the seeds are removed, the chilies are pounded along with other spices to give a wonderful flavor and color.

Fennel seeds: Fennel seeds can be used either whole or ground. They are used in both savory and sweet applications and add a nice sweet anise flavor to the dish. You will commonly find this ingredient as part of the base for curry pastes.

Jasmine rice: Jasmine rice is one of the most popular rices throughout Southeast Asia. It is a long-grain rice with a fragrant, floral aroma. While all Southeast Asian countries produce Jasmine rice, I prefer rice produced in

Thailand, and Three Elephant is all that I use.

MSG: While this ingredient is a little controversial, MSG is a flavor enhancer. If used appropriately, I think it is an amazing ingredient to have in your pantry.

Palm sugar (Eastland): Palm sugar is made from the sap of the sugar palm, which is cooked until most of the moisture is evaporated. You can find this sugar in a spoonable form or in harder discs. Palm sugar is very versatile and adds a nice nutty, sweet flavor to whatever you are cooking. Palm sugar is used in both savory and sweet dishes in Southeast Asian cuisine.

Peanuts (dry roasted, skinless, and unsalted): Peanuts are used to make peanut sauces and to garnish classic dishes throughout Southeast Asia such as Pad Thai (page 161).

Rice flour: Rice flour is a fine white powder that comes from milled rice. Rice flour can be made from different types of rice—glutinous rice and sweet rice. Rice flour is very versatile and can be used in pastries, noodles, dumpling dough, and batters, to name a few. It can also be used as a thickening agent in the same manner as cornstarch.

Rock sugar: Irregular lumps of crystallized pure cane sugar with a clean taste that is less sweet than refined sugar. If substituting white sugar in its place, use half of the amount.

Star anise: Star anise can be used either whole or ground. It has a bitter aniseed flavor, and the flavor is very important to Southeast Asian cooking. The whole stars can be added directly to what you are cooking but must be removed before serving.

Szechuan peppercorns: Szechuan peppercorns aren't actually peppers. They have a fragrant aroma that is similar to lavender, and their famous numbing sensation happens around the mouth. The peppercorns can be used whole or ground.

Tamarind paste: Tamarind is a sticky, sour-tasting fruit that grows in bean-like pods. The paste is often used as a souring agent in Southeast Asian cuisine. While finding fresh tamarind pods can be challenging, blocks of cooked tamarind are somewhat easy to find and can easily be turned into tamarind paste. Avoid buying premade paste, as it loses its fruity, subtle sour flavor and becomes harsher.

Tapioca pearls: Tapioca is a starch that is extracted from the cassava root. It varies in size and can be used in multiple applications but tends to be used in sweet dishes or drinks. It can also be used as a thickener and can absorb whatever flavor it is cooked in.

Tapioca starch or flour: The names are used interchangeably. This is gluten-free. When used in a batter and fried, it helps make things extra crispy.

Toasted rice powder: Toasted rice powder is made from toasted sticky rice that is traditionally pounded by hand in a mortar and pestle. The rice powder can be used as a garnish on top of salads and as a thickener for sauces. It adds texture and nuttiness to dishes such as Pork Laab (page 142).

Turmeric (ground): Ground turmeric is used as a coloring agent as well as a spice. It has a slightly gingery, bitter flavor. It is used in curries, curry powder, and batters.

Vinegar: In a Southeast Asian kitchen, it is not uncommon to find several varieties of vinegar. The pricier ones like rice vinegar are used for marinating and cooking, while the less expensive (and, often, more pungent) kinds, such as distilled white vinegar and apple cider vinegar, are used for pickling vegetables and for dipping sauces.

Rice vinegar (unseasoned): Rice vinegar is milder and sweeter than Western vinegars. It's made from rice. Make sure that it says "unseasoned" on the label.

Distilled white vinegar and apple cider vinegar: Both are used a lot in Filipino cooking and add a clean and distinct flavor, with apple cider vinegar also adding sweetness. They are totally interchangeable. Just add a pinch of white sugar if using distilled white vinegar in a recipe where apple cider vinegar is called for.

Coconut vinegar: This is natural vinegar made from fermented coconut sap. It is very mild and sweet and is used a lot in Philippine cooking. Coconut vinegar is a staple in Southeast Asian and Indian cuisine that is rapidly gaining popularity in the West. Coconut vinegar has a cloudy, white appearance and a slightly milder taste than apple cider vinegar.

White bait (dried): These little fish (baby anchovies) are typically between 1 and 2 inches long. They are usually sun-dried and then fried and used as garnish on top of noodles or rice, or eaten as a snack by themselves served with a chili vinegar dipping sauce.

White pepper: White pepper is used more in Southeast Asia than we use it here in the United States (although black pepper is often used, depending on the country and the dish). White pepper is milder in flavor and has a musty scent. When I call for it in a recipe, I suggest you use it and not black pepper because black pepper will overpower the dish.

Yellow bean sauce: Yellow bean sauce is also commonly known as yellow bean paste or fermented yellow soybean paste. This sauce, which is made from the soybeans that are left over from making soy sauce, is great in stir-fries and marinades.

FRESH HERBS/VEGETABLES

Betel leaves: Betel leaves have a slightly peppery taste and are most often eaten raw. You can also stuff them with ground meat and then grill them. Find them in Asian markets and online at Amazon. I am not a fan of frozen betel leaves because they tend to be too watery. If you can't find fresh betel leaves, I suggest using sesame leaves or even perilla leaves, not the same flavor, but I prefer both over frozen betel.

Calamansi: This is my favorite citrus of all time. It is hard to get them fresh on the East Coast, but you can buy the juice. Make sure to spend the extra dollar and go with a good (more expensive) brand like Boiron. The flavor is similar to a lemon mixed with a key lime. The fruit is smaller (about one-quarter) than a regular lime. It has green skin and an orange color inside. The juice can be used in sauces, deserts, salad dressing, and more.

Chilies: In Southeast Asia, chilies are eaten dried, fried, pickled, and fresh. You'll find different chilies in salads, curries, soups, pastes, dips, and just about everything.

Red Thai bird chili: These chilies tend to be no bigger than 2 inches long and are the mature version of the green Thai bird chili. They are very hot, so a little goes a long way, but the heat is nicely balanced by their fruitiness. Be careful when handling the chilies and make sure to wear gloves.

Green Thai chili: These chilies are milder than the red ones, although they are still spicy.

Long red chili: These chilies are triple the size of the Thai bird and are way less spicy but still add a kick of spice.

Chinese chives/garlic chives (with buds and no buds): These chives are used differently from the way we use regular chives. Instead of slicing them thin, in Southeast Asia they use 1½- to 2-inch pieces. Usually they are stir-fried in a dish and tossed in at the end to add a sweet onion/garlic flavor.

Choy sum: Choy sum is a member of the mustard family and can be distinguished by its small yellow flowerheads and bright green oval leaves. Mild and sweet with crunchy stems and soft leaves, it is perfect for stir-fries, soups, stews, and even curries. If you can't find it, substitute bok choy.

Coriander/cilantro: This herb is fresh and citrusy and probably one of my most favorite things to eat. Everything from the root to the stems to the leaves is edible and I don't let any of it go to waste. The roots are used in marinades and curry pastes, while the stems are used in stocks, and the leaves are used either in a salad or as a garnish.

Culantro (sawtooth coriander): While the flavor and aroma of culantro and cilantro are similar, culantro has a stronger taste. Culantro can handle high heat but also can be eaten raw in salads.

Curry leaves: These leaves are often used in curries and stir-fries. Curry leaves, which look like smaller, more delicate bay leaves, have a uniquely citrusy, nutty aroma that is slightly reminiscent of curry powder.

Daikon: Daikon looks like a white carrot, but it's actually part of the radish family. This vegetable is often pickled, eaten raw, or used in soups. It adds great texture to a dish and can take on whatever flavors it's being infused with while still having a distinct flavor of its own.

Galangal: This important ingredient has a smoother skin than ginger, with a more pungent flavor. It has a citrusy, mustardy taste that adds complexity to dishes. Galangal is very rarely eaten raw and is usually used in curry paste or cut into slices to infuse a dish.

Ginger (mature): This is the most common ingredient you will find in the rhizome family. Ginger can be eaten raw, juiced, cooked, or made into a paste. It is very versatile and can enhance a dish's flavor. If you are going to eat it and not use it to infuse flavor into a dish, you must peel the tough exterior.

Green mango: A green mango is basically an unripe mango. The fruit should be firm and the outside will be green while the inside is white (similar to the green papaya). Green mango is usually sour and only slightly sweet. It is also commonly shredded and used in salads or pickled.

Green papaya: Green papaya is an unripe version of the orange/pink papaya we are used to. The skin is green and the inside meat is white. Make sure the papaya is firm and completely green when selecting it at a supermarket. When shredding papaya for salads, street vendors in Thailand will peel the papaya whole and then, using a large chef's knife or small clever, make a bunch of deep incisions down the entire length of the papaya then slice down crosswise to create shreds. This method can be a bit tricky and slightly dangerous, so I also recommend peeling the papaya and using an Asian julienne peeler (Western julienne peelers don't work well for this). If making pickles, cut the papaya in half lengthwise and then scoop the white seeds out before using. Papaya is usually shredded or sliced thin and used in salads or pickled.

Japanese eggplant: These eggplants are thinner in shape and also have a much thinner skin. They also don't get as bitter as other eggplants do when cooking them. Eggplants are very versatile and can be used in stir-fries, soups, and curries. My favorite way is to grill them and eat them with very little added to it.

Kaffir lime leaves: One of my favorite flavors in Southeast Asian cooking is kaffir lime. It is often hard to find the actual fruit in the States, but you can easily find the leaves either fresh or frozen or dried (although the dried do not have nearly as much flavor). You can use whole kaffir leaves to infuse flavor into soups and curries, or they can be sliced super thin and added to stir-fries or eaten raw in salads. In certain parts of Southeast Asia you may now see these referred to or labeled as makrut or lime leaves. If you can't find the leaves, you can substitute a few teaspoons of finely grated lime zest in their place. It will not be the same, but it will add a touch of the citrus flavor that kaffir adds.

Lemongrass: When choosing lemongrass, choose whole stalks whose bottoms don't look dried out. Lemongrass can be eaten raw if sliced very thin, used to infuse flavor into soups, or as a main ingredient in curry pastes. Avoid using dried or pre-minced lemongrass, as you will lose the fresh lemony flavor.

How to prep lemongrass:
There are two main ways to cook with lemongrass, and each determines how you handle it.

To infuse teas, broths, soups, and braising liquids, trim off the spiky tops and the bases, crush the stalks with the side of a knife to release their aromatic oils, or you can leave the stalks whole or cut them into 1- to 2-inch pieces. Remove the pieces before eating (they tend to be woody) or eat around them.

To use lemongrass in marinades, stir-fries, salads, spice rubs, and curry pastes, trim the top and base of the stalks—you want to use only the bottom 4 to 5 inches. Though lemongrass stalks measure 12 inches or more, almost all of the flavor is contained in the bottom of the stalk. To get to that flavor, cut away the thinner top portion of the stalk and the very woody base. Then peel away the tougher outer layers to get to the more tender part of the stalk. (You can use all of these scraps to make a soothing herbal tea; steep them in boiling water for 5 minutes, then strain.) Even after peeling, lemongrass is quite fibrous, and it's best to either use it whole to infuse flavor and then remove it, or chop it very finely. To make chopping it easier, use a sharp knife and slice it into thin rounds first.

How to store:

To store, wrap in plastic and refrigerate for up to one week or freeze for up to six months.

Long beans (a.k.a. yard beans): Long beans are most similar in flavor and texture to green beans. They can be eaten raw in salads, as a side on their own, or stir-fried and added to soups and curries. American or French green beans can be substituted—just use 1½ times the amount called for in the recipe.

Morning glory: Morning glory (not to be confused with the garden plant of the same name, the seeds of which have hallucinogenic properties) is also known as water spinach, river spinach, Chinese spinach, and Chinese watercress. It is used in stir-fried dishes and soups.

Pandan leaves: I have never been able to find these leaves fresh in the States, only frozen. This leaf has a very unique and distinct flavor that is slightly sweet with floral undertones. There really is nothing comparable, so I do not list a substitute in recipes. It is used in both savory and sweet dishes.

Peppermint: This herb is known for its refreshing pepper flavor. It is used in salads and noodle dishes and adds a brightness and fresh flavor to the dish.

Persian limes (also known as Tahiti limes): Persian limes are used a lot in all Southeast Asian cooking.

Shallots: In Southeast Asian cooking, the shallots used are much smaller than what we are used to in the States. The smaller shallots have a sweeter, milder flavor and are the onion of choice, especially in raw applications. They are used in many different ways and are a main component in curry pastes.

Thai basil (Asian basil): This herb has purple stems and purple buds. Thai basil is spicier and less sweet than Italian basil, with a hint of anise flavor. It goes great in stir-fries, soups, and salads.

Thai garlic: Thai garlic is known for its smaller cloves, thinner skin, and sweeter flavor. Since the skin is much less fibrous than what we are used to in the States, you don't even need to peel it. In Thailand they pound the garlic with the skin on and stir-fry it or deep-fry it as is. Regular white garlic found in all US markets is an acceptable substitute.

Turmeric (fresh), yellow or white: If you can find fresh turmeric, you are in luck. More often than not, you can only find it in its dry powder form, which is completely fine as well. White turmeric is often used raw in a salad, julienned nice and thin, while the yellow turmeric is used in curries and marinades.

Vietnamese mint (laksa leaves) (rau ram): Vietnamese mint is spicy and a bit peppery. The flavor is described as being a cross between spearmint and cilantro, so if you can't find it, just use equal parts of both.

NOODLES

Hokkien noodles: These oiled fresh noodles, made from wheat flour and egg, resemble spaghetti in thickness and are almost meaty in texture. If you have a choice, buy the noodles loose-packed instead of vacuum-packed; they're fresher. To prepare, cook in boiling water for 30 seconds to 1 minute. Drain well and add to dishes such as Nyonya Laksa (page 166).

Pancit palabok noodles: Palabok noodles are similar to rice noodles but are made from cornstarch. They come in different sizes of thickness from thin to thick. They need to be soaked in warm water before cooking. My brand of choice is Super brand; I prefer the thick noodles.

Rice stick noodles (banh pho): This is *the* noodle of choice for Pad Thai (page 161). This noodle is made from rice flour. It's wider and thicker than rice vermicelli and has more elasticity. Soak in warm water until just softened, up to 25 minutes, before using. You do not want noodles to be too soft, or they will get overcooked.

Rice vermicelli: The neutral, virtually flavorless taste of this dried, thin, and translucent noodle, made from extruded rice flour paste, makes it extremely versatile. Common in Chinese and Southeast Asian dishes, it provides texture without bulk to stir-fries, salads, summer rolls, Mee Krob (page 159), and more. Rice vermicelli is sold in large cellophane-wrapped bundles. Before using in stir-fries or other dishes, cover it with hot water and let stand for about 5 minutes, until tender, then drain and pat dry. If adding to a stir-fry or other cooked dish, keep the soaking time on the short side; drain while still al dente.

Chinese egg noodles: These traditional fresh, thin, rounded noodles, made from wheat flour and egg, are found in a number of Asian dishes, including chow mein, and have an addictively chewy texture. They can be cooked in boiling water, then finished another way by adding to either a stir fry or soup or braise. However you use them, be sure not to overcook them when boiling; they should be al dente, like pasta. Check the label to make sure you're buying noodles that get their hue from eggs, not from food coloring.

RICE

Jasmine rice (Three Elephants brand): This is long-grain rice that is very fragrant and commonly served as a side dish in most Southeast Asian meals.

Sticky rice (Cock brand): This short-grain rice is also referred to as glutinous rice (even though there is no gluten in it) that can be used in both savory and sweet applications. Traditionally, the rice must be soaked in water before steaming, but nowadays it can also be cooked in a rice cooker without soaking first. Sticky rice requires less water than regular rice and therefore it is steamed and not boiled.

SINANDOMENG
P 47.00

SINANDOMENG RICE
LAON
P 48.00 /kg

Doña Maria PREMIUM QUALITY RICE
P 75.00 /KG

Mag-Magic Rice
PIGEON JASMINE THAI
P 65.00 /1k

MINDORO PURE
DINORADO
P 55.00 /1kg.

JASMIN THAI HOM
MALI
P 58 1 KILO

Mag-Magic Rice araw-araw!
Blue bird
55.00 kilo

Mag-Magic Rice araw-araw!
KUKU 96
55.00 kilo

GREAT TASTE
DENORADO
P 50.00 /1k

明機器
TEL: 2922615 / 2972008
MING ENG

8 /kg
STAR
KYOKU
JASMINE

2

CONDIMENTS AND BASICS

Condiments are the key to so many dishes in Southeast Asia. They add that pop, that excitement, everything that makes you want to go back for more. My favorite part about most of these condiments is that they keep—sometimes up to a few months in the refrigerator or freezer. That means that if I come home late or have to wake up early and need to throw something together, I have exactly the right sauce to make it something special. For instance:

Chili Jam (page 51), also known as nam prik pao, is a super-versatile condiment found on most tables in Thailand and used a lot in Thai cooking. I like to steam a bunch of clams, toss in some chili jam, and dinner is served. Garlic Oil (page 43) is the secret ingredient in badass salad dressing and not-so-secret in Garlic Rice (page 150). Peanut Sauce (page 48) is most commonly used as a dip for satay, or try thinning it out with a bit of stock or water to coat noodles in it. The more you play around, the more ways you'll find to utilize each and every sauce in here.

My favorite, however, is Isaan Sauce (page 46), a meat dipping sauce from the Isaan region of Thailand. The first time I had it, I was blown away. It took me months to come up with this iteration and in those months of testing, I realized that this was the cuisine I needed to be cooking. It's the perfect mix of sour from the tamarind, earthy from the cilantro root, sweet from the palm sugar, and funky from the fish sauce. Rice powder then adds in a toasty note, and raw shallot keeps it just a little sharp. At the restaurant, we use Isaan sauce mostly as a beef dipping sauce, but at home I swear I put it on everything from grilled chicken to pork to vegetables.

Another thing about Southeast Asian cuisine that I love is that condiments aren't always sauces. In fact, pickles are some of the most important condiments. While sauces tend to add depth, umami, and sometimes heat, pickles add freshness and acidity, complementing the rest of each dish and helping to cleanse the palate. You'll notice that the vinegars we use tend to be banana, coconut, or rice. When you think about it, it makes sense, as banana, coconut, and rice are all staples of Southeast Asian cuisine. By using those vinegars, we're able to intensify those flavors and build some very complex dishes with incredible depth.

I love Atchara (page 57), a pickled green papaya, with fried foods because the clean notes of the green papaya balance out any greasiness. The only danger is that you can eat the two together forever! The same goes for my Cucumber Relish (page 53). The coconut vinegar, almost herbal cucumber, and bright lime make the perfect accompaniment for my Malaysian Beef Curry Puffs (page 77). They're each great solo, but the two are unstoppable together.

CHICKEN STOCK

5 pounds chicken bones, rinsed well

½ large Spanish onion

8-inch piece of fresh ginger, halved

5 scallion white bottoms

3 garlic cloves

When you start a dish with homemade stock, you don't have to worry about sodium levels or strange preservatives. Plus, it is easy to make and lasts months in the freezer.

1. Put the bones into a large pot, cover with cold water by 1 inch, bring to a boil over high heat, and then turn off the heat. Drain the bones into a large colander. Rinse the pot, add the bones back, and add enough cold water to cover by 3 inches.

2. Return the pot to the stove over high heat and bring to a boil. Reduce the heat to low. Add the onion, ginger, scallions, and garlic. Slightly cover the pot and cook, skimming the top occasionally, for 3 hours. Strain the stock into a large bowl and let cool. Transfer to quart containers with lids and keep in the refrigerator for up to 3 days or in the freezer for up to 3 months.

Variation: GINGER-CHICKEN STOCK

3 quarts Chicken Stock

4-inch piece of fresh ginger, sliced

1 tablespoon kosher salt

½ teaspoon MSG

1. Combine the chicken stock, ginger, salt, and MSG in a large saucepan over high heat and bring to a boil. Reduce the heat to low and simmer and cook for 15 minutes. Remove from the heat, cover, and let steep for 45 minutes.

2. Strain the stock into a large bowl and let cool. Transfer to quart containers with lids and keep in the refrigerator for up to 3 days or in the freezer for up to 3 months.

PORK STOCK

5 pounds pork bones, rinsed

1 Spanish onion, halved

4-inch piece of fresh ginger, skin on and cut in half

5 scallions (white parts only)

3 garlic cloves

1. Put the bones in a large stockpot, cover with cold water, bring to a boil over high heat, drain, and return the bones to the pot.

2. Cover the bones again with cold water by 3 inches, bring to a boil over high heat, reduce the heat to low, and add the onion, ginger, scallions, and garlic. Slightly cover the pot and cook for 2½ hours, skimming the top every 30 minutes.

3. Strain the stock and let cool to room temperature. Store the stock, tightly covered in the refrigerator, for up to 3 days or freeze for up to 3 months.

LOBSTER STOCK

YIELDS: 4 QUARTS

2 tablespoons canola oil

5 lobster heads, cleaned and quartered

These are very basic, subtly flavored stocks that can be used interchangeably. They have no aromatics, and their neutral flavor will not take over the other ingredients in the dish. You can purchase lobster heads at your local fish store or counter, and every time you make a shrimp dish (of which there are many in this book), save all the shells that you peel and store them tightly in the freezer in a ziplock bag.

1. Heat the oil in a large, wide pot over high heat until the oil shimmers. Add the lobster heads and cook for about 5 minutes total, until seared well on both sides.

2. Add 5 quarts of cold water and bring to a boil. Reduce the heat to low and simmer until the desired lobster flavor is reached, about 1½ hours.

3. Strain the stock into a large bowl and let cool to room temperature. Use immediately or store tightly covered in the refrigerator for 3 days, or divide into quart containers with lids and freeze up to 3 months.

SHRIMP STOCK

YIELDS: ABOUT 3½ QUARTS

2 tablespoons canola oil

10 cups raw shrimp shells (about 4 pounds), rinsed well

1. Heat the oil in a large, wide pot over high heat until the oil shimmers. Add the shells and cook for about 5 minutes total, until seared well on both sides.

2. Add 5 quarts of cold water and bring to a boil. Reduce the heat to low and simmer until the desired shrimp flavor is reached, about 1½ hours.

3. Strain the stock into a large bowl and let cool to room temperature. Use immediately or store tightly covered in the refrigerator for 3 days, or divide into quart containers with lids and freeze up to 3 months.

THAI CURRY POWDER

THAI CURRY POWDER

YIELDS: 1 QUART

½ cup whole cumin seeds

⅓ cup whole coriander seeds

20 whole star anise

6 cinnamon sticks, pounded into small pieces

2 tablespoons whole cloves

1½ cups ground turmeric

Most Thai curries are made from a spice paste rather than curry powder, but this isn't to say Thai cooks don't use curry powder—they do. While curry powder and curry pastes cannot be used interchangeably, you can use curry powder to whip up a quick curry, or use it as part of a marinade. Curry powders vary from country to country and person to person. Its all about personal preference of spices and proportions. This is the blend that I like to make because I can use it in many different recipes like Khao Soi (page 193), Thai Herbal Sausage with chili relish (page 73), and Grilled Beef in Betel Leaf (page 241), just to name a few. All of the ingredients are easy to find and last for months in your pantry.

1. Combine the cumin, coriander, star anise, cinnamon, and cloves in a large sauté pan and toast over low heat until fragrant. Remove and let cool.

2. Transfer the spices to a spice grinder, in batches, and grind to a fine powder.

3. Pour the spices into a bowl, add the turmeric, and mix to combine. Store in a container with a tight-fitting lid in a cool, dark place for up to 6 months.

TEN-SPICE MIX

YIELDS: ABOUT 1 CUP

¼ cup kosher salt

3 tablespoons five-spice powder

3 tablespoons coriander seeds, toasted and ground (see page 22)

2 tablespoons garlic powder

1 tablespoon chili powder

1 tablespoon white pepper

Pinch of ground galangal (see page 28)

This is my favorite spice mix. I use it for Chicharron (page 62), shrimp and chicken dishes, and anything fried. I just love anything made with five-spice powder! Double or triple the recipe—it keeps tightly covered in the pantry for up to 6 months.

Whisk together the salt, five-spice powder, coriander, garlic powder, chili powder, white pepper, and galangal in a small bowl. Cover and store in a cool, dark place for up to 6 months.

HOUSE DRESSING

YIELDS: ABOUT 2 CUPS

7 fresh Thai chilies, chopped

2 garlic cloves, smashed

1 cup freshly squeezed lime juice

½ cup Squid Brand fish sauce

⅓ cup granulated sugar

I call this "house dressing," and it can be used on any of the salads in this book. At Pig and Khao, it dresses several of my salads, including the Thai Papaya Salad (page 129) and the Red Curry Rice Salad (page 138). It also makes a great dipping sauce for grilled meat and seafood, and you can use it on a typical American lettuce salad, too.

1. Combine the chilies and garlic and ½ cup of the lime juice in a blender and blend until just coarsely chopped. Add the remaining ½ cup lime juice, the fish sauce, sugar, and ¾ cup of cold water and blend until smooth but flecks of the chili are still visible.

2. Transfer the dressing to a container with a tight-fitting lid and store in the refrigerator for up to 5 days.

HOUSE MARINADE

YIELDS: ABOUT 1 QUART

4 garlic cloves

12 cilantro stems, chopped

2 cans unsweetened coconut milk

⅓ cup Squid Brand fish sauce

¼ cup granulated sugar

1 teaspoon kosher salt

¾ teaspoon white pepper

This is one of the standard marinades in Thailand for grilled chicken and pork. It can also be used as an instant marinade for shrimp. The coconut milk acts as a tenderizer for the meat while infusing it with a ton of flavor.

1. Combine the garlic and cilantro stems in a blender, add ½ cup of the coconut milk, and blend until the garlic and cilantro are a paste. Add the remaining coconut milk, fish sauce, sugar, salt, and pepper and blend until smooth.

2. Transfer the marinade to a container with a tight-fitting lid. Use immediately or store in the refrigerator for up to 3 days.

FERMENTED MUSTARD GREENS

YIELDS: ABOUT 3 QUARTS

1 cup jasmine rice

3 quarts warm water

¼ cup plus 1 tablespoon kosher salt

½ cup distilled white vinegar

2 pounds mustard greens, cleaned and trimmed and coarsely chopped into 2-inch pieces

Fermented mustard greens are one of my favorite condiments to have on hand at all times. They add a really nice texture, funk, and saltiness to dishes. I highly recommend you make your own, as the packaged ones you will find in an Asian grocery store are just not as good. I add a little bit of vinegar to the fermenting liquid to help start the process, but what really makes this ferment is the rice and rice rinse water. The mustard greens should be left out in a warm place in an airtight container. The storage temperature will affect the length of time the mustard greens need to ferment.

1. Put the rice into a large bowl, add 1 quart of the water, and mix around with your hand to rinse and remove the starch. Strain the rice through a colander into a large bowl (save the water). Repeat this step two more times. Tie the rice in a large piece of cheesecloth.

2. Add the salt and vinegar to the rice water and stir to combine.

3. Put the mustard greens into a large plastic container and pour the rice water over the top. If the mustard greens are not fully covered, add enough extra warm water to just cover. Weigh down the mustard greens with the rice in the cheesecloth and then put a plate on top to weigh it down further.

4. Cover and wrap the container tightly in plastic wrap and place in a warm place for 5 to 7 days.

5. Transfer the greens to Mason jars and pack tightly. Add some of the brining liquid to cover by 2 inches. Tighten the lids and keep refrigerated. The greens will continue to ferment and will last several months in the refrigerator.

Note:

If the greens are not completely submerged in the water, there is a chance that mold will develop.

TAMARIND PASTE

YIELDS: ABOUT 2 CUPS

1 pound block tamarind pulp
(see page 26)

Tamarind paste is a base for a lot of Southeast Asian recipes such as Isaan Sauce (page 46), Pad Thai (page 161), and Mee Krob (page 159). The taste is similar to a lime—it's fruity and sour, but unlike a lime, it's not acidic. You can purchase tamarind paste, but I prefer to make my own because homemade tamarind paste has a more complex, distinct fruity taste that the store-bought tamarind pastes and concentrates lack, and making your own allows you to have more control over the texture of the paste.

1. Bring 4 cups of water to a boil over high heat in a medium saucepan. Put the tamarind pulp in a large bowl, pour just enough of the boiling water over the pulp to barely cover, and let sit at room temperature for 30 minutes.

2. Gently break the tamarind pulp apart with your hands and mash it so that the fruit (this is the paste) starts to separate from the rough fibers. Leave the water in the bowl while you do this. If the tamarind pulp was just barely covered with water while it soaked in the step above, you should have the perfect amount of water to combine with the pulp. If the mixture seems water-logged, you can pour off a bit of the extra liquid.

3. Pass the pulp through a colander with large holes set over a large bowl, pressing with a rubber spatula to separate the pulp from the fibers. The tamarind paste will separate from the fibers and collect on the other side of the colander or in the bowl.

4. Once you've separated as much of the paste as you can (note: add a bit more hot water to the fibers and press them through the colander a second time if you think you can extract a bit more paste), discard the fibers and store the paste in a nonreactive container. The paste will keep in the refrigerator for 1 week and in the freezer for up to 3 months.

GARLIC OIL/ CRISPY GARLIC

YIELDS: 1 QUART

1 quart canola oil

2 heads garlic, finely chopped
(about 20 cloves)

Crispy garlic and garlic-infused oil are essential condiments in Asia. The crispy garlic can be used as a topping for just about any dish in this cookbook, and the oil is used to cook stir-fries, to flavor soups and sauces, and to drizzle over noodle dishes.

1. Line a large plate with paper towels. Set a strainer over a bowl. Heat the oil in a medium saucepan over medium heat until it just begins to shimmer. Add the garlic and cook, stirring occasionally, until golden brown, 4 to 7 minutes.

2. Immediately strain the oil into the bowl and transfer the garlic to the prepared plate to drain. The garlic will keep for 5 days in a container with a lid. Line the container with a piece of paper towel to absorb any excess oil.

ANNATTO OIL

YIELDS: 2 CUPS

2 cups Garlic Oil (recipe above)

2 tablespoons annatto seeds
(see page 22)

This Filipino oil mostly adds color to food, since it really has no flavor. I use garlic oil so that it adds not only color but flavor, too. Used for grilled meats such as Chicken Inasal with Atchara and Patis Sauce (page 223) and seafood.

1. Combine the oil and annatto seeds in a small saucepan, bring to a simmer over high heat, remove from the heat, and let steep for 30 minutes.

2. Strain the oil into a container with a tight-fitting lid. Store in the refrigerator for up to 1 month.

SCALLION OIL

SCALLION OIL

YIELDS: 2 CUPS

2 cups canola oil

½ cup packed thinly sliced scallions (white and green parts)

1½ teaspoons kosher salt

This oil is used a lot in Vietnamese cooking. It's used in salad dressings like we would use olive oil. I use lots of it in my cooking, and one of my favorite ways is to just spoon it over grilled fish with a drizzle of fish sauce and a squeeze of lime. Using an ice bath to stop the cooking of the scallion will help retain its fresh flavor and keep it green.

1. Fill a large bowl with ice and nestle another slightly smaller bowl into the ice.

2. Put the oil in a medium saucepan and bring to almost smoking over high heat. Add the scallions and salt and remove from the heat. Pour the oil immediately into the bowl sitting on top of the ice and stir until cool.

3. Transfer the mixture to a container with a tight-fitting lid. Store in the refrigerator for up to 1 week.

THAI GREEN SEAFOOD SAUCE

YIELDS: ABOUT 2 CUPS

2 cups chopped cilantro root

15 garlic cloves, smashed

20 green Thai bird chilies, stems removed

½ cup plus 1 tablespoon freshly squeezed lime juice

¼ cup plus 2 tablespoons Squid Brand fish sauce

3 tablespoons palm sugar

I refer to this as the universal grilled seafood sauce of Thailand. Go to any island in the country (and there are many) and you will find vendors grilling fresh-from-the-ocean seafood (scallops, fish, shrimp) and serving it with this super-simple and refreshing green sauce (there is also a red version). It is also great with chicken and pork, too. I love it! If you can't find cilantro root, just substitute chopped cilantro stems.

Combine the cilantro root, garlic, chilies, lime juice, fish sauce, and palm sugar in the bowl of a food processor and process until almost smooth (should have a bit of texture). Scrape into a bowl and store, covered, in the refrigerator for up to 2 weeks.

PATIS SAUCE

YIELDS: 2½ CUPS

1½ cups coconut vinegar

½ cup Squid Brand fish sauce

2 garlic cloves, finely chopped

2 small red Thai bird chilies, thinly sliced

Patis sauce means fish sauce. Patis is to the Filipinos what nam pla (the Thai name for fish sauce) is to the Thais, but fish sauce on its own is not spicy. In the Philippines, dishes are served with a bowl of vinegar infused with chilies and garlic and a separate bowl of fish sauce. The idea is that you mix them together. All that I have done is combined them for you so that you just have one sauce. I serve this as a dipping sauce for grilled meats such as Chicken Inasal with Atchara and Patis Sauce (page 223), smoked fish, and anything fried.

Whisk together the vinegar, fish sauce, garlic, and chilies in a small bowl. Let sit for at least 30 minutes to allow the flavors to meld. The sauce can be stored tightly covered in the refrigerator for up to 1 week.

(JAEW) ISAAN SAUCE

YIELDS: 2 CUPS

¼ cup finely chopped fresh cilantro root or cilantro stems

½ cup Squid Brand fish sauce

⅔ cup freshly squeezed lime juice (6 to 7 limes)

⅓ cup palm sugar

1½ tablespoons Tamarind Paste (store-bought or page 42)

1 tablespoon dried Thai chili flakes

1 teaspoon toasted rice powder

1 heaping tablespoon finely diced shallot

3 fresh kaffir lime leaves, finely chopped

⅛ teaspoon galangal powder (optional)

The food of Isaan is known for being very spicy and pungent, and this famous sauce will fire up your taste buds. Chili flakes and fish sauce add the heat and funk. The sauce pairs beautifully with grilled meats such as beef, which is what I serve it with at Pig and Khao, but it is great with pork and chicken and lamb, too. I love making it in a mortar and pestle because that is the authentic method and the way that I was taught, and also, using a blender changes the mouthfeel. If you do make it in a blender, blend on a low speed so that the chili does not become too pulverized. This is not a smooth sauce; it is meant to have texture. Toasted rice powder adds viscosity and a nutty flavor. I love this sauce. The real name is Jaew, but I call it Isaan Sauce because I had it for the first time in Isaan.

1. Combine the cilantro root in a blender with a splash of fish sauce or lime juice (to help it blend more easily) and blend until smooth. Add the palm sugar and blend for 10 seconds. Add the fish sauce, lime juice, tamarind, and chili flakes and blend until almost smooth (should have a bit of texture).

2. Transfer the mixture to a medium bowl and stir in the rice powder, shallot, and kaffir leaves. Add the galangal powder, if using. Use immediately or let cool to room temperature, cover, and refrigerate for up to 5 days. Remove the sauce from the refrigerator 30 minutes prior to using, to come to room temperature.

LIVER SAUCE

YIELDS: 1 QUART

1 cup apple cider vinegar

½ cup granulated sugar

¼ cup canola oil

10 garlic cloves, sliced

1 medium Spanish onion, finely diced

Two 4.76-ounce cans Flower brand liver pâté

2 teaspoons kosher salt

½ teaspoon freshly ground black pepper

This liver-based sauce, with its savory flavor, is found only in Filipino cooking, and it is always served alongside the classic dish Crispy Pata (Braised Pork Shank, page 235). It also goes really well with any grilled or fried meat. Truth be told, most people in the country just buy the famous bottled version of liver sauce by the Mang Tomas sauce company instead of making it from scratch. This recipe was taught to me by one of my mom's closest friends, and making it always makes me think of him.

1. Combine the vinegar and sugar in a small saucepan, bring to a boil over high heat, and cook, without stirring, until the sugar dissolves, about 2 minutes. Remove from the heat.

2. Heat the oil in a medium saucepan over medium heat until it begins to shimmer. Add the garlic and cook, stirring a few times, until golden brown, about 4 to 5 minutes. Remove the garlic with a slotted spoon and place on a plate lined with paper towels.

3. Add the onions to the pan and cook, stirring a few times, until the onions are soft, about 5 minutes. Add the liver pâté and cook, breaking it up into small pieces with a wooden spoon. Add the salt, pepper, vinegar mixture, fried garlic, and 1 cup of water, bring to a boil, reduce the heat, and simmer and cook, stirring occasionally, until the mixture softens and reduces slightly, about 20 minutes. Remove from the heat and let cool for 5 minutes.

4. Transfer the mixture to a blender and process until smooth. Return to the pan that you cooked it in, bring to a simmer over medium heat, and cook until the sauce begins to thicken to a sauce consistency and coats the back of a spoon, about 10 minutes longer. Transfer to a bowl and let cool to room temperature. The sauce can be stored, tightly covered, in the refrigerator for up to 1 month.

PEANUT SAUCE

YIELDS: ABOUT 4 CUPS

One 13.5-ounce can unsweetened coconut milk

¼ cup canned Thai red curry paste

¾ cup unsweetened natural peanut butter

¼ cup granulated sugar

3 tablespoons apple cider or white wine vinegar

2 tablespoons chili-garlic sauce, such as Huy Fong

1 teaspoon kosher salt

This sauce is often served with satay and summer rolls. Add a bit of water to thin it out and it makes an excellent dressing for salads. My version is on the spicy side, which is how I prefer it, but if you like your food a bit less spicy, just add less of the chili-garlic sauce.

1. Combine the coconut milk, curry paste, peanut butter, sugar, vinegar, chili-garlic sauce, salt, and ½ cup of water in a medium saucepan and bring to a boil over high heat. Reduce the heat to low and simmer for 5 minutes.

2. Remove from the heat and let cool to room temperature. Use immediately or transfer to a container with a tight-fitting lid and refrigerate for up to 1 week.

SOY DIPPING SAUCE

YIELDS: 3 CUPS

2 cups Kikkoman light soy sauce

1 cup apple cider vinegar

¼ cup granulated sugar

1 or 2 Thai chilies, thinly sliced (depending on how spicy you like)

This savory sauce is delicious with Crispy Pata (Braised Pork Shank, page 235) but also goes well with everything from grilled fish, chicken, and beef to vegetables. To lessen the spiciness of the sauce, mix ingredients together just before serving so the chilies don't overwhelm the other flavors.

Whisk together the soy sauce, vinegar, and sugar in a medium bowl, add the chilies, and let sit at room temperature for at least 30 minutes to allow the flavors to meld. Refrigerate in an airtight container for up to 1 week.

GREEN CHILI RELISH

YIELDS: ABOUT 2 CUPS

10 large jalapeño chilies, stems removed

7 Thai green chilies, stems removed

1 banana pepper, stem removed

15 cloves garlic, peeled

3 shallots, peeled

1 tablespoon Thai shrimp paste

½ cup minced cilantro root

Pinch of kosher salt

¼ cup palm sugar

5 tablespoons Red Boat fish sauce

¾ cup fresh lime juice

Also known as nam prik noom. *Nam prik* means relish in Thai, and *noom* refers to the type of chili, which in this case is the long green chili (I use other green chilies in this recipe to add some heat and depth of flavor). This is a northern Thai condiment that goes with just about anything from chicharron to Thai herbal sausage, grilled meats or raw vegetables. My version is just one example of a nam prik, although there are many different variations.

1. Heat a grill to high or a grill pan over high heat until smoking. Grill the chilies, banana pepper, garlic, and shallot until golden brown and slightly charred on both sides. Transfer chilies and banana pepper to a bowl, cover with plastic wrap, and let sit for 10 minutes, then remove the skin.

2. Put the shrimp paste in a sheet of foil, wrap tightly, and grill for 4 minutes on each side.

3. Coarsely chop the chilies, banana pepper, garlic, and shallot on a cutting board.

4. Combine the cilantro root and salt in a mortar and pestle and pound to make a paste. Add the palm sugar and pound until it dissolves. Add the chili mixture, shrimp paste, fish sauce, and lime juice and mix to combine. Serve immediately or refrigerate in a container with a tight-fitting lid for up to 1 week.

NUOC CHAM

YIELDS: 2 CUPS

½ cup coconut vinegar

½ cup granulated sugar

½ cup plus 2 tablespoons Squid Brand fish sauce

¼ cup plus 2 tablespoons freshly squeezed lime juice (2 to 3 limes)

1 large garlic clove, finely chopped

1 or 2 Thai chilies, thinly sliced

This Vietnamese dipping sauce, with its bright and spicy mix of sweet, sour, salty, and bitter flavors, is used as a condiment and dipping sauce to accompany everything from grilled meat and spring rolls to noodle dishes.

Whisk together ½ cup of water, the vinegar, sugar, fish sauce, lime juice, garlic, and chilies in a nonreactive bowl until the sugar dissolves. Use immediately or transfer to a container with a lid and refrigerate for up to 1 week.

CHILI JAM
(NAM PRIK PAO)

YIELDS: ABOUT 3 CUPS

1 cup canola oil

8 medium shallots, thinly sliced

17 dried shrimp, soaked in warm water for 15 minutes, drained, and patted dry with paper towels

50 garlic cloves, thinly sliced

50 whole dried Thai chilies

1 cup plus 2 tablespoons palm sugar

¼ cup homemade Tamarind Paste (page 42)

¼ cup Squid Brand fish sauce, plus more for finishing

There are a million (ok, maybe a hundred) kinds of relishes in Thailand, and this one is definitely one of the most common and the most versatile. It is that perfect combination of sweet, salty, spicy, and acidic that Southeast Asian cooking is known for. I use it as a base for salad dressings and stir it into soups and stir-fries. You can buy store-bought versions, but as with many things, homemade is much better. It is a bit tedious to make, I won't lie, but it lasts for a long time in the refrigerator.

1. Heat the oil in a medium saucepan over medium heat until it reaches 300 degrees F. Line a large plate with paper towels. Fry the shallots in two batches until golden brown and crispy, stirring a few times, about 4 minutes. Remove with a slotted spoon to the prepared plate. Bring the oil back up to 300 degrees F.

2. Add the shrimp to the oil and fry until lightly golden brown and crisp, about 1 minute. Transfer to the plate with the shallots.

3. Add the garlic to the oil and cook, stirring constantly, until light golden brown, 3 to 4 minutes. Transfer to the plate with the shrimp and shallots.

4. Add the chilies to the oil, and fry, stirring a few times until their color deepens slightly and they become fragrant, about 45 seconds to 1 minute. Transfer the oil to a heatproof bowl or measuring cup and let cool, about 10 minutes.

5. Combine the shallots, shrimp, garlic, chilies, and ¼ cup of the reserved oil in a blender and blend until smooth. Transfer the mixture to a medium saucepan, add the palm sugar, tamarind, fish sauce, and 1 cup of water and blend until smooth.

6. Transfer the paste to a medium saucepan and cook over medium heat, stirring often, for 10 minutes. Remove from the heat, let cool to room temperature, and season with more fish sauce, if desired or needed. Store, tightly covered, for up to 1 month in the refrigerator.

SAMBAL BELACAN

YIELDS: 1¼ CUPS

14 fresh red Thai bird chilies, stems removed

5 dried red Thai bird chilies, seeded and soaked in warm water for 30 minutes

6 medium shallots, chopped

1 teaspoon kosher salt

1 teaspoon granulated sugar

1 cup canola oil

1 heaping tablespoon plain Malaysian shrimp paste (see page 20), toasted in foil in the oven, on the grill, or over medium heat on top of the burner for 2 to 3 minutes

Sambal belacan is a hot and spicy chili sauce from Malaysia. The ultimate sambal belacan has to be fiery and savory. Toasting the shrimp paste adds a deeper, slightly smokier flavor. Best served with meat, seafood, or even noodles.

1. Combine the chilies, shallots, salt, sugar, and ½ cup of the oil in a blender and blend until smooth. Add the shrimp paste and blend until combined.

2. Heat the remaining ½ cup of the oil in a medium sauté pan over medium heat and cook the paste, stirring constantly, until it becomes a deep red color, about 5 minutes.

3. Transfer to a bowl, let cool, and then store, tightly covered, in the refrigerator for up to 3 weeks.

CRISPY FRIED SHALLOTS

YIELDS: ABOUT 2½ CUPS

2 cups canola oil

6 large shallots, thinly sliced lengthwise

1 cup rice flour

Kosher salt

1. Heat the oil in a medium saucepan over medium heat until it reaches 300 degrees F on a deep-fry thermometer.

2. Line a rimmed baking sheet with a few layers of paper towels. Spread the shallots on the baking sheet to remove excess moisture.

3. Line a plate with a few layers of paper towels. Put ½ cup of the flour in a large bowl, add half of the shallots, and toss to coat well. Pat off any excess flour and fry until golden brown and crispy, stirring a few times, about 2 minutes. Remove with a slotted spoon to the prepared plate and lightly season with salt. Repeat with the remaining shallots.

CUCUMBER RELISH

2 cups coconut vinegar

1 cup sweet chili sauce

⅓ cup Squid Brand fish sauce

¼ cup freshly squeezed lime juice (about 3 limes)

2 garlic cloves, smashed

½ teaspoon Thai chili flakes

2 teaspoons kosher salt

2 tablespoons finely chopped fresh cilantro leaves

2 pounds (about 10) Kirby cucumbers, halved and sliced into ¼-inch-thick half-moons

I love serving this cucumber relish with Lor Bak (page 79), Malaysian Beef Curry Puffs (page 77), and Red Curry Fish Cakes (page 81).

1. Combine the vinegar, 2 cups of cold water, the chili sauce, fish sauce, lime juice, garlic, chili flakes, salt, and cilantro in a large bowl and whisk together.

2. Put the cucumbers in a medium bowl or container with a tight-fitting lid, pour the pickling solution over the cucumbers, and store, covered, in the refrigerator for at least 5 hours and up to 24 hours. The pickles will keep, tightly covered, in the refrigerator for several weeks.

PICKLED CUCUMBERS

½ cup plus 1 tablespoon distilled white vinegar

2 tablespoons granulated sugar

1¼ teaspoons kosher salt

2 fresh Thai chilies, smashed

1 garlic clove, smashed

1 English cucumber, sliced crosswise into ⅛-inch-thick slices

Most meals in Southeast Asia are garnished with at least one pickled condiment. Cucumbers are one of my favorites and super easy to prepare. They are also good just for snacking on by themselves.

1. Combine the vinegar, 1 cup of water, the sugar, salt, chilies, and garlic in a medium bowl and whisk together.

2. Put the cucumber in a glass jar with a lid or a container with a lid and pour the pickling solution over it. Let cool to room temperature, then cover and refrigerate for at least 8 hours. Store, tightly covered, in the refrigerator for up to 1 month.

**PICKLED DAIKON
AND CARROTS**

PICKLED DAIKON AND CARROTS

YIELDS: ABOUT 1 QUART

2 cups distilled white vinegar

⅓ cup granulated sugar

1½ tablespoons kosher salt

2 large carrots, shredded

1 large daikon, peeled, seeded, and shredded

Daikon is a large white Asian radish that looks similar to a carrot, but unlike a radish, which has a strong, peppery taste, the daikon is mild and sweet with a crispy texture that holds up perfectly when pickled. You will find the combination of daikon and carrot throughout Vietnam used in noodle dishes and on sandwiches.

1. Combine the vinegar, 1½ cups of water, the sugar, and salt in a medium bowl and whisk until dissolved.

2. Combine the carrots and daikon in a bowl, pour the pickling liquid over them, cover, and refrigerate for at least 1 hour and up to 1 week.

PICKLED GREEN MANGO

YIELDS: 1 QUART

1¼ cups distilled white vinegar

¾ cup granulated sugar

1½ tablespoons kosher salt

2 large green mangoes, peeled, pitted, and coarsely shredded

Simpler than Atchara (Pickled Papaya, page 57), Filipinos eat this quick-pickled mango with Crispy Pata (Braised Pork Shank, page 235). Green mango is mango that isn't ripe—it has a slightly sour flavor and a wonderful crunchy texture.

Combine the vinegar, ¾ cup of water, the sugar, and salt in a large bowl and stir until the sugar begins to dissolve. Stir in the mangoes, cover, and refrigerate for at least 1 hour and up to 1 week before serving.

PICKLED CHILIES

PICKLED CHILIES

YIELDS: 1 PINT

1¼ cups apple cider vinegar

1 tablespoon plus 1 teaspoon granulated sugar

2 teaspoons kosher salt

2 cups thinly sliced (¼ inch thick) fresh long red Thai chilies or jalapeño or serrano peppers

These long red Thai chilies are not as spicy as their shorter version. In fact, they are pretty mild, similar to a Fresno (Fresno peppers can make a good substitute if you can't find long red chilies). You can also pickle jalapeño and serrano peppers this way, too.

1. Combine the vinegar, ⅔ cup of water, the sugar, and salt in a medium bowl and whisk until the sugar and salt are dissolved.

2. Put the chilies in a jar with a lid or a container with a tight-fitting lid and pour the pickling solution over them. Cover and let sit at room temperature for 24 hours. Store, tightly covered, in the refrigerator for up to 1 month.

ATCHARA (PICKLED PAPAYA)

YIELDS: ABOUT 1 QUART

3 cups apple cider vinegar

1¼ cups (packed) light brown sugar

1½ tablespoons kosher salt

¼ cup canola oil

1 large Spanish onion, halved and thinly sliced

3-inch piece of fresh ginger, peeled and finely chopped

9 garlic cloves, finely chopped

1 green papaya (about 2 pounds), peeled, seeded, and coarsely shredded

1 pound carrots (about 4 medium or 2 very large), peeled and coarsely shredded

3 tablespoons Squid Brand fish sauce

1 cup golden raisins

This pickled condiment is served alongside any grilled or fried food in the Philippines. Immature green papaya has crisp white flesh with very little flavor and is used mostly for its incredible crunch. Its mild flavor serves as a great backdrop for the powerful flavors of vinegar, ginger, garlic, and fish sauce. Green papaya has a clean taste similar to jicama, which would make a great substitution if green papaya is not available.

1. Whisk together the vinegar, 1 cup of water, the brown sugar, and the salt in a large bowl until the sugar dissolves. Set aside.

2. Heat the oil in a large sauté pan over high heat. Add the onion and ginger and cook until soft, about 4 minutes. Add the garlic and cook for 2 minutes longer. Add the papaya and carrots and cook, stirring occasionally, until slightly soft but still has texture, about 5 minutes.

3. Stir in the pickling liquid, fish sauce, and the raisins and let the mixture cool to room temperature. Transfer the relish to a large container with a tight-fitting lid and refrigerate for at least 24 hours before using. Store the relish in the refrigerator for up to 2 weeks.

3

SNACKS AND STREET FOOD

When I was living in Bangkok, a friend sent me to a street-side spot for grilled meat. It was there, eating this incredible grilled pork neck (a cut we don't see often in the States) with this awesome sauce that I became obsessed with Southeast Asian street food. For weeks, I thought about it and tried to make it over and over. It had all of the elements of a perfect dish—sweet, salty, sour, and hot. Working on that sauce, trying to replicate its balanced flavors day in and day out, inspired me to open Pig and Khao in the first place.

The energy of the streets, the intoxicating smells, the intensity of the flavors that you find on literal corners are an absolute inspiration to me. They remind me why I make the food I do, connect me to my travels and my second home. Across Southeast Asia, street food is the heart of the day to day. While I traveled in Vietnam, Thailand, and Singapore, eating street food is almost all I did. I would start chatting with one friend, learn the name of a stall from that person, seek it out, and then speak to locals while waiting in line for other recommendations.

One of the vendors I read more about after stumbling upon it in Bangkok was run by a woman named Jay Fai who's been making the same phenomenal crab omelets for almost seventy years. They're so good that she has a Michelin star. I was too scared to try to replicate her omelets, but I do make a Thai dish, Broken Mussel Pancake (page 65), that I like to think of as its cousin.

<<

Street food isn't just good—it's also cheap. You can eat for a full day for just ten dollars. In a lot of places, that's cheaper than the ingredients it would take to make a full day's worth of meals. The price and the fact that most people live in fairly small apartments with even smaller kitchens—making it difficult if not impossible to cook meals in—contribute to the popularity of street food. For less than two dollars in Thailand, you can get four or five skewers with all kinds of phenomenal meats.

Street foods, of course, vary by country. In Vietnam and Thailand, they mostly have stalls similar to your classic hot dog stand in New York but full of homemade fermented sausages or spiced peanuts. In Malaysia or Singapore, you'll see more hawker centers. Hawker centers are semi-enclosed buildings housing rows and rows of small food stalls that serve a variety of savory food and desserts, almost always prepared to order. The food is often a bit more elaborate and includes larger noodle dishes. Hawker stalls resemble walk-in closets, cluttered with cooking equipment and ingredients, but don't let their small size fool you: these cramped kitchens are putting out some of the best food in the entire world. I am constantly amazed each time I am there.

In the Philippines, there are more sit-down spots similar to what the United States calls fast casual, but even those are full of snacks like the first recipe in this chapter—irresistible Ten-Spice Chicharron (page 62).

TEN-SPICE CHICHARRON

YIELDS: ABOUT 50 PIECES

One 2-pound piece of pork skin

Kosher salt

6 cups canola oil

Ten-Spice Mix (page 39)

Coconut vinegar, for serving

In the Philippines, people eat these golden-brown fried pigskin snacks dipped in coconut vinegar and use them as a crunchy topping for Pancit Palabok (page 163). In Malaysia and Thailand, chicharrones are used as a garnish. I serve Thai Herbal Sausage (page 73) with these chicharrones, minus the ten-spice mix (I just add more salt at the end). But no matter how you eat them, you will agree that they are delicious. Scraping off as much fat as possible after boiling and chilling the pork skin will produce lighter, puffier, less greasy chicharron.

1. Preheat the oven to 300 degrees F.

2. Put the pork in a large pot, cover with cold water by 2 inches, and add 1 tablespoon of kosher salt. Cover and cook until the skin is fork-tender, about 2 hours.

3. Remove the skin from the water, pat dry with paper towels, and put on a large rimmed baking sheet, skin-side up. Refrigerate, uncovered, until cold, at least 8 hours and up to 24 hours. Once the skin is cold, scrape off as much of the fat as possible using a knife; discard the fat.

4. Cut the skin into 1½ x 1½-inch pieces and lay them on a large rimmed baking sheet, making sure not to overlap the pieces. Place in a dehydrator set at 155 degrees F or in your oven set to its lowest setting (which can be between 150 and 170 degrees F). Allow the skin to "cook" for 12 hours (the skin will look dry and shiny and will be crisp). Remove the skin from the dehydrator or oven. At this point, you can fry the pieces if you wish to eat them immediately, or store in an airtight container and refrigerate.

5. Heat the oil in a large wok or high-sided sauté pan until it registers 375 degrees F on a deep-fry thermometer. Line a rimmed baking sheet with several layers of paper towels.

6. Fry the chicharrones in batches (making sure not to overcrowd the pot) and cook until golden brown, 3 to 5 minutes. Transfer (using a spider) to the prepared baking sheet and let drain for 20 seconds. Transfer the pieces to a large bowl and season with the spice mixture while still hot. Serve with coconut vinegar on the side for dipping.

THAI ROASTED PEANUTS

YIELDS: ABOUT 5 CUPS

4 cups unsalted peanuts

½ cup packed unsweetened shredded coconut

10 fresh kaffir lime leaves, thinly sliced

1 large lemongrass stalk, trimmed (see page 28), and sliced paper thin on a mandolin

¼ teaspoon dried Thai chili flakes

1 teaspoon kosher salt

⅛ teaspoon garlic powder

2 tablespoons Thai sweet chili sauce

I love the familiar Thai flavors of coconut, kaffir, lemongrass, and chili in this recipe. You will find roasted peanuts all over the country freshly made all day on the streets and served hot in bags.

1. Preheat the oven to 350 degrees F. Line a rimmed baking sheet with parchment or a silpat.

2. Combine the peanuts, coconut, kaffir, lemongrass, chili flakes, salt, garlic powder, and chili sauce in a bowl and mix until combined.

3. Spread the mixture onto the prepared baking sheet and bake, turning several times so that the coconut doesn't burn, about 10 minutes. Let cool before serving. Store in a container with tight-fitting lid in a cool, dark place for up to 1 week.

VIETNAMESE RICE CAKES WITH EGGS

SERVES: 4 TO 6

RICE CAKES

2 cups rice flour

3 tablespoons tapioca starch

1 tablespoon kosher salt

1 tablespoon granulated sugar

1 tablespoon canola oil

DIPPING SAUCE

½ cup Kikkoman low-sodium soy sauce

¼ cup apple cider vinegar

2 teaspoons granulated sugar

Freshly squeezed juice of 1 lime

TO SERVE

¼ cup canola oil

1 garlic clove, finely chopped

2 large eggs, whisked until smooth

½ teaspoon finely diced red Thai chili

¼ cup Pickled Daikon and Carrots (page 55)

This is another famous street food in Vietnam (referred to as Bot Chien). For some reason, this dish is not often found in the States so if you want to make a really unique dish that you won't find outside of Vietnam, try this.

1. Make the rice cakes: Whisk together the flour, starch, salt, and sugar in a large bowl until combined. Whisk in 3 cups of water and the oil and continue whisking until smooth.

2. Pour the mixture into a large saucepan and cook over low heat, whisking constantly so that the bottom doesn't burn, until thickened, about 5 minutes. Remove from the heat and let cool for 5 minutes, whisking a few times.

3. Transfer the mixture to a blender in batches and blend until smooth. Transfer to a medium bowl.

4. Fill a pot with 2 inches of water. Make sure your steamer basket fits snugly in (or over) the pot and isn't in danger of tipping over. Also make sure the bottom layer of food sits above the water line and doesn't get submerged. A wok is traditionally used, but I find a shallow skillet works just as well. Add about 2 inches of water to the pan and bring it to a simmer over medium heat.

5. Place the prepared pan inside. Scrape the rice cake mixture into it, making sure to flatten the top evenly. Put the steamer basket over the simmering water and top with the lid. Steam until firm and a toothpick inserted into the center comes out clean, 35 to 45 minutes. Keep an eye on the water level and add more if the pot starts to go dry. Once cool, cut the cooked mixture into 2-inch cubes.

6. Make the dipping sauce: Whisk together the soy sauce, vinegar, sugar, and lime juice in a medium bowl. Let sit at room temperature while you prepare the dish.

7. Line a rimmed baking sheet with several layers of paper towels. Heat 1 tablespoon of the oil in a large nonstick sauté pan and pan-fry the rice cake cubes, in batches, until golden brown and crispy. Transfer to the prepared baking sheet.

8. Heat the remaining ¼ cup oil in a nonstick sauté pan and cook the garlic. Add the eggs, then the cubes of rice cake, and cook until the eggs are no longer wet.

9. Garnish with cilantro leaves and Thai chili and serve with dipping sauce and pickled daikon and carrots.

BROKEN MUSSEL PANCAKE

YIELDS: 1 LARGE PANCAKE
SERVES: 1 TO 2

15 PEI mussels in shells or oysters, such as kumamotos, shucked and patted dry

3 tablespoons tapioca flour

1 tablespoon rice flour

1 tablespoon limestone water (see Note)

1 tablespoon soy sauce

⅛ teaspoon freshly ground white pepper

1 scallion (white and green parts), thinly sliced

½ cup canola oil

1 large egg, beaten until light and fluffy

3 garlic cloves, finely chopped

½ cup bean sprouts

2 tablespoons Shark Brand sriracha

1 tablespoon sweet chili sauce

This crispy/chewy pancake from Thailand (referred to as Hoi Tod) is a small dish or snack food that is enjoyed all day long, and it is also one of my favorite things to eat when I visit. The pancake is made in a flat wok, which means that it is almost always served at a stall that also serves Pad Thai (page 161), another Thai food made on a flat wok. The broken mussel pancake is greasy by nature, which makes it great served with a beer or eaten when you are hungover. Limestone water is authentic to this dish and adds an extra crispness to the pancake.

1. If you are using mussels: Bring 2 cups of water to a boil in a large pot, add the mussels, cover the pot, and cook, shaking the pan a few times until the shells just begin to open, about 20 seconds. Drain in a colander, immediately rinse with cold water to stop the cooking, and remove the mussels from the shell. Drain on paper towels.

2. Whisk together the flours, 5 tablespoons of cold water, the limestone water, soy sauce, and white pepper in a large bowl until just smooth; if too thick, add more water, 1 teaspoon at a time. Fold in the mussels and scallion.

3. Heat the oil in a large seasoned cast-iron pan (or nonstick pan) until the oil begins to shimmer. Add the pancake batter and cook without touching until the bottom begins to set, 30 to 45 seconds. Pour the beaten egg over the top, making sure to fill in any spots that the pancake batter did not fill. Cook for 60 seconds longer, then flip the pancake (it is okay if it breaks) and cook the other side until lightly golden brown and crispy, about 2 minutes longer. Remove the pancake to a serving plate.

4. Add the garlic to the pan and cook until fragrant, about 20 seconds. Stir in the bean sprouts and cook until just heated through, about 30 seconds longer. Top the pancake with the bean sprouts. Mix together the sriracha and chili sauce in a small bowl and serve alongside the pancake.

Note:

To make limestone water, empty the contents of a small container of pink limestone, available from Thai and Southeast Asian markets, into a 2-quart jar and fill with water. Cover the jar tightly with a lid and shake to dissolve the limestone. Let stand 1 to 1½ hours, until the water has almost cleared. Store the mixture in the refrigerator for up to 1 month. You can also substitute 1 cup seltzer water mixed with 2 teaspoons of baking soda.

LUMPIA

YIELDS: 15

4 ounces ground beef

8 ounces ground pork

6 garlic cloves, finely chopped

2 tablespoons finely chopped fresh ginger

½ cup water chestnuts, drained, rinsed, drained again, and cut into small dice

¼ cup finely diced carrots

½ small Spanish onion, finely diced

3 tablespoons low-sodium soy sauce

¾ teaspoon toasted sesame oil

1 teaspoon kosher salt

½ teaspoon freshly ground black pepper

½ teaspoon Thai chili flakes

1 medium scallion, thinly sliced

15 spring roll wrappers (I prefer Wei-Chan), cut in half crosswise on the diagonal

1 large egg whisked with 1 tablespoon water

1 quart peanut or vegetable oil

1½ cups store-bought sweet chili sauce (page 22)

In the Philippines, we have two kinds of spring rolls or, as we call them, lumpia—fresh and fried. The fresh version has an almost crepe-like wrapper. While those are delicious, it's the fried version, Lumpia Shanghai, that always puts a smile on my face. My parents say that's been true since I was a toddler. I can't wait to introduce my son to these delicious snacks as well, and given that they're a staple at every Filipino party, holiday, and birthday, I don't think that will take long. This roll can be filled with whatever you like: beef, pork, or vegetables. The combination in this recipe is my favorite.

1. Put the beef and pork in a large bowl and gently mix to combine.

2. Add the garlic, ginger, water chestnuts, carrot, onion, soy sauce, sesame oil, salt, pepper, chili flakes, and scallion and mix until combined.

3. Line a baking sheet with parchment. Take half of a wrapper and place it on your work surface so that a point is facing you. Place about 2 heaping tablespoons of the filling on the wrapper and spread it out to the edges. Turn up the bottom corner and roll upward. Fold in the left and right corners, making sure the filling is nicely packed, with no air pockets. Continue rolling. Dip your finger in the egg wash, pat it on the remaining corner, and finish rolling the lumpia, sealing the edge. The lumpia should be about ½ inch in diameter. Put the lumpia on the baking sheet. The lumpia can be made to this point and refrigerated, covered with a damp towel, for up to 8 hours or frozen in an airtight container for 2 to 3 weeks.

4. Heat the oil in a wok or high-sided sauté pan over medium heat until it reaches 350 degrees F on a deep-fry thermometer. Line another baking sheet with paper towels. Fry the lumpia in batches of four to six, until golden brown and crispy and the meat is cooked through, for a total of 4 minutes for fresh lumpia and 6 minutes for frozen. Remove with a slotted spoon to the prepared baking sheet. Serve with the sweet chili sauce on the side.

Note:

I find that it helps to separate the wrappers in advance; cover them with a damp paper towel to prevent them from drying out.

CHICKEN SATAY SKEWERS

SERVES: 4 TO 6

¾ cup unsweetened coconut milk

2 heaping tablespoons Red Curry Paste (page 183) or Maesri brand (see page 20)

1 tablespoon Squid Brand fish sauce

1 tablespoon (packed) light brown sugar

1 teaspoon kosher salt

1 teaspoon ground turmeric

2 pounds skinless, boneless chicken thighs, cut into 1-inch pieces

Thirty 8-inch wooden bamboo skewers, soaked in water for at least 30 minutes before use

Canola oil

Peanut Sauce (page 48), for serving

Rice, for serving

Many different countries throughout Southeast Asia have their own version of chicken satay. My recipe is more Thai influenced with its use of coconut milk, fish sauce, and spicy red curry paste. This is a street snack you would find on the side of the road at a street vendor, but you can bring it into your own home and serve it as an addictive appetizer or hors d'oeuvre for a party. You can use canned curry paste if you are short on time. If you prefer your satay spicier, feel free to kick it up a notch and add more chilies to the marinade or sauce. If you can marinate your chicken overnight or even up to 24 hours, the satay will taste even better.

1. Whisk together the coconut milk, curry paste, fish sauce, brown sugar, salt, and turmeric in a large bowl until smooth. Add the chicken and toss well to coat. Cover and refrigerate for at least at least 8 hours and up to 24 hours.

2. Remove the chicken from the marinade and lightly blot with paper towels to remove some of the marinade. Thread each piece of chicken onto a skewer, using three-quarters of the skewer, leaving the bottom half empty so the person has something to hold on to when eating.

3. Preheat the grill to high or a grill pan over high heat. Put the skewers on a baking sheet and drizzle with some of the oil. Grill until cooked through and charred on both sides, about 5 minutes per side. Transfer to a platter and serve with the peanut sauce on the side. Serve with rice of your choice.

FILIPINO BBQ SKEWERS

SERVES: 4 TO 6

½ cup light soy sauce

¼ cup banana ketchup
(see page 20)

¼ cup lemon-lime soda,
such as Sprite

3 tablespoons freshly squeezed
lemon juice

5 garlic cloves, finely chopped

2 teaspoons (packed) light
brown sugar

1 tablespoon finely grated
fresh ginger

¼ teaspoon kosher salt

1½ pounds skinless, boneless
chicken thighs, cut into
1½-inch cubes

Sixteen to twenty 6-inch wooden
bamboo skewers, soaked in water
for at least 30 minutes before use

Canola oil

2 scallions, thinly sliced

¼ cup Crispy Garlic (see page 43)

This is a very popular snack or street food that you will find in the Philippines. The marinade calls for lemon-lime soda because that is what they use in the Philippines. I'm not sure why this ingredient became authentic to the recipe, but my guess is because the acid in soda breaks down the protein in the meat to make it more tender, and the sugar caramelizes it to make it sweeter. If you can't find banana ketchup (also known as banana sauce), just use regular ketchup. Soaking the bamboo skewers for at least 30 minutes in water before using will prevent them from burning on the grill.

1. Combine the soy sauce, ketchup, soda, lemon juice, garlic, brown sugar, ginger, and salt in a large bowl and whisk until smooth. Remove ⅓ cup of the marinade, transfer it to a small bowl, cover, refrigerate, and reserve for grilling.

2. Add the chicken to the remaining marinade and mix until each piece is completely coated. Cover and refrigerate for at least 4 hours and up to 24 hours.

3. Heat a grill to high or a grill pan over high heat. Remove the chicken from the marinade. Thread 3 pieces of the chicken tightly onto each prepared skewer. Drizzle the skewers with a bit of canola oil and grill until charred on both sides and just cooked through, about 4 minutes per side, brushing with the reserved sauce during the last few minutes. Transfer to a platter and garnish with the scallions and crispy garlic.

TOKWAT BABOY

SERVES: 4 TO 6

½ cup coconut vinegar

½ cup Lee Kum Kee Premium Soy Sauce

¼ cup Kikkoman light soy sauce

2 tablespoons palm sugar

1 tablespoon finely diced fresh ginger

Freshly squeezed juice of 1 lime

1 fresh red Thai chili, thinly sliced

⅛ teaspoon five-spice powder

⅛ teaspoon freshly ground black pepper

6 pig ears (about 1½ pounds) or 2 pounds pork belly

2 tablespoons kosher salt

1 quart canola oil

1 cup rice flour

1 pound extra-firm tofu, patted dry and cut into 1-inch dice

1 small red onion, halved and thinly sliced

2 large scallions (white and green parts), thinly sliced

½ cup fresh cilantro leaves

This Filipino snack food is referred to as pulutan, which means anything that goes well with beer or cocktails. Pig ears are not meaty and don't really have a porky flavor, so they take on the flavor of the sauce. They get crispy like chicharron, but they are also chewy. If you can't find pig ears or just don't want to make them, crispy pork belly (my recipe for Braised Pork Belly Adobo is on page 233) will work just fine.

1. Mix together the vinegar, soy sauces, palm sugar, ginger, lime juice, chili, five-spice powder, and pepper in a medium bowl and whisk until the sugar has dissolved. Let rest at room temperature while you prepare the rest of the dish. The sauce can be made 2 days in advance and stored, covered, in the refrigerator.

2. Rinse the pig ears well in cold, salted water and scrape off any excess hair with a knife, if needed. Put the ears in a large pot, cover with cold water by 2 inches, add the salt, and bring the water to a boil over high heat. Reduce the heat to medium-low and cook, covered, for about 2 hours, until tender. Check the water level after 1 hour and add more just to cover, if needed. Drain the ears and let cool. Pat dry with paper towels and slice each ear into thin slices.

3. Heat the oil in a wok or high-sided sauté pan over medium heat until it reaches a temperature of 350 degrees F. Line a rimmed baking sheet with several layers of paper towels.

4. Put the rice flour into a shallow bowl, dredge the pig ear slices, and tap off any excess flour. Fry the slices, in batches, for about 4 minutes, until golden brown and crispy. Transfer to the lined baking sheet.

5. After frying the last batch of the ears, bring the temperature of the oil back up to 350 degrees F. Fry the tofu, in batches, until golden brown. Remove with a slotted spoon to the prepared baking sheet.

6. Combine the pig ear slices, tofu, red onion, scallions, and cilantro in a large bowl. Add enough of the dressing to lightly coat the ears and tofu but not enough to make them soggy. Serve on plates with more dressing on the side, if desired.

FERMENTED SAUSAGE

YIELDS: 2 POUNDS

15 garlic cloves, minced

⅓ cup chopped cilantro root or cilantro stems

1½ tablespoons kosher salt

1¼ tablespoons sugar

¼ teaspoon white pepper

¼ teaspoon pink curing salt

2 pounds coarsely ground pork belly

1 cup cooked Steamed Jasmine Rice (see page 150), cooled

One 4-ounce package natural hog casings, rinsed and dried (see Note)

If you love Thai food and have eaten this sausage (Sai Krok Isan) on the streets in Thailand, this recipe is for you. If you haven't, be prepared to taste a sausage with a unique sour taste (thanks to the fermentation process), which may seem off-putting at first, but believe me, it is delicious. In Thailand, the sausage is served on a plate with cabbage and pieces of ginger on the side, and you simply take a bite of the sausage, then a bite of the cabbage, then a bite of the ginger. To make it easier to eat and more appropriate for a party, you can wrap pieces of the sausage in a cabbage leaf with a slice of ginger. It takes a bit of work to make it, and you need the proper space and environment, but take my word, it's worth it to try it at least once!

1. Using a mortar and pestle or food processor, combine the garlic, cilantro root, salt, sugar, white pepper, and curing salt and pound or process to a smooth paste.

2. Put the pork in a large bowl, add the garlic paste, and mix well to combine. Fold in the rice.

3. Using a stand mixer with the large sausage maker attachment or a regular sausage stuffer, stuff the sausage according to the manufacturer's directions and make links that are 3 inches in length.

4. Hang the sausage in a warm space (about 85 degrees F), uncovered, for 5 days with trays directly underneath to catch any of the moisture that will drip from it.

5. Grill or fry the sausage and serve with cabbage cups, plain julienned ginger, freshly sliced green Thai chili, and unsalted roasted peanuts.

Note:

To prepare casings for stuffing, soak them in cold water with a few teaspoons of white vinegar added for 30 to 45 minutes to remove excess salt and to soften them. Rinse several times by running cold water through the entire length of casing by wrapping an open end of the casing around a faucet and turning on the water—like a water balloon. Store the casings in a tightly sealed container in the refrigerator (not the freezer) for up to 1 year.

Natural hog casings can be purchased in Asian markets and online at Amazon in 4- and 8-ounce packages.

THAI HERBAL SAUSAGE

**YIELDS: ABOUT 5 POUNDS,
10 TO 12 SERVINGS**

¼ cup plus 1 tablespoon Red Curry Paste (page 183) or Maesri brand (see page 20)

1½ teaspoons Thai Curry Powder (page 39)

2 tablespoons Red Boat fish sauce

¼ cup chopped fresh cilantro leaves

1 large stalk finely chopped fresh lemongrass

10 finely chopped fresh kaffir lime leaves

2 teaspoons kosher salt

1 teaspoon granulated sugar

¾ teaspoon freshly ground black pepper

½ teaspoon Thai chili flakes

3 pounds pork shoulder, coarsely ground

12 ounces boneless pork belly, ground

One 4-ounce package natural hog casings, rinsed and dried (see Note)

Canola oil

Green Chili Relish (page 49)

Chicharron (page 62)

Sticky Rice (page 151)

This is a straight-up sausage that needs no fermenting. I love this unique sausage because of the complexity of the flavors. When was the last time that you had sausage flavored with curry powder, curry paste, lemongrass, kaffir leaves, and cilantro? There is no sausage like this anywhere. Ideally this sausage should be served with Sticky Rice (page 151), Green Chili Relish (page 49), and plain salted chicharron.

1. Whisk together the curry paste, curry powder, fish sauce, cilantro, lemongrass, kaffir, salt, sugar, pepper, and chili flakes in a large bowl until smooth. Add the pork and mix gently to combine.

2. Using a stand mixer with the large sausage maker attachment or a regular sausage stuffer, stuff the sausage according to the manufacturer's directions and make links that are 3 inches in length.

3. Preheat the grill to high or grill pan over high heat or heat a few tablespoons of canola oil in a high-sided sauté pan until the oil begins to shimmer. If using a grill or grill pan, brush the sausages with canola oil and grill for 8 to 12 minutes, until golden brown and charred on both sides and just cooked through. If pan-frying, cook for 8 to 12 minutes, until golden brown on both sides and just cooked through

4. Serve with green chili relish, chicharron, and sticky rice.

Note:

Natural hog casings can be purchased in Asian markets and online at Amazon in 4- and 8-ounce packages.

To prepare casings for stuffing, soak them in cold water with a few teaspoons of white vinegar added for 30 to 45 minutes to remove excess salt and to soften them. Rinse several times by running cold water through the entire length of casing by wrapping an open end of the casing around a faucet and turning on the water—like a water balloon. Store the casings in a tightly sealed container in the refrigerator (not the freezer) for up to 1 year.

SUMMER ROLLS WITH JICAMA, CHINESE SAUSAGE, AND EGG

YIELDS: 8 TO 10 ROLLS

¼ cup canola oil

1½ cups thinly sliced jicama

1 cup thinly sliced carrots

Kosher salt

2 garlic cloves, finely chopped

3 Chinese sausages, peeled and cut in half lengthwise

2 large eggs

1 package rice paper (bánh tráng)

½ cup fresh mint leaves, torn

½ cup fresh cilantro leaves

Peanut Sauce (page 48)

In Vietnam, you'll typically find summer rolls that contain shrimp, noodles, and herbs. So, when I came across this variation while traveling there, I was intrigued and quickly ordered one. Even though I know that you can really put anything into a summer roll, I just never thought to use sausage. This is like a summer roll on steroids—so much flavor and texture and that faint flavor of my favorite spice, five-spice, from the prepared Chinese sausages. My favorite brand of Chinese sausage (also known as lap xurong) is Kam Yen Jan and can be purchased at Asian markets or online.

1. Heat 2 tablespoons of the oil in a large nonstick sauté pan over high heat until the oil begins to shimmer. Add the jicama and carrots, season with a bit of salt, and cook until crisp-tender, about 4 minutes. Stir in the garlic and cook for 1 minute longer. Transfer to a large plate to cool.

2. Line a large plate with paper towels. Heat 1 tablespoon of the oil in the same pan over high heat until the oil begins to shimmer. Add the sausages and cook until lightly golden brown and just heated through. Remove with a slotted spoon to the plate lined with paper towels. Wipe the pan with paper towels.

3. Crack the eggs into a medium bowl, season with a pinch of salt, and whisk until light and fluffy. Return the pan to medium-low heat, add the remaining 1 tablespoon of the oil and half of the egg mixture in an even layer, and cook for about a minute, until the bottom is set. Turn the omelet over and continue for 1 more minute, until just cooked through. The eggs should have no color and remain pale. Slide the omelet out onto a cutting board and let cool for 3 minutes. Repeat with the remaining oil and egg. Roll each omelet tightly into a log and cut crosswise into thin strips. Set aside.

4. Wet a clean dish towel with hot water, wring it out, and rub each rice paper one at a time so that it becomes pliable (many people tell you to dunk the paper directly in water, but I don't think that is necessary and it only results in a wet wrapper). Place about ¼ cup of the jicama-carrot mixture, some of the egg ribbons, mint, cilantro, and Chinese sausage along the bottom third of the wrapper. Roll the wrapper up once, fold in the sides, and then roll tightly shut. Cut in half and serve with peanut sauce.

MALAYSIAN BEEF CURRY PUFFS

YIELDS: ABOUT 15

MALAYSIAN MEAT CURRY POWDER

2 tablespoons coriander seeds

2 tablespoons cumin seeds

1 teaspoon whole black peppercorns

1 teaspoon fennel seeds

1 teaspoon ground turmeric

3 whole cloves

2 whole cardamom pods

1 small cinnamon stick

2½ tablespoons Kashmiri chili powder (see headnote)

Every Southeast Asian country has a version of this handheld snack. Even though they look exactly like empanadas, it is the dough in these Malaysian puffs that sets them apart. The classic variation, known as karipap pusing (spiral curry puffs), is made with two separate doughs that are combined to create an incredibly golden brown turnover that is flaky, crispy, and beautiful but complicated to make. I created a dough that is easier and just as delicious. The fillings can be made with any meat or vegetable. And the relish on the side brings a fresh accent.

Kashmiri chili is common in Malaysian cooking. If you can't find it, you can substitute 3 parts sweet paprika to 1 part cayenne.

1. Make the curry powder: Combine the coriander, cumin, peppercorns, fennel, turmeric, cloves, cardamom, and cinnamon stick in a medium sauté pan over medium heat and cook, mixing constantly, for about 2 minutes, until fragrant. Transfer to a plate and let cool for 5 minutes.

2. Put the spice mixture into a coffee grinder and grind to a fine powder. Mix in the chili powder. Transfer to a container with a tight-fitting lid. The spice mixture will last for 6 months stored in a cool, dark place.

3. Make the dough: Combine the flour, salt, and butter in the bowl of a food processor and process for about 8 pulses, until the mixture resembles coarse meal. Add ¼ cup of the water and pulse a few times, then add more water until the dough just comes together and forms a ball.

4. Transfer the dough to a lightly floured surface and knead until soft. Form into a disc, wrap in plastic, and refrigerate for at least 30 minutes and up to 2 days.

5. Make the filling: Line a plate with paper towels. Heat 2 tablespoons of the canola oil in a large sauté pan over medium-low heat until it begins to shimmer. Stir in the potatoes, cover, and cook, stirring occasionally, for about 7 minutes, until soft but no color is achieved. Transfer the potatoes with a slotted spoon to the paper towel–lined plate.

6. Return the pan to the stove, raise the heat to high, add the remaining 1 tablespoon canola oil, and heat until it begins to shimmer. Add the onion and cook for about 5 minutes, until soft. Add the beef and garlic and cook, stirring occasionally, for about 8 minutes, until the meat is golden brown and the juices have evaporated.

RECIPE AND INGREDIENTS CONTINUE

DOUGH

2 cups all-purpose flour, plus more to dust the work surface

½ teaspoon kosher salt

1 cup (2 sticks) cold unsalted butter, cut into small pieces

½ cup ice water

BEEF FILLING

3 tablespoons canola oil

½ to ¾ small Russet potato, peeled and cut into ¼-inch dice (should yield 1 cup)

1 small Spanish onion, diced

½ pound ground chuck 80/20

2 garlic cloves, finely chopped

1 tablespoon Malaysian Meat Curry Powder

2 tablespoons Squid Brand fish sauce

1 tablespoon granulated sugar

¼ teaspoon Thai chili flakes

6 fresh curry leaves, thinly sliced

2 tablespoons freshly squeezed lime juice (1 to 2 limes)

¼ cup finely chopped fresh cilantro

TO SERVE

Canola oil

1 batch Cucumber Relish (page 53)

7. Stir in the potatoes, curry powder, fish sauce, sugar, chili flakes, and curry leaves and cook for 3 more minutes, until the flavors meld, adding a few splashes of water if the mixture becomes too dry. Remove from the heat and stir in the lime juice and cilantro. Transfer to a large plate or rimmed baking pan and let cool completely before stuffing the curry puffs. This will yield about 2 cups of filling. You will need about 1¾ cups to fill the puffs. Eat the remaining filling or store tightly covered in the refrigerator for 2 days and stir it into scrambled eggs.

8. Remove the dough from the refrigerator and divide it in half. Wrap the other half and return it to the refrigerator. Lightly flour a surface, put the dough on top, and lightly flour the top. Roll out the dough into a large circle ⅛ inch thick. Cut out 4½-inch circles using a ring cutter or ramekin (should get 7 circles without rerolling).

9. Transfer the circles to a baking sheet lined with parchment paper and refrigerate for about 15 minutes, until chilled. Repeat with the remaining dough and transfer those circles to another baking sheet lined with parchment and chill in the refrigerator for 15 minutes.

10. Lightly flour a surface again and gently roll out one circle at a time, making sure that each is 4½ inches wide. Place a circle of dough in your palm and place 2 tablespoons of the meat filling in the center. Fold the dough into a semicircle and seal by pressing and pleating the edges together. Return the puffs to the parchment paper–lined baking sheet and chill in the refrigerator until firm, at least 15 minutes and up to 24 hours.

11. Fry the curry puffs: Heat 3 inches of oil in a large wok or high-sided sauté pan until it reaches 350 degrees F on a deep-fry thermometer. Line a rimmed baking sheet with several layers of paper towels.

12. Fry the puffs in batches for about 5 minutes, until golden brown. Remove using a spider and let drain on the prepared baking sheet. Repeat with the remaining dough. Serve with the cucumber relish on the side.

13. Freeze curry puffs separately and only pack them together once they are fully frozen to prevent them from sticking together.

LOR BAK

YIELDS: 20

3 tablespoons sweet soy sauce

2 teaspoons soy sauce

2 teaspoons canola oil

1 teaspoon granulated sugar

1 teaspoon mushroom powder
(see Note)

1 teaspoon toasted sesame oil

¼ teaspoon white pepper

¼ teaspoon five-spice powder

1 small shallot, finely diced

2 garlic cloves, finely chopped

¾ pound ground pork 80/20

⅓ cup finely diced water chestnuts

¼ cup finely chopped scallion

¼ cup finely chopped fresh cilantro
leaves

1 tablespoon cornstarch

20 sheets tofu skin

1 quart canola oil

This finger food from Malaysia is quite similar to a spring roll except that the wrapper is made from tofu skin and not wheat flour, something that I have not seen elsewhere. The tofu skin gives the roll an airier texture. You will see long rolls of lor bak at the hawker stalls in Penang with all kinds of different fillings. This is my favorite. I love adding water chestnuts to fillings for added crunch and texture.

1. Mix together the soy sauces, oil, sugar, mushroom powder, sesame oil, white pepper, five-spice powder, shallot, and garlic in a large bowl until combined. Add the pork, water chestnuts, scallion, and cilantro and mix until just combined. Cover and refrigerate for at least 1 hour to allow the flavors to meld.

2. Whisk together the cornstarch and 2 tablespoons of water in a small bowl until smooth, to make a slurry.

3. Lay one sheet of tofu skin on a flat surface. Lightly dab it with some water to soften it. Spoon 2 scant tablespoons of the mixture onto the center of the sheet, fold in the two sides, and roll up tightly. Seal the edges with the cornstarch slurry. Store any leftover filling, tightly covered, in the refrigerator and stir it into eggs for an omelet or scrambled eggs for breakfast.

4. Line a rimmed baking sheet with several layers of paper towels. Heat the oil in a deep fryer or a Dutch oven over medium heat until it reaches 350 degrees F. Fry the rolls in batches, turning once, for 3 to 5 minutes, until golden brown, crispy, and cooked through. Drain on the prepared baking sheet. Let cool slightly, then cut each roll into several pieces and serve.

Note:

Mushroom powder can be found in Asian markets. Alternately, you can grind dried shiitake mushroom in a coffee grinder. Store the remaining powder in a container with a tight-fitting lid.

RED CURRY FISH CAKES

YIELDS: 12 TO 15

12 ounces red snapper or tilapia fillet

3 ice cubes

3 tablespoons Red Curry Paste (page 183) or Maesri brand (see page 20)

1 large egg

2 tablespoons Red Boat fish sauce

2 teaspoons granulated sugar

2 tablespoons fresh kaffir lime leaves (about 4), finely chopped

2 long beans or 5 green beans, thinly sliced

¼ cup chopped fresh Thai basil leaves

½ cup canola oil

Cucumber Relish (page 53) or sweet chili sauce

This is the first Thai dish (other than Pad Thai) that I learned to make! I love these tiny pop-in-your-mouth cakes full of flavor and crunch. They are slightly spicy from the red curry paste and they have this springy texture that I love. The cucumber relish brightens up the dish. You will find them all over the streets in Thailand. Typically, the cakes are deep-fried, but pan-frying them yields just as good a texture and is less messy. If you can't find snapper or aren't a fan, tilapia works really well, too.

1. Thirty minutes before preparing the recipe, place the bowl and blade of the food processor in the freezer. Fifteen minutes before preparing the recipe, put the fish on a plate and place in the freezer.

2. Put the ice cubes in the bowl of a food processor and process to a fine powder. Add the snapper, curry paste, egg, fish sauce, and sugar and process for about 2 minutes, until the mixture is totally smooth and becomes thick and springy, stopping a few times to scrape down the sides of the bowl.

3. Scrape the mixture into a large bowl and fold in the kaffir leaves, long beans, and basil.

4. Heat the oil in a large nonstick or cast-iron pan over high heat until the oil begins to shimmer. Line a baking sheet with paper towels.

5. Put 2 tablespoons of the paste in the pan and flatten using a spatula. Fry for about 4 minutes per side, until golden brown on both sides and just cooked through. Serve with cucumber relish or sweet chili sauce on the side.

THAI FRIED CHICKEN

SERVES: 4

MARINADE

3 pounds chicken (combined, drumsticks and thighs, bone in and skin on)

5 garlic cloves, peeled

1 teaspoon coriander seeds

1 teaspoon whole white peppercorns

¼ cup chopped fresh cilantro root or cilantro stems

2 tablespoons Squid Brand fish sauce

2 tablespoons oyster sauce

2 teaspoons kosher salt

1 teaspoon granulated sugar

1 tablespoon MSG

FRYING

2½ cups rice flour

1 teaspoon kosher salt

1 teaspoon MSG

1 cup limestone water (see page 65)

6 cups canola oil

3 fresh pandan leaves (see page 31)

Crispy Fried Shallots (page 52)

Store-bought sweet chili sauce

I was taught to make Thai fried chicken years ago by a random street food vendor on the streets of Bangkok. I wish that I remembered his name so I could give him a shout-out! But no worries, just because I don't remember his name doesn't mean that I don't remember all of his secrets.

Thai Fried Chicken is all about the crispness. Unlike Western-style fried chicken, where the coating is thick and tasty, but the chicken beneath can be bland, Thai Fried Chicken features a crisp coating *and* deeply flavored meat. Scoring the chicken before applying the marinade paste allows the flavor to penetrate down to the bone (secret #1). Also, using limestone water (see page 65) in the batter is the way to get teeth-shattering crisp chicken that will stay that way for a while (secret #2). You can find pink limestone online, or substitute seltzer mixed with baking soda instead. The seltzer–baking soda option will not be as crisp, but it will still be delicious. A natural mineral water made with pink limestone is widely used in batters for fried foods and pastries as a key ingredient that promotes crispiness.

1. Marinate the chicken: Pat the chicken dry with paper towels. Using a sharp knife, make shallow parallel cuts in one direction, about ½ inch apart. Rotate the chicken and make another set of cuts at angles to the first set, crossing at about 45 degrees to make a crosshatch pattern.

2. Pound the garlic, coriander, white peppercorns, cilantro, fish sauce, oyster sauce, salt, sugar, and MSG in a mortar and pestle until it becomes a smooth paste, or combine all of the ingredients in the bowl of a food processor and process until smooth.

3. Rub some of the marinade onto each piece of chicken, making sure to cover the entire piece. Place the chicken on a baking rack set over a baking sheet and refrigerate, uncovered, for at least 6 hours and up to 24 hours. Remove the chicken from the refrigerator 1 hour before frying to take the chill off. Doing this will keep the coating from getting too dark before the chicken is cooked through.

4. Fry the chicken: Whisk ½ cup of the rice flour, the salt, and the MSG together. Slowly whisk in the limestone water and continue to whisk until smooth.

RECIPE CONTINUES

5. Put the remaining 2 cups rice flour in a large baking dish.

6. Heat the oil in a large wok or high-sided sauté pan until it reaches 350 degrees F. Once it reaches temperature, add the pandan leaves.

7. While the oil is heating, dip each piece of chicken into the batter, making sure to evenly coat it. Immediately dredge in the flour and shake off any excess. Put on a baking rack set over a baking sheet and repeat with the remaining chicken. Let sit at room temperature for 15 minutes.

8. Line another baking sheet with paper towels. Fry the chicken in batches, turning a few times, for about 12 minutes, until it is golden brown on both sides and just cooked through. Remove with a spider to the baking sheet. Repeat with the remaining chicken. Serve on a platter, topped with crispy fried shallots and sweet chili sauce on the side.

MOO PING

2 garlic cloves

¼ cup packed chopped fresh cilantro root or cilantro stems

One 15-ounce can Chaokoh coconut milk, well stirred

2 tablespoons plus 1 tablespoon palm sugar

2 tablespoons Squid Brand fish sauce

2 tablespoons soy sauce

1 tablespoon oyster sauce

¼ cup chopped fresh cilantro root or cilantro stems

¼ teaspoon white pepper

½ teaspoon baking soda

2 pounds pork shoulder, excess fat trimmed and cut across the grain into ½-inch slices

Thirty 6-inch wooden bamboo skewers (see Note)

Canola oil

Sticky Rice (page 151)

Isaan Sauce (page 46)

Note:

Soaking the skewers in cold water for 30 minutes before using will prevent them from burning on the grill.

Moo means "pork" and *ping* means "skewer" in Thai, and so here you have the quintessential recipe for pork skewers. The marinade is very traditional for skewered meats in Thailand—the sweet of the coconut milk and sugar caramelize when grilled, giving that all-important texture, while oyster sauce and fish sauce add color and umami.

I still remember the first time I had one of these pork skewers on my first trip to Thailand. I was told by the locals that there's only one place to get the best Moo Ping—from a guy known as the Moo Ping King on Silom Street in Bangkok. Moo Ping King's late-night stall is open from 11:00 p.m. to 3:00 a.m. and there's always has a line of drunk kids waiting for his skewers. I happily waited that night and discovered the stall was absolutely worth the hype—the skewers were one of the best things that I have ever eaten. The pork is best cooked over charcoal, but a gas grill or grill pan will work, too. The King serves his with only Sticky Rice (page 151) and Isaan Sauce (page 46) and that is how I suggest you serve yours, too.

1. Combine the garlic and cilantro in a mortar and pestle and pound to a paste or combine in a mini food processor and process until smooth.

2. Transfer the garlic paste to a large bowl. Add the coconut milk, palm sugar, fish sauce, soy sauce, oyster sauce, cilantro, white pepper, and baking soda and whisk until smooth and the sugar has dissolved. Remove 1 cup of the marinade to a small bowl. Cover and reserve the rest of the marinade in the refrigerator until ready to grill the pork.

3. Add the pork to the 1 cup of marinade and toss to coat each piece of pork. Cover and marinate in the refrigerator for at least 3 hours and up to 24 hours.

4. Remove the pork from the marinade. Thread 4 to 6 pieces of the pork onto each skewer and place them on a baking sheet. Brush the meat on both sides with canola oil.

5. Heat a charcoal or gas grill according to the manufacturer's suggestion or heat a grill pan over high heat. Grill the pork for about 4 minutes per side, until golden brown on both sides and cooked to medium-well doneness, brushing with some of the reserved marinade occasionally. Serve warm with sticky rice and Isaan sauce.

4

COCKTAILS AND BEVERAGES

I love an ice-cold beer when it's hot and humid out. Sometimes that means I'm in New York and other times I'm in Southeast Asia. At Pig and Khao, we really want to transport you, and in the summer the weather plays into that. We can't always import beer from overseas, but we shoot for light and refreshing, like the beers most Southeast Asian countries produce locally. Sometimes it's so hot that they even add ice—but we save the ice for our cocktails.

Now, cocktails aren't huge in Southeast Asia. Sure, they are served in fancy restaurants and cocktail bars, but for the most part those places are for tourists. The locals are big rum drinkers because of the abundance of sugarcane, but if you ask for something like a rum and Coke, the bartender will give you just that—a shot of rum and a bottle of Coke. We were inspired by our friends at Black Crescent two doors down to go a little more upscale with cocktails (cocktails are also a really good way to utilize the extra ingredients that I have hanging around the kitchen!) and to create fun drinks that also go well with my food.

While they are not authentic, our cocktails are definitely inspired by Southeast Asian flavors. Our Spicy Pakwan Cocktail (page 103), for example, is a nod to all of the fresh fruit juices you can get from vendors on the street. *Pakwan* means "watermelon" in Tagalog, so of course that's the base. We add lime, sherry, and spicy tequila, and you have a crazy-refreshing drink.

Another foolproof way to add some Southeast Asian flair to classic cocktails is by using flavored simple syrups. We invented our Curry-Ginger Simple Syrup (see page 88) when we were trying to come up with a rum-based drink at one point and found some curry leaves leftover in the kitchen. We added them with a bit of fresh ginger to some sugar, melted it all together, and mixed it with rum and lemon juice. Voilà, a delicious and completely unique drink component.

Simple syrups are the perfect blank slate, so take inspiration from your favorite dishes or leftover herbs and spices and get going. Once you've found a few recipes you like, try them with nonalcoholic drinks like iced tea, iced coffee, lemonade, or even a splash of seltzer or club soda for homemade soda such as Cilantro Soda (page 91).

SIMPLE SYRUPS

Simple syrup is simply equal parts water and sugar mixed together and used to sweeten cold drinks. The sky is the limit with flavorings and the following are some of my favorites. I use them in specific cocktails in this book, but you can also mix them with seltzer to create your own homemade sodas.

CLASSIC SIMPLE SYRUP

Yields: 2 cups

2 cups granulated sugar

Combine the sugar and 2 cups of cold water in a small saucepan and bring to a boil over high heat. Cook until the sugar has completely dissolved. Let cool to room temperature. Transfer to a container with a tight-fitting lid and keep in the refrigerator for up to 1 month.

DEMERARA SIMPLE SYRUP

Yields: 2 cups

2 cups demerara sugar

Combine the sugar and 2 cups of cold water in a small saucepan and bring to a boil over high heat. Cook until the sugar has completely dissolved. Let cool to room temperature. Transfer to a container with a tight-fitting lid and keep in the refrigerator for up to 1 month.

CINNAMON SIMPLE SYRUP

Yields: 2 cups

3 cinnamon sticks   2 cups hot simple syrup

1. Put the cinnamon in a small sauté pan over low heat and cook for about 2 minutes, shaking the pan several times until the sticks are fragrant and the color deepens.

2. Add the simple syrup, remove from the heat, and let steep for 1 hour. Transfer to a container with a tight-fitting lid and refrigerate for up to 1 month.

LEMONGRASS SYRUP

Yields: 1 quart

4 cups granulated sugar   4 stalks lemongrass, trimmed, bruised, and coarsely chopped

1. Combine the sugar and 4 cups of water in a medium saucepan, bring to a boil over high heat, and cook for about 5 minutes, until the sugar has completely melted. Add the lemongrass, remove from the heat, and let steep for 1 hour at room temperature.

2. Strain into a container with a tight-fitting lid and refrigerate for up to 1 month.

CURRY-GINGER SIMPLE SYRUP

Yields: 2 cups

2 cups granulated sugar

1 cup packed fresh curry leaves

One 3-inch piece of fresh ginger, sliced into 1-inch pieces

1. Combine the sugar and 2 cups of water in a medium saucepan, bring to a boil over high heat, and cook for about 2 minutes, until the sugar has completely melted. Add the curry leaves and ginger, remove from the heat, and let steep for 2 hours at room temperature.

2. Strain the syrup into a container with a tight-fitting lid and refrigerate for up to 1 month.

FRESH COCONUT MILK

YIELDS: ABOUT 2 CUPS

1 fresh coconut (1½ to 2 pounds), opened, liquid reserved, peeled, and coarsely grated (see Tip)

If you have never had fresh coconut milk, you must try it! There is nothing that compares. Curries and dressings and ceviches all taste better when made with freshly made coconut milk.

1. Measure the grated coconut and measure the same amount of water. Put the water and any of the liquid saved from the opening of the coconut in a large saucepan and bring to a simmer over low heat.

2. Put the shredded coconut in a large bowl, pour the warm water over it, and let it sit for a few minutes until cool enough to handle. Begin massaging the coconut with your hands and continue for about 5 minutes.

3. Strain the mixture through a strainer lined with cheesecloth, pressing down hard to get every last drop. Store in a container with a tight-fitting lid in the refrigerator for up to 3 days or freeze for up to 1 month. Thaw before using.

TIP:
When buying fresh coconuts, a heavier one is better because it has a lot of liquid. Check around the eyes, and if there is mold, do not buy.

CILANTRO SODA

CILANTRO SODA

SERVES: 1

¼ cup loosely packed fresh cilantro leaves

2 tablespoons Lemongrass Syrup (page 88)

2 tablespoons freshly squeezed lemon juice

Ice cubes

Very cold club soda

This is one of our nonalcholic drinks at Pig and Khao, and it brings the delicious flavors of Southeast Asia into a homemade soda. I use a ton of cilantro in my cooking, and this is a great way to use up any leftover herbs I have hanging out in my refrigerator. Fresh Thai basil or mint would work really well, too.

Combine the cilantro, lemongrass syrup, and lemon juice in a pint glass and muddle for a few seconds. Add ice cubes and fill to the top with club soda.

BANGKOK FIRE

SERVES: 1

¼ cup whisky

2 tablespoons freshly squeezed lemon juice

2 tablespoons Thai Chili Honey (recipe follows)

Ice cubes

Lemon wedge

When I was living in Bangkok, I had my first "gold rush" cocktail, which is whisky, honey, and lime juice. I became obsessed with this drink and would have it every time I would visit my friends' restaurant Eat Me (which was often). I'm a huge fan of any cocktail that is spicy, and this is a play on those beloved gold rushes I enjoyed in Bangkok.

Combine the whisky, lemon juice, honey, and a few ice cubes in a cocktail shaker and shake for 10 seconds. Strain over the ice into a cocktail glass and garnish with a lemon wedge.

THAI CHILI HONEY

Yields: 2 cups

2 cups clover honey

1 teaspoon Thai chili flakes

1. Stir together the honey and chili flakes in a small saucepan and bring to a boil over high heat. Remove from the heat and let cool to room temperature.

2. Strain the honey into a container with a lid and let sit in a cool, dark place for up to 1 month.

HORCHATA

SERVES: 1

¼ cup Allspice-Infused Rum
(recipe follows)

¼ cup Horchata Milk
(recipe follows)

2 tablespoons Demerara Simple
Syrup (page 88)

Ice cubes

2 tablespoons toasted
coconut chips

This is not your classic horchata from Mexico, which is made with rice milk, and you would not find this in Southeast Asia. Instead, it is a version of horchata that I serve as a cocktail at my restaurants because I think it goes well with my menu (especially spicier dishes). The coconut fat mellows the flavors in your mouth, like cow's milk does with chilies in Mexican cooking.

Combine the rum, horchata milk, simple syrup, and a few ice cubes in a cocktail shaker and shake for 10 seconds. Pour into a highball glass filled with ice cubes and garnish with the coconut chips.

ALLSPICE-INFUSED RUM

Yields: 2 cups

2 cups dark rum

2 tablespoons whole allspice berries

Combine the rum and allspice in a container with a tight-fitting lid and let sit at room temperature for at least 2 days and up to 2 weeks.

HORCHATA MILK

Yields: 2 cups

One 14-ounce can coconut milk

½ teaspoon ground Ceylon cinnamon

2 tablespoons Demerara Simple Syrup (page 88)

Whisk together the coconut milk, cinnamon, and simple syrup in a medium bowl until smooth. Transfer to a container with a lid and refrigerate until cold, about 1 hour. The horchata will keep in the refrigerator for up to 1 week.

RUM AND HYDE

SERVES: 1

¼ cup dark rum

2 tablespoons freshly squeezed lemon juice

1¾ tablespoons Curry-Ginger Simple Syrup (page 88)

Ice cubes

Curry leaf, for garnish

This is my husband's creation, and the Curry-Ginger Simple Syrup (page 88) is what makes it so special. He had it in a small speakeasy right around the corner from a famous place known for its chili crab in Kuala Lumpur. He loved the crab, but he was obsessed with this cocktail and the interesting flavor that the curry leaf gives. He vowed to bring it back to the States, and the great thing about it is that it includes ingredients that I always have a lot of just hanging around (which is how many of my cocktails are created). The nutty, pungent aroma of the curry leaf and the spiciness of the ginger blend well with the sweetness of the rum and create a cocktail that goes perfectly with my food.

Combine the rum, lemon juice, simple syrup, and a few ice cubes in a cocktail shaker and shake for 10 seconds. Strain into a rocks glass filled with ice and garnish with curry leaf.

THAI BASIL DAIQUIRI

SERVES: 1

¼ cup Thai Basil–Infused Rum (recipe follows)

2 tablespoons Classic Simple Syrup (page 88)

2 tablespoons freshly squeezed lemon juice

Ice cubes

Here is a simple American classic exploding with Asian flavors and made with the spirit of choice in Southeast Asia, rum. Szechuan peppercorn adds a touch of heat, and the Thai basil gives it a peppery herbaceousness.

Combine the rum, simple syrup, lemon juice, and a few ice cubes in a cocktail shaker and shake for 10 seconds. Strain into a martini glass.

THAI BASIL-INFUSED RUM

Yields: About 1 quart

1 bottle Cruzan Rum

1 pint fresh Thai basil leaves

1 teaspoon Szechuan peppercorns

1. Combine the rum, basil, and peppercorns in a glass container with a tight-fitting lid and let sit at room temperature, in a cool, dark place, for at least 48 hours and up to 7 days.

2. Strain twice into a clean container and store in a cool, dark place for up to 6 months.

MIND ON MY MONEY

1 teaspoon green Chartreuse

Ice cubes

1½ ounces Brockmans Gin

½ ounce Aperol

¾ ounce Candied Orange and
Orange-Basil Syrup (recipe follows)

¾ ounce freshly squeezed
lime juice

Candied orange peel
(recipe follows), for garnish

Thai basil leaf, for garnish

This is a gin and juice type that is perfect for summer. I use Brockmans Gin, which has a citrus-forward taste, as well as Aperol, which goes great with the citrus notes, while adding some bitterness and sweetness (and amazing color). The super-flavorful Candied Orange and Orange-Basil Syrup (page 98) brings in the Asian feel. That, along with freshly squeezed lime juice, represents the "juice" portion of the cocktail. The spray (or rinse) of green Chartreuse pulls the sweetness back just enough to make it a well-balanced, refreshing summer cocktail. Note: The candied orange and syrup need to be made at least 1 day in advance. Always keep some on hand to whip up this refreshing drink in an instant.

1. Splash the Chartreuse in a coupe glass and fill with ice. Let sit while you prepare the cocktail.

2. Fill a cocktail shaker with ice, then add the gin, Aperol, syrup, and lime juice and shake for 10 seconds.

3. Roll the Chartreuse/ice in the glass so that the entire glass is coated, then dump it into a sink. Strain the cocktail into the glass and garnish with candied orange peel and basil leaf.

RECIPE CONTINUES

CANDIED ORANGE AND ORANGE-BASIL SYRUP

Yields: About 2 cups

2 thick-skinned oranges

2½ cups granulated sugar

¼ cup fresh Thai basil leaves, torn and tied in a piece of cheesecloth

1. Quarter each orange, remove the peel, and transfer the peel to a medium saucepan. Cover with cold water by 2 inches, bring to a boil over high heat, and drain. Repeat this step two more times. Drain well. When cool enough to handle, scrape off the pith using a spoon or sharp paring knife and thinly slice the peels lengthwise.

2. While the orange peels are being blanched, combine 2 cups of the sugar, 1 cup of water, and the Thai basil in a medium saucepan; bring to a boil over high heat; and cook until the sugar dissolves. Add the orange peels, reduce the heat to low, and cook for about 45 minutes, until the peels are very soft and translucent.

3. Line a baking sheet with wax paper or parchment paper and sprinkle with ¼ cup of the remaining sugar. Remove the peels with a slotted spoon and place on the prepared baking sheet, sprinkle the remaining ¼ cup sugar over the peels, and toss to combine. Discard the cheesecloth with the basil in it and transfer the syrup to a container with a lid. Refrigerate until cold, at least 2 hours and up to 24 hours. The syrup will keep for up to 1 month in the refrigerator.

4. Let the peels sit, uncovered, for at least 8 hours and up to 24 hours. The candied orange peels will last, tightly covered in a container and stored in a cool, dry place, for up to 1 month or in the refrigerator for up to 2 months.

PERFECT STORM

SERVES: 1

PERFECT STORM BASE (MEDLEY)

2 ounces Flor de Caña 7 yr (rum)

1 ounce Velvet Falernum

1 ounce Benedictine

1 ounce allspice dram

1 ounce Toasted Cinnamon Simple Syrup (page 88)

TO SERVE

Ice cubes

2 ounces Amontillado sherry

¾ ounce freshly squeezed lemon juice

½ ounce Perfect Storm Base

½ ounce Curry-Ginger Simple Syrup (page 88)

½ ounce Gosling's rum

Lime wedge, for garnish

This is my dream version of a Dark and Stormy cocktail that has a rum base. The spices and the Curry-Ginger Simple Syrup (page 88) complement many of the dishes in this book.

1. Make the medley: Mix together the rum, Falernum, Benedictine, dram, and simple syrup in a bowl. Cover and refrigerate for at least 1 hour and up to 24 hours—this allows the flavors to meld. The mixture will last, tightly covered, in the refrigerator for up to 1 month.

2. Make the cocktail: Fill a cocktail shaker with ice cubes, add the sherry, lemon juice, the perfect storm base, simple syrup, and rum and shake for 10 seconds. Fill a highball glass with ice, strain the cocktail into the glass, and top off with rum. Garnish with a lime wedge.

LOWER EAST SIDE

LOWER EAST SIDE

SERVES: 1

6 ice cubes

1½ ounces Old Overholt Whiskey

¾ ounce Antica Vermouth

½ ounce Cynar

2 drops habanero bitters

A twist on a classic Manhattan. I named this cocktail the Lower East Side because of the location of my restaurant Pig and Khao. I especially like this recipe because of the habanero bitters that add a unique flavor in addition to just a touch of heat to this iconic cocktail.

Add the ice cubes to a cocktail shaker. Add the whisky, vermouth, Cynar, and bitters. Stir for 10 seconds. Serve straight up in a rocks glass.

STINKY PEAT

SERVES: 1

CHAMOMILE-INFUSED OLD OVERHOLT

2 cups Old Overholt Whiskey

1 chamomile tea bag

TO SERVE

2 ounces chamomile-infused Old Overholt

½ ounce St-Germain

2 dashes orange bitters

Ice cubes

1 tablespoon Laphroaig Scotch

2-inch piece of fresh lemon peel

Tea plays such an important role in Southeast Asia, and so I wanted to create a cocktail that could incorporate this ingredient. I'm not a huge fan of Scotch, but I do love using it as a rinse for the peaty (hence the name) aroma that it brings.

1. To make the infusion: Combine the whisky and tea bag in a container with a lid and let infuse at room temperature for 8 hours. Remove the tea bag and discard.

2. To serve: Combine the whisky, the St-Germain, orange bitters, and ice in a shaker glass and stir vigorously for 5 seconds.

3. Rinse a rocks glass with the Laphroaig. Wipe the glass with the lemon peel, strain the mixture into the glass, and serve straight up.

SPICY PAKWAN COCKTAIL

SERVES: 1

1 tablespoon dry Thai chili flakes

1-liter bottle Lunazul tequila

2 ounces freshly squeezed lime juice

Kosher salt

Ice cubes

1 ounce Thai chili–infused tequila

1 ounce Manzanilla sherry

1 ounce fresh watermelon juice

¾ ounce Classic Simple Syrup (page 88)

Wedge of fresh watermelon, for garnish

Pakwan means "watermelon" in Tagalog. Watermelon juice is the drink of choice throughout Southeast Asia, so we had to have at least one cocktail with it as a base. This is one of my favorites and one that I find myself having one or two of at the end of a shift. We make our own chili-infused tequila at the restaurant, but if you don't feel like making your own, you can add a few dashes of Thai hot sauce to the cocktail before you shake.

1. Add the Thai chili flakes to the tequila and let infuse for at least 8 hours before using.

2. Pour 1 ounce of the lime juice and ¼ cup of kosher salt onto two separate small plates. Dip the rim of a highball glass into the lime juice, then press into the salt. Fill the glass with ice cubes.

3. Combine the tequila, sherry, watermelon juice, the remaining lime juice, and simple syrup in a cocktail shaker filled with ice and shake for 10 seconds. Strain into the highball glass and garnish with a piece of watermelon.

5

BREAKFAST AND BRUNCH

Breakfast is the most important meal of the day in Southeast Asia. Unlike in the States, everyone eats it, but the concept of "breakfast food" is very different. Instead of bacon and pancakes, think fish and noodles and soup. At first, it may seem weird to eat this kind of food in the morning, but you need to understand that what is eaten for a specific meal in Southeast Asia is much less set in stone than it is in much of the Western world. In most of Southeast Asia, you can pretty much eat the same foods for breakfast as you might eat for lunch or for dinner. In fact, many of the breakfast dishes are made using leftovers from the night before.

The base for most of these dishes is rice or noodles. They're easy to access, cheap, and fun to add flavor to. Growing up, garlic rice was my favorite breakfast. I'd add scrambled eggs or maybe dried fish for a perfect and hearty way to start the day.

Breakfast in Southeast Asia is basically food we love to eat at any other time of the day. Take Banh Xeo (page 117)—it's almost like a crispy crepe. The batter is made with rice flour and coconut milk that bubbles up in the shape of the pan in screaming-hot oil. I like to fill mine with shrimp and crispy bacon and then I top it off with all kinds of fresh herbs. It's delicious for breakfast but works for lunch or even as an appetizer.

While brunch honestly isn't a thing in Southeast Asia, a lot of the dishes work because they are so versatile. Banh mi? At Piggyback NYC, I turned mine into a cross between the classic and a bacon, egg, and cheese. I replaced the bacon with braised pork belly, kept the egg fried so you get that luscious yolk dressing throughout the whole sandwich, and replaced the cheese with something equally rich and salty—chicken liver pâté.

Even though breakfast sweets aren't huge in Southeast Asian food, there are two that are, and both just happen to be my favorite. One is almost like a dessert—Champorado (page 115). It's a Filipino rice pudding with chocolate. When I was growing up, my mom would actually sub out the rice with oatmeal and serve it warm. I went back to the classic rice for the restaurant, but had to add my own twist—crispy bacon, which gives it not only a bit of texture but that amazing sweet/savory flavor that Americans seem to love at breakfast. The other is our Kaya Jam Toast (page 121)—a dish made of Ja bread and coconut custard that I learned to make in Singapore—so for those people who like sweet over savory for breakfast, these two options are sure to keep everyone happy.

COOKING EGGS

Eggs in Asia are used differently than in the United States. In the United States, we typically eat them for breakfast with a side of bacon and toast or on a biscuit with a slice of melted cheese. Eggs are eaten for breakfast in Asia, too, but are most often prepared scrambled in fried rice; steamed to create a silky custard; whisked into hot broth to create a soup; hard-cooked and cured in green tea or soy sauce; or soft-cooked and served atop a steaming bowl of ramen. Duck eggs and quail eggs are used a lot in Southeast Asian cooking, too.

FRIED EGGS

Erase all French technique that you were either taught in culinary school or learned by watching Julia Child or reading her cookbooks. Southeast Asian cooking is not about low and slow when it comes to food preparation, and eggs are no different. These eggs are literally fried.

Yields: 1

¼ cup canola oil

1 large egg

Kosher salt

Line a plate with paper towels. Heat the oil in a small nonstick pan over high heat until it begins to shimmer. Crack the egg carefully into a small ramekin, being careful not to break the yolk, then gently slide the egg into the hot oil, standing back as far as possible (the oil will splatter). For sunny-side up, cook the egg for about 1½ minutes, until the white is set, the edges are golden brown, and the yolk is still slightly loose. For over easy, instead of gently turning, I skip the flip and just baste the top with the oil until the yellow is slightly set but still runny. Transfer the egg, yolk-side up, to the paper towel–lined plate and season with salt.

POACHED EGGS

These are pretty classic and totally the way that I learned to make them during my French training at CIA.

Yields: 4

4 large eggs

2 tablespoons distilled white vinegar

Kosher salt, optional, depending on recipe

1. Line a plate with paper towels. Bring 2 inches of water to a boil in a medium high-sided sauté pan over high heat. Reduce the heat to a simmer (medium-low heat) and add the vinegar.

2. Crack the eggs, individually, into a small ramekin, making sure not to break the yolk. Slide the eggs, one at a time, into the simmering water and cook for 3 minutes, spooning the simmering water over the eggs until the white is set and the yolk is still runny.

3. Gently remove the eggs with a slotted spoon and lay them on the paper towel–lined plate to dry.

MEDIUM-COOKED EGGS

I garnish a lot of dishes with these eggs. You will also find them in your bowl of ramen. Follow these directions, and you will have a perfectly medium-cooked (kind of jammy in the center) egg every time.

Yields: 4

4 large eggs

Prepare a bowl of ice water. Bring a medium pot of water to a boil over high heat. Carefully lower the eggs into the boiling water and cook the eggs for exactly 6 minutes (set a timer). Drain the eggs and immediately plunge them into the ice water. Let the eggs sit for about 10 minutes, until cold. Immediately peel them and remove them from the water, dry them off, and refrigerate them in a bowl for up to 2 days.

HARD-COOKED EGGS

Follow the above directions but let cook for 9 minutes.

COOKED SOY-CURED EGGS

Yields: 12

1 dozen large eggs

1½ cups Lee Kum Kee Premium Soy Sauce

1 cup sake

¾ cup granulated sugar

1. Prepare an ice bath using a large bowl. Set aside.

2. Bring a large pot of water to a boil over high heat. Carefully add the eggs and cook for exactly 8 minutes. Drain and plunge the eggs immediately into the ice bath and let sit for 10 minutes.

3. Whisk together the soy, sake, and sugar in a large bowl until the sugar dissolves. Once the eggs are chilled, carefully peel them and add them to the soy mixture. Cover and refrigerate for at least 12 hours and up to 24 hours.

THAI FRIED EGG SALAD

SERVES: 2 TO 4

DRESSING

½ cup freshly squeezed lime juice

¼ cup plus 1 tablespoon Squid Brand fish sauce

½ teaspoon maggi sauce (see page 20)

2 tablespoons palm sugar

1 red Thai chili, thinly sliced

1 green Thai chili, thinly sliced

EGGS

½ cup canola oil

8 large eggs, room temperature

4 garlic cloves, thinly sliced

1 large shallot, thinly sliced

White pepper

½ cup fresh cilantro leaves

In Thailand, this dish is referred to as Yam Khai Dao, which means "fried egg salad." Like all Southeast Asian salads, this isn't a salad as we Americans know salads, and it is not similar to our egg salad, which is dressed in mayonnaise. The egg is cooked at high heat in a good amount of oil to get those crunchy edges. It is traditionally eaten with Steamed Jasmine Rice (see page 150) or Sticky Rice (page 151), but hey, you can have it with toast, too! I like to keep my eggs at room temperature before frying them because the whites spread well. Green Thai chilies are less spicy than the red and add a slightly herbaceous flavor, and honestly I include both because that is how I was taught. You can use both or just use one!

1. Make the dressing: Whisk together the lime juice, fish sauce, maggi, and palm sugar until the sugar dissolves. Stir in the chilies and let sit at room temperature while you prepare the eggs. The dressing can be made 2 days in advance and stored, tightly covered, in the refrigerator.

2. Make the eggs: In a skillet or high-sided nonstick sauté pan, heat the oil over high heat until almost smoking. Add the eggs, 2 or 3 at a time, and cook for 2 to 3 minutes, until the white is crispy around the edges but the yolk is still runny.

3. Transfer to a plate, pour a few heaping tablespoons of the dressing over the eggs, and garnish the top with a few slices of the garlic, shallot, a pinch of white pepper, and some of the cilantro leaves.

BRAISED PORK BELLY BANH MI WITH FRIED EGG

YIELDS: 8 SANDWICHES

BRAISED PORK BELLY

⅔ cup Kikkoman light soy sauce

¼ cup kosher salt

¼ cup apple cider vinegar

6 bay leaves

2 star anise

2 tablespoons granulated sugar

5 garlic cloves, smashed

1 teaspoon ground black peppercorns

3 pounds boneless pork belly, skin on

CHICKEN LIVER PÂTÉ

1 pound chicken livers, cleaned, rinsed well, and patted dry

¼ teaspoon pink salt

¼ teaspoon kosher salt

¼ teaspoon white pepper

¼ teaspoon MSG

1 tablespoon five-spice powder

¼ cup (½ stick) unsalted butter, cubed, plus 3 tablespoons unsalted butter, diced

1 large shallot, finely diced

Banh mi is a sandwich found in Vietnam. The chicken liver pâté and the baguette used to create this sandwich are signs of the French influence that can be found in many classic Vietnamese dishes. There are many variations of this sandwich throughout the country (cold cuts, fried fish) but not as often one that includes pork belly and fried egg. That is pretty much my spin, and it works perfectly on my brunch menu at Piggyback NYC. Making chicken liver pâté is really easy, but if you don't have the time, feel free to buy it prepared—just add a touch of five-spice powder to it to get that Vietnamese flavor.

1. Prepare the pork belly: Preheat the oven to 325 degrees F.

2. Combine 12 cups of water, the soy sauce, salt, vinegar, bay leaves, star anise, sugar, garlic, and peppercorns in a large pot and whisk. Add the pork belly, fat-side up, and bring to a boil over high heat. Cover and cook in the oven for about 2½ hours, until just fork tender but not falling apart.

3. Prepare the chicken liver pâté: Put the chicken livers in a large bowl, add the pink salt, kosher salt, white pepper, MSG, and five-spice powder and toss well to combine.

4. Line a plate with paper towels. Heat 2 tablespoons of the diced butter in a large sauté pan over medium heat until the mixture just begins to shimmer. Add the chicken livers and cook, stirring several times, for about 6 minutes, until lightly golden brown and almost cooked through (they should still be pink in the center). Remove with a slotted spoon to the paper towel–lined plate.

5. Add the remaining 1 tablespoon of diced butter to the pan and heat again over medium heat until it begins to shimmer. Add the shallots and garlic and cook for about 4 minutes, until soft. Stir in the bourbon and cook for about 2 minutes, until completely reduced. Add the cream, soy sauces, and salt and bring to a simmer. Return the chicken livers to the pan and cook for 30 seconds. Remove from the heat and let cool slightly.

6. Transfer the mixture to a blender, add the gelatin, and gently pulse to combine. Remove the lid to let any steam out, return the lid, and pulse a few more times. Blend until smooth. Blend in the cubed butter piece by piece until combined.

RECIPE AND INGREDIENTS CONTINUE

3 garlic cloves, finely chopped

¼ cup bourbon

¼ cup heavy cream

2 tablespoons Kecap Manis sweet soy sauce

1 tablespoon Lee Kum Kee Premium Soy Sauce

½ teaspoon kosher salt

1½ sheets gelatin, soaked in ice-cold water for 5 minutes until soft and drained or 1½ teaspoons powdered gelatin soaked in 1 tablespoon cold water in a small ramekin until soft

TO SERVE

2 cups plus 1 tablespoon canola oil

½ cup maggi sauce (see page 20)

Eight 9-inch crusty baguettes

1 cup Sriracha Mayonnaise (recipe follows)

2 cups Pickled Daikon and Carrots (page 55), drained

80 fresh cilantro leaves

2 large jalapeño chilies, thinly sliced crosswise

12 Fried Eggs (see page 106) (optional)

7. Transfer the mixture to an 8-inch baking dish. Cover and refrigerate until firm, at least 4 hours and up to 24 hours. The liver can be made up to 3 days in advance. Keep it tightly covered.

8. Remove the pork belly from the braising liquid, transfer to a baking sheet, and let cool to room temperature, about 30 minutes. Let cool, uncovered, in the refrigerator for at least 8 hours and up to 24 hours. Once the belly is cold, slice crosswise into 8 equal pieces. The pork can be stored, tightly covered, for up to 1 week in the refrigerator.

9. Assemble the banh mi: Heat the oil in a large high-sided sauté pan over medium heat until it begins to shimmer. Line a baking sheet with paper towels. Fry the pork in the oil, a few slices at a time, about 2 minutes per side, until golden brown and crispy on each side. Transfer the pork, using a slotted spoon, to the prepared baking sheet. Brush the top of each slice with some of the maggi sauce.

10. If the bread is fresh and crusty, use as is. If the bread is a day old, heat an oven to 350 degrees F, put the bread on a baking sheet, and bake in the oven for 5 minutes or until just crispy.

11. Spread the chicken liver on the bottom of each baguette. Spread the mayonnaise on the top half of the baguette. Put 4 slices of the pork belly on top of the chicken liver pâté and top the pork with some of the pickled vegetables, cilantro leaves, and slices of jalapeño. Top each with a fried egg, if desired, and eat immediately.

SRIRACHA MAYONNAISE

Yields: About 1¼ cups

1 cup Kewpie brand mayonnaise

3 tablespoons sriracha

Squeeze of fresh lime juice

Whisk together the mayonnaise, sriracha, and lime juice in a small bowl. Cover and refrigerate for at least 30 minutes and up to 24 hours to allow the flavors to meld.

THAI PORK OMELET

SERVES: 4

8 large eggs

4 ounces ground pork

5 garlic cloves, finely chopped

1 medium scallion, thinly sliced

½ teaspoon white pepper

2 teaspoons soy sauce

¾ cup canola oil

½ cup fresh cilantro leaves

Shark brand sriracha, for serving

The first time that I ate one of these omelets was on the street in Thailand. I had never eaten a deep-fried egg and I was shocked that it was crispy but still tender. My mind was blown, and my low and slow egg cooking that my French training taught me was turned on its ear. Two important tips: Whisk the eggs well until light and frothy and uniform in color and make sure that the oil is smoking-hot.

1. Put the eggs in a large bowl and whisk until light and frothy and uniform in color. Stir in the pork, garlic, scallion, white pepper, and soy sauce until combined.

2. Heat the oil in a 12-inch wok or a high-sided sauté pan over medium heat until it begins to shimmer. Carefully pour the mixture into the hot oil and cook for about 1½ minutes, until it begins to puff up and the bottom becomes golden brown. Carefully flip the omelet over and continue cooking until the other side is golden brown and the omelet is cooked through.

3. Carefully turn the omelet out onto paper towels to drain the fat. Divide into 4 pieces. Garnish with the cilantro and serve with sriracha on the side.

PORK TOCINO

SERVES: 8

1 cup pineapple juice

⅔ cup (packed) light brown sugar

½ cup Kikkoman light soy sauce

1 tablespoon finely chopped fresh garlic

1 tablespoon annatto powder

2 tablespoons kosher salt

2 pounds pork butt, thinly sliced across the grain

¼ cup canola oil

1 recipe Garlic Rice (page 150)

8 sunny-side up eggs (see Fried Eggs, page 106)

2 scallions, thinly sliced

This is another great pork dish from the Philippines that is usually eaten for breakfast and sometimes lunch, which makes it a great brunch dish. It is typically served with Garlic Rice (page 150) and a fried egg. The prepared version found in the Philippines is bright red and made with artificial colors. For this all-natural version, I've replaced artificial colors and preservatives with annatto powder and pineapple juice. The key to taking this dish to the next level is allowing the meat to marinate for a minimum of 24 hours. The pineapple in the marinade will break down the meat, and the sugar and salt will cure it.

1. Whisk together the pineapple juice, brown sugar, soy sauce, garlic, annatto, and salt in a bowl until the brown sugar and salt have dissolved.

2. Add the pork slices and toss to coat in the marinade. Transfer to a large plastic bag with a ziplock top, press out the air, and seal. Put the bag into a bowl (in case of leaks), place in the refrigerator, and marinate the pork for a minimum of 24 hours (48 hours is preferable).

3. Remove the meat from the marinade and pat dry on paper towels. Heat 2 tablespoons of the oil in a large sauté pan over high heat until the oil begins to shimmer. Cook the pork in batches for about 2 minutes per side, until golden brown on both sides and just heated through. Repeat, using more oil.

4. Spoon the rice into shallow bowls or onto plates. Top with several slices of the pork and then an egg. Garnish with the scallions.

CHAMPORADO

1 cup sticky rice

1½ cups whole milk

1 can unsweetened Chaokoh coconut milk

¼ cup Dutch-processed cocoa powder

1 cup granulated sugar

1 ounce bittersweet chocolate, finely chopped

2 teaspoons kosher salt

Crispy bacon, chopped

Chocolate for breakfast may sound like a dream. Champorado is that dream realized, and it was a favorite of mine growing up. My mom made quick-cooking oatmeal instead of sticky rice, and you can eat it that way, too, but it's prepared with rice in the Philippines. I love both versions.

In some regions of the Philippines, it is classically served topped with tuyo (dried salted fish similar to anchovy), but I use crispy bacon, which mimics that umami flavor and is more palatable to the American diner.

1. Combine the rice and 1¼ cups of water in a medium saucepan and bring to a boil over high heat. Reduce the heat to medium-low and continue cooking for about 14 minutes, until the water is almost completely absorbed.

2. While the rice is cooking, whisk together the milk, coconut milk, and cocoa powder in a large bowl until smooth.

3. Add the milk mixture to the rice and cook, stirring often, for about 10 minutes, until the mixture is thickened and the rice is very soft. Stir in the sugar, chocolate, and salt and cook 5 minutes longer. Serve in a bowl topped with crispy bacon.

BANH XEO

SERVES: 4

1 cup rice flour

1½ teaspoons ground turmeric

¾ teaspoon kosher salt

¼ cup light beer (such as Bud, Bud Light, or Corona)

⅓ cup unsweetened coconut milk

½ cup canola oil

16 large shrimp, peeled and deveined and tails removed

2 scallions, thinly sliced

4 ounces mung bean sprouts

½ cup crispy bacon bits (see Note)

⅓ cup Pickled Daikon and Carrots (page 55)

¼ cup fresh cilantro leaves

16 fresh Thai basil leaves, torn

16 fresh mint leaves, torn

Red lettuce leaves

Nuoc Cham (page 49)

This dish hails from Vietnam, where it is referred to as a sizzling crepe due to the noise that is made when the batter hits the hot oil in the pan. It is eaten primarily for breakfast, but you will see it served by street vendors for lunch, snacks, and even dinner sometimes . . . although not as a main course but more as an appetizer.

I was taught how to make my version by a well-known restaurateur and chef named Chef Vy, who owns several restaurants and a cooking school in Hoi An. Google Chef Vy in Vietnam to read about this remarkable woman.

Traditionally, you would not find this dish with bacon; I use bacon to make it more breakfast-like for my American customers. Typically, it would include leftover pork bits from other dishes or a combination of pork and shrimp. Vegetarians can just add vegetables. The addition of herbs and lettuce makes this dish lighter, which is very representative of Vietnamese food.

1. Whisk together the flour, turmeric, and salt in a large bowl until combined. Whisk together ½ cup of water, the beer, and the coconut milk in a second large bowl until smooth. Add the wet ingredients to the dry ingredients and whisk until just smooth. Let the batter rest while you prepare the filling.

2. Line a plate with paper towels. Heat 2 tablespoons of the oil in a large nonstick pan over high heat. Add 4 of the shrimp and cook for 20 seconds. Pour ½ cup of the batter into the pan, making sure that it coats the bottom. Add a quarter of the scallion and a quarter of the bean sprouts to one side of the crepe. Reduce the heat to medium-low, cover the pan, and cook for about 2 minutes, until the shrimp are just cooked through. Remove the lid and cook until the bottom is nice and crispy, 6 minutes. Transfer the crepe to the plate lined with paper towels to drain. Put a quarter of the bacon, daikon, cilantro leaves, Thai basil, and mint leaves on the same side as the bean sprouts. Fold in half to make a semicircle. Repeat to make the remaining 3 crepes.

3. To serve: Cut up the banh xeo into pieces, wrap in lettuce leaves, and dip into the nuoc cham.

Note:

To make the crispy bacon bits, heat 1 tablespoon of canola oil over medium heat in a medium sauté pan. Add 6 slices of thin bacon and cook for about 8 minutes, until golden brown and crisp on both sides. Transfer to a plate lined with paper towels, let cool for 5 minutes, and finely chop with a chef's knife.

BEEF TAPA

SERVES: 4

¼ cup Kikkoman light soy sauce

2 tablespoons granulated sugar

1 tablespoon coconut vinegar

3 tablespoons canola oil, plus more for cooking

1 teaspoon kosher salt

½ teaspoon freshly ground black pepper

3 cloves finely chopped garlic

1 pound nicely marbled sirloin steak, sliced ¼ inch thick

Garlic Rice (page 150)

8 sunny-side up eggs (see Fried Eggs, page 106)

This very popular breakfast dish was most likely created as a way to preserve meat before refrigeration. It's very similar to Pork Tocino (page 114) minus the pineapple, and using beef instead of pork. This Filipino beef dish needs a minimum marinating time of 24 hours in the refrigerator to get its jerky-like texture. Coconut vinegar is the vinegar of choice in the Philippines and is milder than distilled white vinegar or apple cider vinegar, but if you can't find coconut vinegar, just use apple cider vinegar and decrease the amount by half. This dish is typically served with a generous portion of Garlic Rice (page 150) and Fried Eggs (see page 106).

1. Whisk together the soy sauce, sugar, vinegar, 1 tablespoon of the oil, salt, and pepper in a large bowl. Add the garlic and beef and toss to coat in the marinade. Cover and refrigerate for at least 24 hour (2 days is ideal).

2. Heat 2 tablespoons of the oil in a large sauté pan or wok over high heat until the oil begins to shimmer. Add half of the beef to the pan and cook for about 5 minutes, until golden brown and just cooked through. Repeat with the remaining meat, adding a bit more oil, if needed.

3. Serve the meat over garlic rice and top with two sunny-side up eggs.

KAYA JAM TOAST

YIELDS: ABOUT 2 CUPS

1 cup Chaokoh unsweetened coconut milk

1 cup granulated sugar

4 fresh pandan leaves

3 large eggs

3 large egg yolks

Pinch of kosher salt

8 slices brioche, sliced ¼ inch thick

¼ cup (½ stick) very cold unsalted butter, cut into 4 pieces, then sliced into 4 thin slices each, plus 6 tablespoons cold unsalted butter, cut into tablespoons

8 Poached Eggs (see page 106)

Dark soy sauce, for garnish

White pepper, for garnish

You can get kaya jam toast anywhere in Singapore. While it is referred to as a jam, it is more of a custard or curd made from eggs, sugar, and coconut milk, and flavored with pandan leaves. Pandan leaf is used in a lot of desserts in Southeast Asia as well as in some savory dishes, too. Only available frozen in the United States, its flavor is totally unique and almost impossible to describe. I suggest trying it and deciding for yourself.

1. Whisk together the coconut milk and ½ cup of the sugar in a medium saucepan. Tie the pandan leaves together and add to the pot, bring to a simmer over high heat, and cook for about 2 minutes, until the sugar has dissolved. Remove from the heat, cover, and let steep for 20 minutes. Remove the pandan leaves and squeeze out all of the liquid from them into the pot.

2. Prepare an ice bath by filling a large bowl with ice cubes and a few cups of cold water. Nestle a medium stainless steel bowl into the ice.

3. Fill a medium saucepan with 2 inches of water and bring to a simmer over high heat. Whisk together the eggs, egg yolks, salt, and the remaining ½ cup sugar in a stainless steel bowl that will fit over the pot until smooth. Whisk in the milk mixture and place the bowl on top of the pot with the simmering water. Cook, whisking constantly, until the mixture is very thick. Remove it from the heat every now and then so that the custard does not get too hot and curdle. This can take between 10 and 20 minutes (maybe longer) depending on how hot the water becomes.

4. Strain the mixture through a fine mesh strainer into the bowl set inside the ice bath and stir for about 10 minutes, until the mixture cools slightly. Cover and refrigerate until completely chilled.

5. Slather each slice of bread with about 2 tablespoons of the kaya jam and divide the cold sliced butter among 4 of the slices. Place the 4 remaining slices on top of the buttered slices, jam-side down, and press down.

6. Heat 3 tablespoons of the remaining butter in a large nonstick pan over medium heat until it begins to shimmer. Add two of the sandwiches and cook for about 2 minutes, until the bottoms are golden brown. Turn over and continue cooking again until the bottom is golden brown. Remove and slice in half on the bias. Repeat with the remaining 3 tablespoons of butter and bread. Serve with 2 poached eggs on the side, drizzled with dark soy sauce and sprinkled with white pepper.

ARROZ CALDO

SERVES: 8

¼ cup canola oil

1 pound skinless, boneless chicken thighs

1 medium Spanish onion, finely diced

One 3-inch piece of fresh ginger, peeled and finely diced

6 garlic cloves, finely chopped

1 cup jasmine rice

1 cup sticky rice

8 cups homemade Chicken Stock (page 36) or low-sodium canned chicken stock or broth

2 tablespoons Red Boat fish sauce

1 teaspoon freshly ground black pepper

Calamansi or freshly squeezed lemon juice to taste

POSSIBLE GARNISHES

Poached Eggs (see page 106)

Hard-Cooked or Cooked Soy-Cured Eggs (see page 107)

Crispy Garlic (see page 43)

Crispy Fried Shallots (page 52)

1 scallion, thinly sliced

Soy sauce

Every Southeast Asian country makes a version of congee, which is essentially a rice porridge made by boiling rice in a great deal of water until it breaks down into a pudding-like consistency. This is the Filipino variation, and has a very pronounced ginger flavor.

This hearty meal is typically eaten for breakfast (but would make a filling dinner, too) and is made with rice left over from dinner the night before. It's heavy and rich, and designed to fill you up for a full workday ahead. The base is perfect for any garnishes—see the list below—and I use them all. I use both jasmine and sticky rice because I love the contrast of textures, but if you decide to use just one, go with 2 cups of cooked jasmine rice. A squeeze of citrus juice (calamansi or lemon) helps add a bit of freshness.

1. Heat the oil in a large stockpot over high heat until the oil begins to shimmer. Add the chicken and cook for about 3 minutes per side, until golden brown (but not cooked through—it will continue to cook in the broth). Remove the chicken to a plate.

2. Add the onion, ginger, and garlic and cook for about 4 minutes, until soft. Add the rice and cook, stirring a few times, for about 2 minutes, until lightly toasted.

3. Add the chicken stock and 8 cups of water, return the chicken to the pot, bring to a boil, reduce the heat to low, cover the pan, and cook for about 20 minutes, until the chicken is just cooked through, stirring occasionally so the rice doesn't burn at the bottom. Remove the chicken from the pot, shred it using two forks into bite-size pieces, and return it to the pot.

4. Continue cooking for about 30 to 40 minutes, until the rice is thick. Season with the fish sauce, pepper, and juice.

5. Serve in bowls as is or with any of the garnishes.

SMOKED CHICKEN MAMI

SERVES: 4

CHICKEN BROTH
Yields: 2 quarts (8 cups)

8 pounds chicken bones

1 large Spanish onion, halved

One 2-inch piece of fresh ginger, chopped, plus one 1-inch piece, chopped

4 scallions, chopped

3 bay leaves

2 teaspoons whole black peppercorns

¾ cup Squid Brand fish sauce

⅓ cup rock sugar or 3 tablespoons granulated sugar

6 garlic cloves, smashed

1½ teaspoons MSG

SOUP

Kosher salt and pepper

⅛ teaspoon Thai chili flakes

¼ cup Garlic Oil (page 43) or 1 large garlic clove, smashed

Freshly squeezed juice of 1 lime

1¼ pounds ramen noodles

2 tablespoons canola oil

1 pound skin-on, boneless chicken thighs

I refer to this as Filipino Ramen. Instant versions can be found in every convenience and grocery store throughout the country. Traditional chicken mami is not smoked, but I love the depth of flavor smoking the chicken bones gives to the broth, and, like all good soups, a rich, flavorful broth is key. I smoke my bones after roasting them, and if you have an outdoor smoker or a well-ventilated kitchen, I suggest that you do this, too. But if filling up your house with the scent of smoked chicken bones is not your thing, then just roast them—it will still be delicious. If you can't find ramen noodles, lo mein noodles will work.

1. Make the broth: Preheat the oven 350 degrees F.

2. Spread the bones on a full baking sheet or divide between two large baking sheets and roast, turning a few times, for about 45 minutes, until golden brown.

3. After roasting, you can smoke the bones. If using an indoor smoker to smoke the bones: Remove the bones from the oven and, using tongs, transfer as many as will fit to the rack that sits on top of the drip tray that comes with the indoor smoker. (If you can't fit them all, just smoke some of them; it will add great flavor.) Add ¼ cup of soaked chips to the bottom of the smoker. Heat the smoker over low-medium heat on a stovetop burner. Once smoke starts to appear (usually after 5 to 10 seconds), slide the lid to close and let it smoke. Smoke the bones for 15 minutes. Remove from the heat and let sit in the tray, covered, for 15 minutes longer.

4. If using an outdoor smoker, prepare your smoker according to the manufacturer's directions. Add 1 cup of soaked chips to the smoker. Put the bones on a baking rack set over a baking sheet or baking pan (whichever fits in your smoker) and smoke for 30 minutes. Remove the bones.

5. Transfer the bones to a large stockpot, add 16 cups of water, and bring to a boil over high heat. Add the onion, the 2-inch piece of ginger, the scallions, bay leaves, peppercorns, fish sauce, sugar, and garlic. Return to a boil, reduce the heat to low, and simmer for about 5 hours, until reduced to about 10 cups and the stock has really great flavor.

RECIPE AND INGREDIENTS CONTINUE

4 ounces bean sprouts

4 ounces baby bok choy

½ cup Crispy Fried Shallots
(page 52)

¼ cup Crispy Garlic (see page 43)

3 scallions (white parts only),
thinly sliced on the bias

¼ cup fresh cilantro leaves

4 Cooked Soy-Cured Eggs
(page 107), optional

6. Strain the stock into a large pot. Add the remaining 1-inch piece of ginger and the MSG. Bring to a boil over high heat, reduce the heat to low, and cook for about 30 minutes longer, until reduced to 8 cups. Strain the stock again in a large bowl and let it sit until it comes to room temperature and the fat begins to rise to the top. Skim some of the fat off the top of the stock using a ladle and discard. The stock can be stored in the refrigerator tightly covered for up to 3 days and frozen for up to 3 months.

7. Make the soup: Heat 6 cups of the broth in a large saucepan over low heat. Add the salt and black pepper to taste, the chili flakes, and the garlic oil. Keep the broth warm. Add the lime juice just before serving.

8. Bring a large pot of water to a boil. Add the ramen. Cook for 2 minutes, until done. Drain.

9. While the water is coming to a boil for the ramen, heat the canola oil in a large sauté pan over high heat until the oil shimmers. Season the chicken on both sides with salt and pepper and cook for about 5 minutes per side, until golden brown on both sides and just cooked through. Remove from the heat and let rest for 5 minutes. Thinly slice crosswise.

10. Divide the bean sprouts, bok choy, and ramen among four large bowls and pour 1½ cups of the broth on top of each bowl. Fan slices of the chicken on top of the noodles. Garnish the top with some of the shallots, garlic, scallion, and cilantro leaves and a soy-cured egg, if desired.

6

SALADS

These salads aren't your classic Caesar or Cobb. They're not lettuce with topping and dressings but rather full dishes unto themselves. They run the gamut from eggplant-based to bean-based to pork-based. Some are vegetable heavy, as you may expect. Others shine with fresh herbs. Not all salads are created equal—especially not if you compare the umami bombs of the Southeast Asian varieties with their Western counterparts. While many Asian salads rely on more meats and seafood than greens, the dressing creates the main flavors. Think fish sauce, garlic, shallot, citrus, and lots of fresh herbs.

To some, that could be stretching the definition of salad, but if you think about it, it's the same idea as what we consider a salad: several ingredients are tossed into a bowl with a dressing.

My favorite salad is Pork Laab (page 142)—it's ground pork with fish sauce, fresh lime juice, red onions, herbs, and the most important ingredient: rice powder! Rice powder is made from sticky rice that has been toasted and pounded in a mortar and pestle to a powder and has a texture that's between coarse and fine. It adds a nuttiness, and it also helps thicken up an overly loose sauce or dressing. Pork Laab is very distinct to Thai cuisine. It's so good that you'll never want a lettuce-based salad again.

Salads in Southeast Asia really reflect the cuisines of the individual countries. In Vietnam, the salad dishes tend to be herb-heavy and fresh, with lots of texture like my Vietnmese Papaya and Crispy Taro Salad (page 135), which is packed with lots of crispy green papaya and fried taro, two varieties of fresh mint, and a handful of cilantro leaves. Thai salads are fresh with lots of textures too, but they also tend to be a bit more bold thanks to the addition of fresh chili peppers, like in my Thai Crispy Catfish Salad with Green Mango (page 139), which has pounded red Thai chilies for heat and cashews for crunch. In Malaysia, there are pickles in a lot of salads. The best part of my Grilled Pineapple and Shrimp Salad (page 133), for example, is the Pickled Cucumbers (page 53). You'd never expect it, but it's the perfect balance to the smoke from the grilled fruit and the sweetness from the shrimp and coconut.

I love using salads as a blank canvas to try out new combinations. I use them to bring together dishes I've found on the street, or I'll create completely new dishes by playing with Southeast Asian techniques and more Western ingredients. That's how I came up with my Grilled Pork Jowl with Fried Brussels Sprouts Salad (page 131) actually. I wanted to create a dish with Brussels sprouts, and I realized that if I crisped them up, they'd be the perfect accompaniment to my braised and grilled pork jowl. They're strong enough to play off of the char of the pork jowl and add an awesome element of texture.

Salads, like all of Southeast Asian cuisine, are all about balance. Once you master a few of the recipes in this chapter, you'll be able to create a few of your own.

THAI PAPAYA SALAD
(SOM TUM)

SERVES: 4

3 garlic cloves, smashed

6 fresh red Thai chilies, stems removed

⅓ cup palm sugar

2 tablespoons Squid Brand fish sauce

1 cup plus 2 tablespoons freshly squeezed lime juice (about 9 limes)

½ pound long beans, cut on bias into 1-inch pieces, or haricots verts, cut in half

1 green papaya, peeled and shredded (see Note)

12 cherry tomatoes, cut in half

¼ cup roasted unsalted peanuts

¼ cup dried shrimp

This is probably the most famous Thai salad. It's one that most people have eaten and is super easy to make. Classically, it is made in a clay mortar and pestle, which will bruise the ingredients and not pound them to a paste. This makes a really great picnic salad and is delicious served with Thai Grilled Chicken (page 221) and Sticky Rice (page 151). The larger green (unripe) papaya can usually be found in Asian markets—you want to find one that is rock hard, with no give at all.

1. To make in a mortar and pestle: Combine the garlic and chilies in a large mortar and pestle and pound to a chunky paste. Add the palm sugar, fish sauce, and lime juice and keep pounding until the sugar dissolves.

2. Add the long beans, papaya, and tomatoes to the mortar and lightly pound the salad, making sure that everything is coated in the dressing. Add 2 tablespoons of the peanuts and the dried shrimp and pound a bit more (the peanuts should remain chunky.) At this point you can adjust the seasoning: if you like it saltier, add a bit more fish sauce; if you like it sour, add a bit more lime juice. Transfer to a platter or shallow bowl and make sure to get all of the dressing out. Garnish with the remaining 2 tablespoons peanuts.

3. To make in a food processor: Combine the garlic, chilies, palm sugar, fish sauce, and lime juice and pulse until coarsely chopped and the sugar begins to dissolve. Taste for seasoning and add more fish sauce for saltier or lime juice for more sour. Combine the beans, papaya, tomato, all but 2 tablespoons of the peanuts, and the dried shrimp in a large bowl and add the dressing and massage the ingredients for 2 minutes.

4. Transfer to a platter or shallow bowl and garnish with the remaining 2 tablespoons peanuts.

*How to shred a papaya
Use a julienne peeler to grate the papaya: Simply peel, halve, and remove the seeds and grate each half into a bowl.

The best way to shred a papaya takes some practice but is really the best way, especially for salads. To do so, peel the papaya whole and just make many long cuts deep into the flesh using a chef's knife, then thinly slice off the top layer into a bowl. Continue until all of the papaya is shredded.

GRILLED PORK JOWL WITH FRIED BRUSSELS SPROUTS SALAD

SERVES: 4

BRAISED PORK JOWL

1¼ pounds cleaned pork jowl, excess fat trimmed (leave ¼ inch of fat attached)

¼ cup Squid Brand fish sauce

2 teaspoons granulated sugar

½ teaspoon white pepper

¼ cup canola oil

SALAD

6 cups canola oil

1 pound Brussels sprouts, trimmed and halved or quartered, depending on their size

Kosher salt

2 large shallots, thinly sliced lengthwise

¼ cup fresh mint leaves

¼ cup fresh cilantro leaves

1 tablespoon rice powder, plus more for garnish

1 cup House Dressing (page 40)

This salad is a version of a dish that is made with pork neck in Thailand. The authentic dish is not served with Brussels sprouts, but I like using Brussels sprouts because they add a bit of crunch. If you can't find pork jowl, use pork shoulder—it is not as fatty, but it is an acceptable substitute.

Pork jowl needs to be cleaned, and I suggest just having your butcher do it for you.

1. Make the pork jowl: Put the pork jowl in a bowl. Add the fish sauce, sugar, and white pepper and toss to coat it in the mixture. Cover and let it marinate in the refrigerator for at least 4 hours and up to 24 hours.

2. Preheat the oven to 300 degrees F. Transfer the jowl to a pot and add enough cold water to just cover the top. Cover and cook for about 2 hours, until tender but not falling apart. Remove from the braising liquid and let cool.

3. Heat a grill to high or grill pan over high heat. Brush the jowl with the oil and grill until charred on both sides. Remove and let cool slightly before slicing thinly.

4. Make the salad: Line a baking sheet with a few layers of paper towels. Heat the oil in a deep fryer or large Dutch oven over medium heat until it reaches 350 degrees F.

5. Fry the Brussels sprouts in batches (be careful—Brussels sprouts will pop when they are first added to the hot oil). Remove the sprouts with a slotted spoon to the prepared baking sheet and immediately season with some salt. Repeat with the remaining sprouts.

6. While the sprouts are frying, combine the shallots, mint, cilantro, rice powder, sliced pork jowl, and Brussels sprouts. Add the dressing and mix well to combine. Transfer to a platter and garnish with rice powder.

POMELO SALAD WITH SHRIMP

SERVES: 4

3 garlic cloves, smashed

2 fresh red Thai chilies, stems removed

1 cup plus 2 tablespoons freshly squeezed lime juice (about 9 limes)

⅓ cup palm sugar

½ cup Red Boat fish sauce

¼ cup canola oil

16 dried shrimp, reconstituted in water, drained, and dried on paper towels

2 pomelos, peeled and segments cut into small pieces (see Note)

24 large shrimp, peeled, deveined, poached, and tails removed

1 shallot, thinly sliced

¼ cup torn fresh cilantro leaves

¼ cup torn fresh mint leaves

½ cup toasted unsweetened coconut flakes

¼ cup whole roasted unsalted peanuts

Pomelo is a fruit similar to grapefruit, but it is not as tart and has a thicker skin. I love this dish because the flavor from the pomelo, shrimp, and lime; the texture of the nuts; the umami from the fried dried shrimp; and the palm sugar sweetness come together to hit all of your senses. It's everything I love about Thai salads: simple in preparation but unbelievably complex flavors. The shrimp can be grilled, stir-fried, or poached, whatever you like. If you are not in the mood to deal with the dried shrimp, just leave it out—you will still get texture from the peanuts.

1. Combine the garlic, chilies, lime juice, and palm sugar in a blender and blend until smooth and the sugar dissolves. Add the fish sauce and blend until combined.

2. Heat the oil in a small sauté pan over high heat until the oil is shimmering. Add the dried shrimp and cook for about 4 minutes, stirring a few times until lightly golden brown and crispy. Drain on paper towels.

3. Combine the pomelos, both shrimp, the shallot, cilantro, and mint in a large bowl. Add the dressing and toss to combine. Just before serving top with the coconut and peanuts.

Note:

To prepare the pomelo: Slice the top and bottom off the pomelo where the pith meets the flesh. The stem end will be thicker than the bottom of the pomelo.

Use a sharp knife to score four cuts in the peel from the top to bottom at equal distances around the pomelo. Do not cut into the flesh, cut the peel only. Peel off the skin.

Follow the natural segments of the pomelo to pry it in half. Remove the papery wall membranes from each segment being careful to keep the segments as whole as possible. If needed, use a paring knife to remove the tough part of the pith.

GRILLED PINEAPPLE AND SHRIMP SALAD

SERVES: 4 TO 6

DRESSING

2 red Thai chilies, thinly sliced

2 garlic cloves, finely chopped

¼ cup granulated sugar

¾ cup freshly squeezed lime juice (about 6 limes)

½ cup Red Boat fish sauce

⅓ cup Scallion Oil (page 45)

SALAD

24 large shrimp (21–25), shelled and deveined

1 small ripe pineapple, sliced lengthwise into ½-inch-thick slices, core discarded

¼ cup canola oil

½ cup Pickled Cucumbers (page 53)

1 small red onion, halved and thinly sliced

1 cup torn fresh cilantro leaves

½ cup torn fresh mint leaves

½ cup whole roasted unsalted peanuts

⅓ cup coconut flakes, lightly toasted

2 tablespoons Crispy Garlic (page 43)

2 tablespoons Crispy Fried Shallots (page 52)

A sure sign that this salad hails from Malaysia is the addition of pickled vegetables, since most salads from Southeast Asia contain fresh vegetables. It's similar to the Pomelo Salad with Shrimp (page 132) in that both contain fruit and nuts, but the pineapple and coconut give a natural punch of sweetness. Grilling the pineapple adds a touch of smoke and intensifies the flavor. Coconut adds more texture. I prefer the larger coconut flakes in this salad, but if you can't find them, feel free to use shredded coconut. This salad is light and refreshing and perfect for an outdoor barbecue.

1. Make the dressing: Combine the chilies and garlic in a mortar and pestle and pound to a coarse paste. Add the sugar and lime and pound until the sugar is dissolved. Stir in the fish sauce. Whisk in the scallion oil.

2. Let the dressing sit while you prepare the salad to allow the flavors to meld. The dressing can be made up to 3 days in advance and stored, covered, in the refrigerator.

3. Make the salad: Prepare an ice bath in a large bowl. Bring a large pot of water to a boil over high heat, add the shrimp, remove from the heat, and poach for about 2 minutes, until just cooked through. Remove the shrimp with a slotted spoon and transfer to the ice bath. Let cool for about 5 minutes. Drain well and pat dry. Remove the tail and slice each shrimp in half lengthwise.

4. Heat a grill to high heat or a grill pan over high heat. Brush the pineapple on both sides with some of the oil. Grill on both sides for about 2 minutes per side, until just slightly charred but not cooked through. Remove and let cool, then cut crosswise into thin slices.

5. Combine the shrimp, pineapple, cucumbers, onion, cilantro, and mint in a large bowl. Add ½ cup of the dressing and toss well to combine. Transfer to a serving bowl or platter and garnish the top with the peanuts, coconut, crispy garlic, and shallots.

VIETNAMESE PAPAYA AND CRISPY TARO SALAD

SERVES: 4

¾ cup freshly squeezed lime juice (about 6 limes)

½ cup Red Boat fish sauce

¼ cup granulated sugar

⅓ cup Scallion Oil (page 45)

2 garlic cloves, finely chopped

3 red Thai chilies, thinly sliced

1 cup House Marinade (page 40)

12 ounces skinless, boneless chicken thighs

Canola oil

1 cup thinly sliced sticks of taro (or cut into julienne)

Kosher salt

Freshly ground black pepper

1 medium green papaya, shredded (see page 129)

2 large carrots, shredded

¼ cup torn fresh Vietnamese mint leaves (see page 32)

¼ cup torn fresh American mint leaves

¼ cup fresh cilantro leaves

¼ cup Crispy Fried Shallots (page 52)

2 tablespoons chopped roasted unsalted peanuts

The first time I ate this salad was in a small restaurant hidden down a tiny alleyway in Hoi An, Vietnam, aptly called Secret Garden. What I love about this salad, as opposed to other papaya salads (every country in Southeast Asia has its own version), is the amount of texture going on. Crispy shallots and peanuts are pretty common, but the addition of fried taro adds a whole other level of texture and flavor. Secret Garden serves their version with shrimp, but I like to use chicken. Feel free to substitute shrimp, calamari, or tofu, or omit the protein altogether and you'll still have one delicious, refreshing salad.

There are many versions of papaya salad in Vietnam, but this one with taro is one of my favorites. I love taro—it adds a great, long-lasting crisp texture, and the flavor is pretty neutral with just a slightly nutty taste. Rinsing off some of the starch in cold water before frying it will guarantee crispy texture. Vietnamese mint leaves, or laksa, are stronger and more peppery than American spearmint. If you can't find laksa (or rau ram, as it is referred to in Vietnam), just increase the amount of spearmint and cilantro in the recipe by 2 tablespoons each.

1. Combine the lime juice, fish sauce, and sugar in a small bowl and whisk until the sugar dissolves. Whisk in the scallion oil, garlic, and chilies. Let the dressing sit while you prepare the salad to allow the flavors to meld. The dressing can be made up to 3 days in advance and stored, covered, in the refrigerator. Combine the house marinade and chicken in a medium bowl and stir to coat. Let marinate for at least 30 minutes and up to 12 hours or overnight.

2. Heat 1 cup of canola oil in a medium saucepan over high heat until it reaches 350 degrees F on a deep-fry thermometer. Line a plate with paper towels. Add half of the taro and fry for about 2 minutes, until golden brown and crispy. Transfer with a slotted spoon to the prepared plate and sprinkle with a bit of salt and pepper. Repeat with the remaining taro.

3. Heat a grill to high, or grill pan or nonstick pan over high heat. Remove the chicken from the marinade and cook the chicken for about 5 minutes per side, until golden brown on both sides and just cooked through. Transfer to a cutting board, let rest 5 minutes, then thinly slice.

4. Combine the chicken, papaya, carrots, mint, cilantro, shallots, and peanuts in a large bowl. Add half of the dressing and toss well to coat everything. Transfer to a serving bowl or platter. Add more dressing and garnish with crispy taro, crispy shallots, and more peanuts, if desired.

THAI GREEN MANGO SALAD

SERVES: 4

This is similar to the Thai Papaya Salad (page 129), but I use coconut milk in the dressing and cashews instead of peanuts, which adds a richness. (And if you can't find green mango, you can definitely use green papaya.) For some reason I see more cashews paired with green mango and peanuts paired with papaya in Southeast Asia, so I tend to do the same thing when I am developing my recipes. The lemongrass and kaffir add a floral note, and the herbs add a green freshness. Any light-flavored protein such as chicken, shrimp, or white fish pairs well with this salad.

DRESSING

4 fresh red Thai chilies, chopped

2 garlic cloves, chopped

¼ cup palm sugar or 3 tablespoons golden sugar or granulated sugar

¼ cup plus 2 tablespoons freshly squeezed lime juice (from 3 to 4 limes)

¼ cup plus 2 tablespoons Squid Brand fish sauce

3 tablespoons fresh or canned unsweetened coconut milk

CHICKEN

4 cilantro stems or cilantro roots

3 garlic cloves, chopped

½ teaspoon kosher salt, plus more for grilling

One 13.5-ounce can unsweetened coconut milk

2 tablespoons Squid Brand fish sauce

3 tablespoons granulated white sugar

⅛ teaspoon white pepper

1¼ pounds skinless, boneless chicken thighs or breasts

SALAD

2 green mangoes, peeled and shredded with Asian julienne peeler

¼ cup unsalted roasted cashews

1 shallot, thinly sliced

2 lemongrass stalks, trimmed and thinly sliced (page 28)

¼ cup loosely packed fresh mint leaves

¼ cup loosely packed fresh cilantro leaves

2 tablespoons fried dry shrimp (see Note)

2 tablespoons fresh kaffir lime leaves, thinly sliced

1. Make the dressing: If you are making the dressing in a mortar and pestle: Combine the chilies and garlic and pound until a chunky paste forms. Add the sugar and pound until it begins to dissolve. Mix in the lime juice, fish sauce, and coconut milk until smooth. If you are making the dressing in a blender: Combine the chilies, garlic, sugar, lime juice, and fish sauce in a blender and blend until smooth.

2. Transfer the dressing to a bowl and whisk in the coconut milk until combined. The dressing will keep, covered in the refrigerator, for up to 1 week.

3. Make the chicken: Combine the cilantro stems, garlic, salt, coconut milk, fish sauce, sugar, and white pepper in a blender and blend until smooth.

4. Put the chicken in a 9-inch baking dish; add the marinade, cover, and marinate in the refrigerator for at least 4 hours and up to 24 hours. The longer it marinates, the better the flavor.

5. Heat a grill to high or a grill pan over high heat. Remove the chicken from the marinade and pat dry with paper towels. Season lightly on both sides with kosher salt and grill for about 4 minutes per side, until golden brown and charred on both sides and just cooked through. Remove and let rest for 5 minutes before slicing.

6. Make the salad: Combine the mango, cashews, shallot, lemongrass, mint, cilantro, dried shrimp, and kaffir lime leaves in a large bowl. Add the dressing and toss to coat.

7. Transfer the salad to a large platter and top with the sliced chicken.

Note:

Soak 2 tablespoons dried shrimp in warm water for 15 minutes. Drain, pat dry with paper towels, and toast in a dry pan over high heat until crispy, about 5 minutes.

RED CURRY RICE SALAD

SERVES: 4 TO 6

RICE BALLS

4 cups cooked Steamed Jasmine Rice (see page 150; which is 2 cups dried)

¼ cup Red Curry Paste (page 183) or prepared store-bought

4 fresh kaffir lime leaves, thinly sliced

1 to 2 tablespoons Squid Brand fish sauce, depending on your taste

4 cups vegetable or peanut oil

SALAD

12 ounces ground pork

1 tablespoon peanut or vegetable oil

2 garlic cloves, finely chopped

Fish sauce to taste

Freshly squeezed juice of 2 small limes

⅛ teaspoon chili flakes

⅛ teaspoon galangal powder

1 small shallot, thinly sliced

1-inch piece of fresh ginger, peeled and thinly sliced

15 fresh mint leaves, thinly sliced

16 fresh cilantro leaves, chopped

1 small red Thai chili, thinly sliced

¼ cup roasted unsalted peanuts

24 leaves Bibb lettuce

This is one of those dishes that I not only love to eat but also love to make. It's a play on one of my favorite Thai dishes, Pork Laab (page 142), and the translation would be something along the lines of fermented cured pork and fried curry rice, but this dish is something more than that. It takes the most interesting textures from each dish and plays them off each other, the crispy rice and the succulent meat, the bright sauce and the heat from the curry. While most traditional restaurants would serve these dishes with a plate of raw vegetables to cool the palate, I opt for lettuce cups to make the experience a bit more interactive.

1. Combine the rice, curry paste, and kaffir lime leaves in a large bowl. Season with fish sauce to taste. Form the rice mixture into small balls (about 2 tablespoons each of packed rice) and flatten them. Line a baking sheet with paper towels.

2. Heat the oil in a medium Dutch oven over medium heat until it registers 325 degrees F on a deep-fry thermometer.

3. Make the salad: While the oil is heating, put 1 cup of water in a medium high-sided sauté pan or saucepan and bring to a boil over high heat. Add the pork and cook, stirring constantly, for about 7 minutes, until cooked through. Remove from the heat and drain off the excess water.

4. Line a plate with paper towels. Heat the oil in a small sauté pan over medium heat until it begins to shimmer. Add the garlic and cook, stirring a few times until lightly golden brown and crispy, about 2 minutes. Remove with a slotted spoon to the paper towel–lined plate and set aside.

5. Transfer the cooked pork to a large bowl and add the fish sauce, lime juice, chili flakes, and galangal powder. Taste for seasoning and add more of any or each if you desire.

6. Fry the rice balls, in batches, for about 3 minutes, until lightly golden brown and crispy. Remove the rice balls with a slotted spoon to the prepared baking sheet. Repeat with the remaining rice.

7. Combine the shallot, ginger, mint, cilantro, Thai chili, peanuts, and crispy garlic and mix together. Break up the curry rice balls into small pieces and add that to the salad.

8. Serve with the lettuce cups on the side.

THAI CRISPY CATFISH SALAD WITH GREEN MANGO
(YUM PLA DOOK FOO)

SERVES: 4

2 Thai chilies, thinly sliced

3 garlic cloves, finely chopped

⅓ cup palm sugar

1 cup plus 2 tablespoons freshly squeezed lime juice (about 8 limes)

½ cup Red Boat fish sauce

1 large green mango, peeled and shredded

⅓ cup whole roasted unsalted cashews

¼ cup torn fresh cilantro leaves

6 fresh mint leaves, torn

1 pound catfish fillets

Canola oil

8 ounces smoked trout, flaked with a fork

This salad hails from the Mekong region in Thailand, where catfish is one of the most common and popular fish. Traditionally, the catfish is cooked over a charcoal grill to help it pick up a smoky flavor before it is pounded into a fluffy mixture by using a mortar and pestle (sorry, a mixer or food processor just won't work) and fried until lightly golden brown and crispy. A grill pan will work if you don't own a grill, or you can poach or pan-sear the fish—the smoked trout bumps up the smoke taste on its own. If you aren't a fan of catfish, you can substitute tilapia.

1. Combine the chilies and garlic in a mortar and pestle and pound to a coarse paste. Add the sugar and lime juice and pound until the sugar is dissolved. Stir in the fish sauce. The dressing can be made up to 3 days in advance and stored, tightly covered, in the refrigerator.

2. Combine the mango, cashews, cilantro, mint, and dressing in a large bowl and mix to combine. Let the salad sit at room temperature while you prepare the fish, to allow the flavors to meld.

3. Heat a grill to high or a grill pan or nonstick pan over high heat. Brush the fillets on both sides with the oil and cook for about 5 minutes per side, until golden brown and just cooked through. Remove and let cool. Flake the fish into bite-size pieces with a fork. Transfer to a large bowl and add the trout.

4. Line a sheet pan with a few layers of paper towels. Begin pounding the fish, in batches, in a mortar and pestle until it becomes light and fluffy. Once all the fish has been pounded, break it up with your hands to make sure there are no large clumps. Transfer the fish to the prepared sheet pan to get rid of any additional moisture.

5. Line another sheet pan with a few layers of paper towels. Fill a wok or a high-sided sauté pan a third of the way with oil and heat it over medium heat until it reaches 380 degrees F on a deep-fry thermometer.

RECIPE CONTINUES

6. Divide the fish into four equal portions (about 8 ounces each). Fry one portion of the fish at a time. While the fish is frying, it will all connect and make one large fluffy circle of fish. It will take 3 to 4 minutes to cook. Then either remove it as a full circle or fold it in half. Drain on a paper towel. Repeat with the remaining portions, adding more oil if needed and allowing it to come up to temperature.

7. Serve one disk per person on a large plate topped with some of the salad and Steamed Jasmine Rice (see page 150) or Sticky Rice (see page 151) on the side.

PORK LAAB

SERVES: 4

1 pound ground pork 90/10

Freshly squeezed juice of 8 limes (about 1 cup)

¼ cup Squid Brand fish sauce

2 teaspoons Thai chili flakes (or more if you like spicy)

1 tablespoon granulated sugar (if the limes are very tart, add more sugar to balance)

1 shallot, thinly sliced

¼ cup plus 1 tablespoon rice powder

1 large scallion (white parts and green parts), thinly sliced

¼ cup torn fresh cilantro leaves

¼ cup torn fresh mint leaves

1 tablespoon Crispy Garlic (see page 43)

Laab is the unofficial dish of Laos that made its way over to Thailand, which kind of makes it the unofficial dish of both countries. Laab can be made with chicken, beef, and even catfish. But my favorite way to make it is with pork. Cooking pork in water gets rid of some of the fat and gives the meat a silkier texture than searing it in oil does.

The star of this dish is the rice powder . . . yes, the rice powder. It gives it that distinctive nutty flavor and adds incredible texture. The more you add the better, in my opinion. I love this served with Sticky Rice (page 151) and a variety of raw vegetables such as cabbage, long beans, and cucumbers.

1. Bring 1 cup of water to a boil in a large high-sided sauté pan. Add the pork and cook, stirring and breaking it up with a wooden spoon, for about 5 minutes, until it is just cooked through and no pink remains. Transfer to a colander and drain well.

2. Whisk together the lime juice, fish sauce, chili flakes, sugar, and shallot in a large bowl.

3. Transfer the pork to the bowl and mix well to combine. Stir in ¼ cup of the rice powder.

4. Transfer to a serving bowl and stir in the scallion, cilantro, and mint. Garnish with the crispy garlic and the remaining 1 tablespoon rice powder.

BURMESE EGGPLANT SALAD

SERVES: 6

1½ pounds (about 6) Japanese eggplant

¼ cup Garlic Oil (page 43)

⅓ cup Red Boat fish sauce

½ cup freshly squeezed lime juice

½ cup roasted peanuts, chopped

½ teaspoon dried Thai chili flakes

¼ cup finely chopped fresh cilantro leaves

¼ cup finely chopped fresh mint leaves

1 teaspoon dried shrimp powder

Crispy Fried Shallots (page 52), for garnish

2 cups shrimp chips, for serving

I learned to make this dish in a stilted house on Inle Lake in Myanmar (which used to be called Burma). My husband and I had been touring the lake for a week, eating and exploring. One of the dishes that had caught my eye was an eggplant salad we'd seen all over, so our tour guide organized an afternoon with a local woman who'd grown up making it. I love how simple this dish is, how it uses the eggplant as a base for the incredibly focused play and balance of flavors. While we ate it on rice chips in Myanmar, we like to serve it with shrimp chips at the restaurant for a little fun.

1. Preheat the grill to high or a grill pan over high heat.

2. Prick the entire surface of each eggplant with a fork (this will keep them from exploding on the grill) and brush with 2 tablespoons of the garlic oil.

3. Put the eggplant on the grill and cook for about 10 minutes total, until very soft and the surface is golden brown and slightly charred. Remove the eggplant to a plate and let them cool slightly. Slice the eggplant in half and scoop out the flesh onto a cutting board. Coarsely chop the flesh and discard the skins. Transfer the eggplant to a large bowl.

4. Add the fish sauce, remaining 2 tablespoons garlic oil, the lime juice, peanuts, chili flakes, cilantro, mint, and shrimp powder and mix until combined. Garnish with fried shallots. Serve with the shrimp chips on the side.

BURMESE TOMATO SALAD

SERVES: 4

1 pound fresh, ripe, beefsteak tomatoes, cored and wedged

1 teaspoon kosher salt

¼ cup freshly squeezed lime juice (2 to 3 limes)

3 tablespoons Garlic Oil (page 43)

1 tablespoon Red Boat fish sauce

1 teaspoon granulated sugar

¼ to ½ teaspoon Thai chili flakes, depending on how spicy you like your food

¾ pound haricots verts, blanched and cut in half on the bias

½ small red onion, thinly sliced

¼ cup torn fresh mint leaves

¼ cup torn fresh cilantro leaves

3 tablespoons roasted unsalted peanuts

This salad is delicious and refreshing served alongside the protein of your choice. Or, you can eat it just as a meal all on its own. You can use heirloom tomatoes, cherry tomatoes, beefsteak tomatoes, or plum tomatoes—just use the best and ripest that you can find. The longer this salad sits, the better it is, so allow it to marinate at room temperature for at least 30 minutes and up to 4 hours before serving.

1. Combine the tomatoes and salt in a large bowl and let them marinate at room temperature for 30 minutes.

2. While the tomatoes are marinating, whisk together the lime juice, garlic oil, fish sauce, sugar, and chili flakes in a small bowl.

3. Add the haricots verts, onion, mint, and cilantro to the tomatoes. Add the dressing and mix well to combine. Let sit at room temperature for at least 30 minutes and up to 1 hour before serving. Garnish with the peanuts just before serving. The salad can be made 4 hours in advance and stored, tightly covered, in the refrigerator. If you are doing this, do not add the peanuts until you serve it.

YUM WOON SEN
(BEAN THREAD SALAD)

SERVES: 4

DRESSING

¾ cup Red Boat fish sauce

Freshly squeezed juice of 6 limes (about ¾ cup)

2 garlic cloves, finely chopped

2 tablespoons palm sugar

4 Thai red chilies, thinly sliced

SALAD

16 large shrimp (21–25), shelled and deveined

10 ounces dried cellophane noodles, soaked in warm water for 30 minutes, drained, and cut with scissors

¼ cup Garlic Oil (page 43)

¼ cup canola oil

⅓ cup dried shrimp, soaked in warm water for 30 minutes, drained well, and dried on paper towels

10 ounces ground pork 90/10

1 teaspoon Thai red chili flakes

½ cup lightly packed fresh cilantro leaves

3 scallions, thinly sliced

¼ cup fresh Chinese celery leaves or regular celery leaves

⅓ cup roasted unsalted peanuts, chopped

2 tablespoons Crispy Garlic (see page 43)

This Thai salad is a great dish to bring to a potluck dinner because it is best served at room temperature and the longer it sits, the better it tastes. It is also one of the only salads in this book that contains noodles. Cellophane noodles are also referred to as glass or mung bean noodles, so keep that in mind when shopping for them. The pork can also be substituted with ground chicken in case you don't eat pork or are looking to make this dish even healthier. This is my version of Yum Woon Sen, so the ingredient measurements are tailored to my preferences of sour/sweet/spicy/salty. Feel free to make adjustments to the recipe to suit your tastes—add fish sauce to make it more salty, more lime juice to make it more sour. I love the pungent, slightly peppery flavor that Chinese celery leaves give this dish, but if you can't find them, Western celery will work just fine.

1. Make the dressing: Whisk together the fish sauce, lime juice, garlic, palm sugar, and chilies in a medium bowl until the sugar has dissolved. Taste for seasoning, adding more lime juice or fish sauce or sugar, if desired.

2. Make the salad: Bring a large pot of water to a boil. Add the shrimp and cook for about 30 seconds, stirring a few times, until just cooked through. Remove the shrimp to a colander and rinse with cold water to stop the cooking.

3. Bring the water back to a boil. Add the noodles to the pot and cook for 30 seconds. Drain well, run under cold water to stop cooking, transfer to a large bowl, and toss with the garlic oil.

4. When the shrimp are cool enough to handle, slice them in half lengthwise and add to the bowl with the noodles.

5. Line a plate with paper towels. Heat the canola oil in a small sauté pan over high heat until the oil shimmers. Add the dried shrimp and cook for about 4 minutes, stirring a few times, until golden brown and crispy. Transfer to the plate to drain.

6. Bring 1 cup of water to a boil in a large sauté pan over high heat. Add the pork and cook for about 7 minutes, breaking up the pork with a spoon so that there are no large clumps, until just cooked through and no pink remains. Drain well and add the pork to the bowl with the noodles and shrimp.

7. Add the dressing and stir well to combine. Add the fried dried shrimp, chili flakes, cilantro, scallions, and celery leaves. Transfer to a serving bowl or platter and garnish with the peanuts and crispy garlic.

7

RICE AND NOODLES

Rice is the backbone of all Southeast Asian cuisine. Rice is the filler, the palate cleanser, the cooling agent for things that are too spicy, and the vehicle for all sauces. It's a necessity with every meal. Dishes are seasoned with the intention to be eaten with rice, which some might find to be too bold on their own. Rice is eaten not only with savory dishes, but it is a main component in desserts as well. Almost every dish at Pig and Khao is served with a side of Steamed Jasmine Rice (see page 150) or Coconut Rice (see page 150). At Pig and Khao, as well as at home, I use a rice cooker, and if you make a lot of rice or will be cooking from this book a lot, then I recommend that you buy one and prepare these recipes according to the manufacturer's directions. If you make or eat rice less than once a week, then use the stove top method below. Follow the directions exactly and you will create perfect rice every time.

Noodles: I am obsessed with noodles. While my obsession started in Italy with pasta, I've begun a much deeper dive into the noodles of Southeast Asia. When you think of Southeast Asian cooking and noodles, thin rice noodles like bun bo or pho may come to mind, or the most famous and well-known Southeast Asian noodle dish of all: Pad Thai (page 161). But what you may not realize is there is a stunning diversity of Southeast Asian noodles.

Similar to Italian noodles, Asian noodles come in all kinds of shapes and sizes. The commonly known thin noodles are often used for stir-fry dishes or soups, but you also have medium- and thick-cut rice noodles like the laksa noodles that I use for spicy noodle soup. Beyond that, you'll see full sheets of noodles or even incredible hand-pulled noodles. These all have fascinating uses that vary from country to country.

Not only do the shapes vary, but the ingredients do, too. Vietnamese cuisine relies primarily on rice noodles because rice is so plentiful. But in other countries, you'll find noodles made not just from rice, but from tapioca or mung bean flour, too. There's also a wide range of textures, from silky to slippery to chewy, that contrast the dishes they're served with. The texture, however, doesn't come just from the ingredients in the noodle but from how it is cooked. Sometimes noodles get a quick dunk in hot water like in the Pancit Palabok (page 163) (noodles cooked in a fish or seafood broth with egg, chicharron, shrimp, and smoked fish flakes). Sometimes they get cooked two different ways in one dish, like in Khao Soi (page 193), in which some of the noodles are cooked and then added to the broth and the remaining noodles are deep-fried in oil. It's an amazing study in textures and it's so fun to see what you can do with one ingredient and two methods of heat application.

I will let you in on one secret, though: While the cooking methods for Southeast Asian noodles are all over the place, there's one thing they have in common. The water is never salted. I think it's because the sauces are so flavorful that you just don't need it.

SIMPLE RICES

Whether providing the perfect canvas for other flavors and textures to shine or playing a starring role in dishes such as Rice Balls (see page 138) or Arroz Caldo (page 122), there is no denying rice's importance in Southeast Asian cuisine. These are my favorite preparations that appear in just about every recipe in this book.

STEAMED JASMINE RICE

2 cups jasmine rice
(I prefer Three Elephant brand)

1. Put the rice into a colander and rinse with cold water until the water runs clear. Drain well.

2. In a medium saucepan with a tight-fitting lid, combine the rice and 2 cups of cold water and bring to a boil over high heat. Stir once, cover, and reduce the heat to low.

3. Simmer for 18 minutes. (Do not lift the lid or stir.) Remove from the heat and let stand, covered, for 5 minutes; serve.

COCONUT RICE

1 cup Chaokoh unsweetened coconut milk

⅓ cup granulated sugar

2 teaspoons kosher salt

1 recipe Steamed Jasmine Rice (recipe above)

1. Combine the coconut milk, sugar, and salt in a small saucepan and bring to a simmer over low heat. Cook until the sugar is dissolved, about 5 minutes.

2. Transfer the jasmine rice to a large bowl and fluff with a fork. Add the coconut milk mixture and fold to combine. Cover the bowl with plastic wrap and let the rice sit for about 10 minutes to allow the mixture to be absorbed.

GARLIC RICE

1 recipe Steamed Jasmine Rice (recipe opposite), made 1 to 12 hours in advance

2 tablespoons canola oil

2 tablespoons (about 4 cloves) finely chopped garlic

1 teaspoon Filipino shrimp paste (I prefer Barrio Fiesta brand)

Kosher salt

1. Spread the rice onto a sheet pan in an even layer and refrigerate, uncovered, for at least 1 hour and up to 12 hours. You want to dry out the rice so it's not mushy when you fry it. Be sure to break it up when ready to use so the rice grains are separated.

2. Heat the oil in a large sauté pan over medium heat. Add the garlic and shrimp paste and cook, stirring constantly, for about 1 minute, until the garlic is soft and fragrant. Add the rice and cook for about 5 minutes, stirring constantly until heated through; season with salt to taste.

STICKY RICE

2 cups sticky rice (glutinous or sweet rice, preferably long-grain)

Sticky rice, a.k.a. glutinous rice, is a sweet Asian rice that becomes sticky when cooked. The key to perfect DIY sticky rice is not only buying the right kind of rice but also cooking it correctly. What is the right kind? Look for bags labeled "long-grain sticky rice," "sweet rice," or "glutinous rice." If it isn't available in the rice aisle of your neighborhood market, check the ethnic foods section. Still no luck? Head to a nearby Asian or international grocer or try online.

The old-school (classic, if you will) way to make sticky rice is to steam it. Of course, you can cook it in a pot on the stove or in a rice cooker, but this is how I learned to make it when I was a child and how I make it to this day.

1. Put the rice in a large pot and cover by 4 inches with cold water. Soak the rice for at least 6 hours and up to 12 hours. Drain the rice through a mesh strainer.

2. Pour the rice into a steamer basket. Boil a few inches of water over high heat in a wok or a pot large enough to fit the steamer basket. Make sure that the rice does not dip down into the water. Cover and steam for 25 minutes and eat.

3. If you do not have a steamer basket: Drain the rice using a fine mesh sieve or colander (line with cheesecloth if the colander holes are too large). Place the rice over a pot of rapidly simmering water (don't allow water to touch the sieve) and steam, covered, for 15 minutes.

4. Remove the lid and flip the rice over. Continue steaming, covered, for 10 minutes, until the rice is translucent and glossy. Taste to make sure the rice is completely cooked; it may take up to 10 minutes more. Remove from the heat, then cover and let rest for 5 minutes.

YELLOW INDONESIAN COCONUT RICE

SERVES: 4 TO 6

1¾ cups jasmine rice, rinsed well and drained

2 cups Chaokoh unsweetened coconut milk

1 teaspoon ground turmeric

4 whole fresh kaffir lime leaves

2 stalks lemongrass, trimmed and bruised (see page 28)

4 thin slices galangal

1 teaspoon kosher salt

This coconut rice is a much more savory and aromatic version of my other coconut rice recipe. I love the lemongrass and kaffir being infused into this rice, and the color courtesy of turmeric is beautiful. This is a perfect side to any grilled or fried meat or seafood.

1. To make in a rice cooker: Combine the rice, coconut milk, turmeric, kaffir leaves, lemongrass, galangal, and salt in the bowl of a rice cooker and cook according to the manufacturer's directions. Discard the kaffir, lemongrass, and galangal.

2. To make on top of the stove: Combine all of the ingredients in a pot over high heat, bring to a boil, reduce the heat, cover, and simmer for 15 to 20 minutes, until the liquid is absorbed and rice is cooked through. Remove from the heat and let sit, covered, for another 10 minutes. Remove the lid and discard the kaffir, lemongrass, and galangal.

MEE GORENG

SERVES: 4

SAUCE

½ cup ketchup

3 tablespoons sweet chili sauce

2 tablespoons dark soy sauce

1½ tablespoons sambal oelek sauce

1 tablespoon Squid Brand fish sauce

½ teaspoon Thai chili flakes

NOODLES

1 cup plus 2 tablespoons canola oil

8 large shrimp (21–25), peeled, cleaned, and deveined

1 large Yukon Gold potato, diced and blanched

8 ounces firm tofu, drained on paper towels and diced

2 large eggs

2 shallots, thinly sliced

3 garlic cloves, chopped

1 pound Chinese egg noodles, blanched in boiling water, drained, rinsed with cold water, and drained again

2 ounces bean sprouts

¼ cup Chinese chives or regular chives

Fresh cilantro leaves, for garnish

This dish is Malaysian/Singaporean. I learned how to make this dish when I visited Kuala Lumpur with my husband a couple of years back. We were staying in the Majestic Hotel, and I was learning how to cook with some of the local hotel chefs. I found this dish really interesting because it has ketchup in the sauce, which I found a little odd at first because you don't see ketchup in Southeast Asian cooking that often. The ketchup works in harmony with the sweet chili, soy, and sambal, and it is just delicious.

1. Make the sauce: Whisk together the ketchup, chili sauce, soy sauce, sambal, fish sauce, and chili flakes in a large bowl. The sauce can be made up to 3 days in advance and stored, tightly covered, in the refrigerator.

2. Make the noodles: Heat a large sauté pan or wok over high heat. Add 2 tablespoons of the oil and heat until shimmering. Add the shrimp and cook for about 1 minute per side, until golden brown on both sides and just cooked through. Transfer to a large plate.

3. Add 2 tablespoons of oil to the pan, add the potato, and cook for about 4 minutes, until the potatoes are lightly golden brown on both sides. Transfer to a bowl.

4. Heat 2 tablespoons more oil until shimmering, add the tofu, and cook for about 2 minutes per side, until golden brown on both sides and very crispy. Transfer to the bowl with the potatoes.

5. Heat the remaining ¾ cup oil in the pan. Add the eggs and let sit 30 seconds before stirring. Add the shallots and cook for about 2 minutes. Add the garlic and cook for 30 seconds. Add the noodles, 1 cup of the sauce, and potatoes and cook, stirring constantly, for about 2 minutes, until the noodles absorb the sauce. Remove from the heat and stir in the bean sprouts, chives, and cilantro. Transfer to bowls and top each with 2 shrimp and additional cilantro leaves.

SHAN

SERVES: 4 TO 6

This dish is from Myanmar (formerly known as Burma) and it was my favorite discovery when I traveled there. My husband and I stayed around Inle Lake (in the Shan State) for about 5 days. We spent the whole time with an amazing tour guide named Cho Cho, who took us to different markets, restaurants, and street stalls. She introduced me to these noodles and set up a cooking lesson for me to learn how to make them. The sauce uses the key ingredients in Myanmar cooking: onions, garlic, ginger, and tomatoes. Traditionally, it is made with sticky rice noodles, but they are difficult to source in the States. Regular rice noodles work well, too.

SHAN SAUCE

2 tablespoons canola oil

⅛ teaspoon ground turmeric

1 medium Spanish onion, finely diced

One 2-inch piece of fresh ginger, minced

4 garlic cloves, finely chopped

1¼ cups homemade Chicken Stock (page 36) or low-sodium canned chicken broth or stock

1 cup pureed fresh plum tomatoes

¼ cup Kikkoman light soy sauce

1 small star anise, ground

6 whole black peppercorns, ground

3 whole cloves, ground

½ teaspoon Thai chili flakes

Pinch of MSG

CHICKEN

3 tablespoons canola oil

½ teaspoon ground turmeric

1 pound ground chicken 80/20

1 teaspoon kosher salt

ASSEMBLE

2 cups homemade Chicken Stock (page 36) or low-sodium canned chicken stock or broth

One 2-inch piece of fresh ginger, smashed

¾ teaspoon kosher salt

Pinch of MSG

2 teaspoons Squid Brand fish sauce

Freshly squeezed lime juice to taste

1 pound fresh rice noodles

6 ounces bean sprouts

½ cup Fermented Mustard Greens (page 41) or store-bought

⅓ cup choy sum, leaves sliced thin

⅓ cup roasted, unsalted peanuts, chopped

2 scallions, thinly sliced on the bias

1. Make the sauce: Heat the oil in a medium saucepan over high heat. Add the turmeric and cook for 10 seconds. Add the onion and ginger and cook for about 5 minutes, until soft. Add the garlic and cook for 1 minute.

2. Add the chicken stock, tomatoes, soy sauce, star anise, peppercorns, cloves, chili flakes, and MSG. Bring to a boil. Reduce the heat and simmer and cook, stirring occasionally, for about 20 minutes, until reduced by half.

3. Prepare the chicken: While the sauce is reducing, heat the oil in a large sauté pan over medium heat until it begins to shimmer. Add the turmeric and cook, stirring constantly, for about 30 seconds, until the color deepens and it becomes fragrant.

4. Add the chicken, season with the salt, and cook for about 8 minutes, until just cooked through. Transfer the chicken to a large bowl to cool. In a small bowl, reserve the pan drippings for the shan sauce.

5. Add the chicken and the reserved pan drippings to the sauce and stir until combined. Keep warm.

6. To assemble: Combine the chicken stock, ginger, salt, and MSG in a small saucepan. Bring to a boil over high heat, remove from the heat, cover, and let steep for 10 minutes. Discard the ginger.

7. Add the stock to the shan sauce. Add the fish sauce and lime juice to taste. Keep warm over low heat.

8. Bring a large pot of water to a boil over high heat. Add the noodles and cook for 15 seconds. Drain well.

9. In the bottom of a large shallow bowl, add the bean sprouts, mustard greens, and choy sum. Pour the sauce over and top with the noodles. Garnish with the peanuts and scallions.

SHRIMP PASTE FRIED RICE WITH SWEET PORK, GREEN MANGO, EGG STRIPS, LONG BEANS, AND SHALLOTS

SERVES: 4

SWEET PORK

1 tablespoon canola oil

½ cup thinly sliced shallots (about 3 large shallots)

⅓ cup palm sugar

¾ pound pork belly, cut in half crosswise and cut into thin pieces that are 2 inches long

1 tablespoon dark soy sauce

2 teaspoons Lee Kum Kee Premium Soy Sauce

1 tablespoon Squid Brand fish sauce

1 teaspoon maggi sauce (see page 20)

SHRIMP PASTE RICE

1 recipe Steamed Jasmine Rice (see page 150)

1½ tablespoons high-quality Thai shrimp paste

3 tablespoons canola oil

3 garlic cloves, finely chopped

Unless you get lucky and happen to fall into an authentic (and I mean truly authentic) Thai restaurant in the States, you are unlikely to see a shrimp paste fried rice (khao kluk kapi), so when I find a restaurant that serves it, I get very excited. Unlike a typical fried rice that has everything mixed in, this version keeps the ingredients separate. It is absolutely stunning to look at, and it is like an explosion of flavors and textures in your mouth.

Shrimp paste fried rice on its own is funky, yes, but it is also very plain, so it depends on all of the condiments served with it. This is my favorite way to serve shrimp paste fried rice, but feel free to play around with using different vegetables and meats. The possibilities are endless. Shrimp paste can be hard to break up at times, so adding a little warm water to it before adding it to a dish makes it easier to incorporate.

1. Make the pork: Heat the oil in a medium high-sided sauté pan over medium-low heat. Add the shallots and cook, stirring occasionally, for about 25 minutes, until the shallots begin to turn golden brown and caramelize.

2. Add the palm sugar and cook, stirring constantly, for about 5 minutes, until the sugar begins to caramelize and turn a deep golden brown (but doesn't burn). Add the pork and 1 cup of water (the sugar will harden but will melt again over the heat) and cook for about 5 minutes.

3. Add the soy sauces, fish sauce, and maggi sauce and continue cooking over low heat for about 30 minutes, until the pork is tender.

4. Make the shrimp paste rice: One day before you plan on making this dish, prepare the rice as directed on page 150. Once cooked and fluffed, transfer the rice to a sheet pan in an even layer and let it cool to room temperature. Then place it in the refrigerator, uncovered, to dry out overnight.

5. The next day, mix together the shrimp paste and 2 tablespoons of warm water in a small bowl (if you add the shrimp paste directly to the pan, it is hard to break up and will leave clumps in your rice) and mix with a fork until smooth.

RECIPE AND INGREDIENTS CONTINUE

TO SERVE

2 large eggs

Kosher salt

Nonstick cooking spray or
1 teaspoon canola oil

2 large shallots, halved and
thinly sliced

4 fresh Thai chilies, thinly sliced

1 large green mango, peeled
and thinly shredded with Asian
julienne peeler

¼ cup roasted, unsalted peanuts

2 tablespoons dried shrimp

2 limes, cut into wedges

6. Heat the oil in a large sauté pan or wok over high heat. Add the garlic and cook for 30 seconds. Add the shrimp paste and cook for 30 seconds. Add the rice and mix well to make sure everything is incorporated. Cook for about 10 minutes, until just heated through.

7. To assemble: Whisk the eggs in a large bowl until light and fluffy and the color is uniform. Season with ¼ teaspoon of salt.

8. Spray a 12-inch nonstick pan with cooking spray. Heat the pan over medium heat. Add half of the eggs, swirling to make sure that they coat the bottom of the pan. Cook for about 2 minutes, until they are 75 percent cooked through (you do not want color on the eggs). Carefully flip over the eggs and continue cooking on the other side for about 30 seconds. Remove the eggs from the heat and slide them onto a cutting board. Repeat with the remaining eggs. Let cool for 5 minutes. Roll the eggs up tightly and cut crosswise into thin strips.

9. Mound the rice in the center of a large bowl. Arrange the pork, eggs, shallots, chilies, mango, peanuts, and shrimp around the outside. When ready to eat, toss everything together, squeeze the lime over the top, and gently mix again.

MEE KROB

SERVES: 4

¼ cup plus 2 tablespoons Tamarind Paste (page 42)

¼ cup palm sugar

3 tablespoons Squid Brand fish sauce

2 tablespoons tomato paste

1½ tablespoons yellow soybean sauce

½ teaspoon Thai chili flakes

Freshly squeezed juice of 1 lime

4 cups plus 2 tablespoons canola oil

6 ounces dried thin rice vermicelli noodles

5 ounces firm tofu, drained, patted dry, and cut into small dice

2 large eggs

1 large garlic clove, finely chopped

1 small shallot, finely diced

6 ounces ground pork 80/20

8 large shrimp (21–25), peeled, deveined, and finely diced

1 cup bean sprouts

5 Chinese chives (garlic chives), cut into 1-inch pieces

This noodle dish had a moment in the late '90s and I'm hoping it will make a comeback. While there might seem like a lot of ingredients, it is still fairly simple. There is a lot of texturing going on in this dish and a lot of complex flavors. I especially love the use of yellow soybean sauce, which adds a little bit of funk and umami.

1. Combine the tamarind paste, palm sugar, fish sauce, tomato paste, soybean sauce, and chili flakes in a medium saucepan and cook over medium heat for about 5 minutes, until the sugar has melted and the sauce thickens slightly. Remove from the heat and whisk in the lime juice. Let cool.

2. Heat 4 cups of the oil over high heat in a wok or high-sided sauté pan until it reaches 350 degrees F on a deep-fry thermometer. Line a baking sheet with several layers of paper towels.

3. Add the rice noodles and fry them, flipping them over, until they puff up. This should take just a few seconds. Remove with a slotted spoon or spider to one side of the prepared baking sheet to drain.

4. After the noodles have cooked, make sure that the oil returns to 350 degrees F and add the tofu and cook for about 3 minutes, until golden brown and crispy, turning a few times. Remove with a slotted spoon or spider to drain on the other side of the baking sheet.

5. Again, return the oil to 350 degrees F. Whisk the eggs until smooth. Hold a chinois over the oil and pour the eggs through it directly into the oil to create strands of eggs. Cook for about 1½ minutes, until the eggs are golden brown. Remove with a spider or slotted spoon to the baking sheet lined with paper towels. (Alternately, beat the eggs until smooth, pour into a measuring glass, and slowly pour the eggs in a steady stream into the oil to create strands, cooking for about 1½ minutes.)

6. Heat the remaining 2 tablespoons oil in a large sauté pan over high heat. Add the garlic and shallot and cook for about 45 seconds, until soft (do not let them burn). Add the pork and cook until almost cooked through; it will be slightly pink. Add the shrimp and cook until both are fully cooked through, about 5 minutes longer. Remove from the heat and stir in the sauce.

7. Transfer the pork mixture to a large bowl, add the fried noodles, tofu, eggs, bean sprouts, and garlic chives, and gently mix to combine.

PAD THAI

SERVES: 4

1¼ cups Tamarind Paste (page 42)

¾ cup Squid Brand fish sauce

1 cup palm sugar

¼ cup (packed) light brown sugar

3 tablespoons rendered pork fat (*not* lard) or canola oil

12 large shrimp, peeled and deveined

2 shallots, thinly sliced

2 large eggs

8 ounces flat rice noodles, soaked in room-temperature water for at least 25 minutes, until soft, drained well, and cut with scissors

¼ cup finely diced preserved radish

¼ cup smoked tofu, cut into small dice

¼ cup roasted, unsalted peanuts, chopped

¼ teaspoon Thai chili flakes

¼ cup Chinese chives (or regular chives), finely chopped

1 cup raw bean sprouts

2 limes, cut into wedges

This is probably the most well-known dish that comes from Thailand and rightfully so. A good Pad Thai is something truly special. Unfortunately, I've had my fair share of bad ones. What I love about Pad Thai is that it combines all of the contrasting flavors you want and expect when you have Thai food: sweet, spicy, sour, and salty.

1. Combine the tamarind paste, fish sauce, palm sugar, and brown sugar in a medium saucepan over medium heat and cook just until the sugar has dissolved. Do not boil and do not reduce the mixture. If by chance it reduces, add a splash of water.

2. Heat the pork fat in a large cast-iron pan or wok over high heat. Add the shrimp and sear on one side until golden. Transfer to a plate.

3. Reduce the heat to medium and add the shallots. Cook for 10 seconds, then add the eggs and cook for 20 to 30 seconds to let set, then break up, stirring constantly. Deglaze the pan with some of the sauce. Add the noodles, preserved radish, tofu, 2 tablespoons of the peanuts, and the chili flakes. Stir to coat. Add the shrimp back to pan and add the Chinese chives and ½ cup of the bean sprouts. Cook for 1 minute longer.

4. Transfer the mixture to a platter or bowls. Squeeze 2 of the lime wedges over the top and the remaining 2 tablespoons peanuts, and the remaining ½ cup bean sprouts. Serve with additional lime wedges on the side.

PANCIT PALABOK

SERVES: 4 TO 6

SAUCE

¼ cup canola oil

6 garlic cloves, finely chopped

2 teaspoons annatto powder

½ cup plus 1 tablespoon
Squid Brand fish sauce

3 cups Lobster Stock (page 37) or
Shrimp Stock (page 37)

1 cup Pork Stock (page 36), or
substitute homemade Chicken
Stock (page 36) or low-sodium
canned chicken stock

NOODLES

1 pound palabok noodles

1½ tablespoons smoked fish flakes

½ cup coarsely crushed chicharron

Juice of 1 lemon, or more to taste,
plus lemon wedges for serving

1 tablespoon Red Boat fish sauce

20 large shrimp (21–25), peeled
and deveined

2 tablespoons canola oil

Kosher salt

2 Thai chilies, thinly sliced

½ cup fresh cilantro leaves

2 scallions (green parts only),
thinly sliced on the bias

2 medium boiled eggs, peeled and
cut into quarters

1 tablespoon Crispy Garlic
(see page 43) (optional)

Pancit means "noodle" in Tagalog and is very popular in the Philippines. This pancit consists of noodles smothered in a flavorful sauce and topped with a luscious mishmash of smoked fish flakes, crushed pork cracklings, grilled shrimp, fried garlic bits, hard-boiled eggs, and sliced scallions. I learned about this dish when I was in my twenties when my mom's good friend taught me how to make it. I kicked my version up a notch by using lobster stock, and if you wanna get really fancy, add some uni (sea urchin) on top as a garnish. Make sure you use the thicker palabok noodles (see page 20).

1. Make the sauce: Heat the oil in a large saucepan over medium heat until the oil begins to shimmer. Add the garlic and cook for 3 to 4 minutes, until lightly golden brown. Add the annatto powder and fish sauce and cook for 1 minute.

2. Add the lobster stock and pork stock, bring to a boil, reduce to a simmer, and cook for 15 minutes. Remove from the heat and cover to keep warm. The sauce can be made 3 days in advance and stored, tightly covered, in the refrigerator.

3. Make the noodles: Soak the noodles in warm water until they are soft. Drain. Bring a large pot of water to a boil over high heat. Add the soaked and drained noodles and cook for about 1 minute, until tender. Drain.

4. While the water is coming to a boil, bring the sauce to a simmer in a large high-sided sauté pan or wok over medium heat. Add the noodles and stir well to combine. Cook the noodles in the sauce until absorbed. Take off the heat and mix in three-quarters of the fish flakes and the chicharron. Add the lemon juice and fish sauce and toss the noodles thoroughly using tongs or two large spoons.

5. While the noodles are cooking in the sauce, heat a grill pan over high heat, toss the shrimp in the oil in a large bowl, and season with salt. Grill the shrimp for about 2 minutes per side, until slightly charred and just cooked through. Transfer to a plate.

6. Stir the noodles well again, add the shrimp, chilies, cilantro, and scallions, and transfer to a large serving bowl. Garnish with the eggs, crispy garlic, if using, lemon wedges, and the remaining chicharron and fish flakes.

LOSHU FUN

SERVES: 4 TO 6

½ pound shiitake mushrooms, stems removed and thinly sliced

4 tablespoons canola oil

Kosher salt

8 ounces fresh pearl noodles (also known as silver needle noodles)

½ pound ground pork 80/20

1 tablespoon Kikkoman light soy sauce

1 tablespoon Lee Kum Kee Premium Soy Sauce

⅛ teaspoon white pepper

1 tablespoon cornstarch

Pinch of MSG

6 garlic cloves, finely chopped

2 red Thai chilies, thinly sliced

One 1½-inch piece of fresh ginger, finely minced

2 tablespoons thinly sliced Chinese chives

2 large eggs

¼ cup fresh cilantro leaves

Freshly squeezed juice of 1 lime

Malaysia's favorite street noodle dish. I had it for the first time when my husband and I were visiting Kuala Lumpur several years ago. I was in line (a long line, which is always as good sign) at a food court and just decided to order what the guy in front of me was ordering loshu. Raw egg adds richness and shiitake gives additional umami and a meaty texture to the dish. Pearl noodles (also known as silver needle noodles or rat tails) are made from rice and tapioca flour and have a soft, chewy texture and a neutral flavor that allows them to stand up to the sauce and strong flavors of this dish.

1. Preheat the oven to 400 degrees F.

2. In a large bowl, toss the mushrooms with 2 tablespoons of the oil and season with salt. Spread the mushrooms on a rimmed baking sheet and roast for about 35 minutes, stirring a few times, until golden brown and soft. Remove the pan to a cooling rack. Reduce the heat of the oven to 350 degrees F and place two 8-inch clay pots or two 8-inch cast-iron skillets or an enamel-coated Dutch oven on the middle rack to heat through while you prepare the rest of the dish.

3. Put the noodles in a large bowl and cover with warm tap water. Let sit for 10 minutes. Gently press on the noodles to separate them, then drain in a colander and set aside.

4. Mix together the pork, soy sauces, white pepper, cornstarch, and MSG in a large bowl. Heat the remaining 2 tablespoons oil in a large high-sided sauté pan over high heat until the oil begins to shimmer. Add the pork and cook for about 5 minutes, breaking up the meat so that there are no large clumps, until lightly golden brown and almost cooked through. Add the garlic, chilies, and ginger and continue cooking until they are soft and the pork is completely cooked through, about 2 minutes longer.

5. Add the mushrooms to the pork mixture and stir to combine. Add the noodles and sauce and cook for about 3 minutes, stirring several times until soft; add the chives. Remove the pots from the oven using oven mitts. Divide the noodle-and-pork mixture between the two pots, make an indentation in the center, and crack an egg into each. Garnish with the cilantro and squeeze lime juice over all. Serve immediately.

NYONYA LAKSA

YIELDS: 4 TO 6

SAMBAL

¼ cup shrimp paste

10 dried Thai chilies, seeded and soaked in warm water for 30 minutes

8 fresh red Thai chilies

2 teaspoons kosher salt

2 teaspoons granulated sugar

⅔ cup canola oil

BROTH

6 dried Thai chilies, seeded and soaked in warm water for 30 minutes

24 dried shrimp, soaked in warm water for 30 minutes

4 garlic cloves, chopped

1 medium shallot, chopped

1 medium stalk lemongrass, trimmed, bruised, and thinly sliced

1-inch piece of fresh galangal, peeled and diced

6 candlenuts or macadamia nuts

2½ tablespoons granulated sugar plus more to taste

1½ tablespoons kosher salt

1½ teaspoons coriander seeds, toasted (see page 22)

½ teaspoon white pepper

½ teaspoon ground turmeric

½ cup canola oil

Most people familiar with Southeast Asian cuisine are familiar with this noodle soup from Singapore and Malaysia. Those really in the know know that there are two distinct versions of this dish—Laksa Lemak or Nyonya, with a coconut milk base, and Assam or Penang Laksa, which is sour and has no coconut milk. It will come as no surprise that both versions are delicious, but this coconut milk version is richer and more palatable for Westerners than the Penang/Assam version, which is super fishy and funky. The last time I visited Singapore, I visited a hawker stall that was famous for its laksa and I learned that the key to their broth is a little bit of evaporated milk. When I got home, I tweaked my old recipe, and the evaporated milk really did take this dish to the next level. Wrapping the shrimp paste in foil (or banana leaves, if you have them) and grilling it adds a touch of smokiness and deepens the flavor.

1. Make the sambal: Wrap the shrimp paste in a double piece of foil or banana leaves. Heat a grill or grill pan over high heat and grill the packet for 4 minutes on each side. Remove and let cool.

2. Combine the shrimp paste, chilies, salt, sugar, and ⅓ cup of the oil in a blender and blend until smooth.

3. Heat the remaining ⅓ cup oil in a medium pan over medium heat until the oil begins to shimmer. Add the paste mixture and cook, stirring constantly, for about 5 minutes, until it becomes a deep red color. Transfer to a bowl and let cool. The paste will keep in the refrigerator, tightly covered, for up to 1 month.

4. Make the broth: Combine the chilies, dried shrimp, garlic, shallot, lemongrass, galangal, nuts, and a few tablespoons of the chili and shrimp soaking liquid in the bowl of a blender and pulse until the mixture is coarsely chopped. Add the sugar, salt, coriander, white pepper, and turmeric and process until a paste has formed, scraping the bottom and sides of the processor bowl. Scrape into a bowl.

5. Heat the oil in a large saucepan over medium-high heat until the oil begins to shimmer. Add the paste and cook, stirring constantly, for about 5 minutes, until the color deepens and the rawness of the shallot, garlic, and lemongrass is cooked out. Add the fish sauce and coconut milk and cook for 15 minutes, stirring constantly. Add the stock, bring to a boil, reduce the heat to low, and simmer for

2 tablespoons Squid Brand fish sauce, plus more to taste

One-and-a-half 14-ounce cans Chaokoh coconut milk

1 quart Lobster Stock (page 37), Shrimp Stock (page 37), or Chicken Stock (page 36)

ASSEMBLE

16 large shrimp (21–25 size), peeled and deveined

20 tofu puffs (see Note)

One 3-count pack Chinese fried fish cake, sliced into ¼-inch-thick slices

½ pound dried medium-thick rice noodles

½ pound Hokkien noodles (see page 32)

1 cup fresh laksa leaves (also known as Vietnamese mint)

1 cup bean sprouts

½ cup fresh cilantro leaves

4 teaspoons Sambal

1 lime, quartered

20 minutes longer. Taste for seasoning and add more salt or sugar, if needed.

6. To assemble: Bring the broth to a simmer in the Dutch oven. Bring a large pot of water to a boil.

7. Add the shrimp to the broth and cook for about 3 minutes, until just cooked through. Using a slotted spoon, transfer the shrimp to a bowl.

8. Add the tofu puffs to the broth and cook for about 5 minutes, until they absorb the broth flavor. Remove with a slotted spoon to another bowl. Add the fish cake and cook for 10 seconds and remove to the bowl with the tofu.

9. Cook the rice noodles for about 4 minutes, until just tender. Drain the noodles using a spider and divide among 4 large bowls.

10. Bring the water back up to a boil and add the Hokkien noodles and cook for about 1 minute, until just tender. Drain the noodles and divide among the bowls with the noodles in them.

11. Divide the shrimp, tofu puffs, fish cake, mint leaves, bean sprouts, and cilantro leaves among the bowls and ladle the broth over each bowl, filling almost to the top. Drizzle each bowl with 1 teaspoon of the sambal and serve lime wedges on the side.

Note:

Tofu puffs are essential for a truly great Laksa; they are just tofu that's been deep-fried, and yes, they are as spongey as they look. Which makes them perfect vehicles to soak up the glorious coconut broth and so you experience a moment of pure bliss when you bite into the tofu puff and all that juice squirts into your mouth. You'll find them in the refrigerated section of Asian markets.

PAD SEE EW

SERVES: 4

12 ounces beef sirloin, thinly sliced across the grain

4 teaspoons soy sauce

2 teaspoons baking soda

3 tablespoons sweet dark soy sauce

3 tablespoons oyster sauce

4 teaspoons Lee Kum Kee Premium Soy Sauce

2 teaspoons granulated sugar

¼ cup canola oil

3 large eggs

3 garlic cloves, finely chopped

16 ounces fresh flat rice noodles, cut in ½-inch-thick noodles lengthwise

3 cups choy sum, coarsely chopped

1 cup bean sprouts

4 Pickled Chilies, thinly sliced, plus 2 tablespoons of the pickling liquid (page 57)

¼ teaspoon white pepper

½ cup chopped fresh cilantro leaves

Thai dried chili flakes, to taste

If Pad Thai is the most famous noodle dish from Thailand, then this is certainly the second most famous noodle dish. The key to making Pad See Ew is to be sure your wok is really hot so you get that smoky char flavor. A hot wok also helps the rice noodles and sauce cook fast together so the noodles don't get overcooked. I love the sweet, spicy, and salty qualities of these noodles with the freshness of Thai basil. Serving this dish with a side of pickled chilies is a must!

1. Put the beef in a bowl, add the soy sauce and baking soda, and mix to combine well. Let marinate at room temperature for 15 minutes.

2. Whisk together the dark soy sauce, oyster sauce, premium soy sauce, and sugar in a small bowl.

3. Bring a medium pot of water to a boil. Add the beef and cook for 20 seconds, stirring once. Drain the beef, transfer to a large plate in a single layer, and leave in the refrigerator until cooled, about 10 minutes (this will stop the beef from overcooking). This step can be done several hours in advance.

4. Cook the dish in two batches: Heat half of the oil in a large cast-iron pan or flat wok over high heat until the oil begins to shimmer. Add half of the eggs (being careful because it will splatter). Let the eggs sit until they just begin to set, about 30 seconds, then, using a spatula, scramble them. Add half of the garlic and cook for 20 seconds longer. Stir in half of the noodles, beef, and sauce and cook, stirring constantly, for 2 minutes. Add half of the choy sum and cook until it just begins to wilt. Remove from the heat and stir in half of the bean sprouts, chilies, pickling juice, and white pepper and transfer to a shallow bowl or platter. Repeat the process with the remaining ingredients. Garnish with the cilantro and chili flakes.

BUN BO NAM BO

SERVES: 6

Bun means "noodles." *Bo* means "beef." *Nam Bo* means "from the sphere of the south." So, Bun Bo Nam Bo is essentially stir-fried beef with rice noodles Southern Vietnamese–style. What I love about this dish is that it has so many textures and layers of flavors going on, starting with the marinated lemongrass beef, the spice-infused broth, and then all of the different herbs and garnishes.

INFUSED BROTH

2 cups homemade beef broth or canned low-sodium beef stock or beef broth

½ medium Spanish onion, charred

One 1½-inch piece of fresh ginger, charred

2 garlic cloves, smashed

1 whole star anise

3 whole cloves

3 whole black peppercorns

1 cinnamon stick

2 tablespoons rock sugar

3 tablespoons Squid Brand fish sauce

1 teaspoon salt

3 scallions

MARINATED BEEF

2 tablespoons Red Boat fish sauce

1½ tablespoons finely chopped lemongrass

1 tablespoon plus ¼ cup canola oil

1 tablespoon oyster sauce

1 tablespoon granulated sugar

¼ teaspoon MSG

¼ teaspoon salt

⅛ teaspoon freshly ground black pepper

1 pound strip loin or skirt or flank steak, sliced thinly across the grain

3 garlic cloves, finely chopped

2 Thai chilies, sliced thin

TO SERVE

24 ounces rice stick noodles, soaked for 1 hour

1 heaping tablespoon oyster sauce

Scant 1 tablespoon Squid Brand fish sauce

¼ cup freshly squeezed lime juice

12 ounces mung bean sprouts, for garnish

½ cup fresh cilantro leaves, for garnish

½ cup fresh Vietnamese mint leaves, for garnish

8 fresh shiso leaves, thinly sliced, for garnish

2 tablespoons Crispy Garlic (see page 43), for garnish

¼ cup Crispy Fried Shallots (page 52), for garnish

⅓ cup roasted unsalted peanuts, for garnish

Thinly sliced daikon and papaya, for garnish

1. Make the broth: Combine the broth, 1 cup water, the onion, ginger, garlic, star anise, cloves, peppercorns, cinnamon stick, sugar, fish sauce, salt, and scallions in a large stockpot over high heat, bring to a boil, reduce the heat to low, and simmer,

RECIPE CONTINUES

covered, for 2 hours. The broth can be made up to 3 days in advance and stored, tightly covered, in the refrigerator.

2. Prepare the beef: Whisk together the fish sauce, lemongrass, 1 tablespoon of the oil, the oyster sauce, sugar, MSG, salt, and pepper in a large bowl until combined. Add the beef and mix well to coat completely. Cover and marinate in the refrigerator for at least 4 hours and up to 12 hours.

3. Remove the beef from the marinade. Heat the remaining ¼ cup oil in a large wok or cast-iron pan over high heat until the oil begins to shimmer. Add the beef and cook for about 1 minute, until golden brown on one side. Add the garlic and Thai chilies and cook for 1 minute longer.

4. Bring a large pot of water to a boil over high heat. Add the noodles and cook until tender and chewy, 30 to 60 seconds. Drain and rinse with cold water. Leave the noodles in the colander at room temperature.

5. Bring the broth to a boil over high heat. Add the broth to the meat, turn the heat off, and stir in the oyster sauce, fish sauce, and lime juice.

6. Divide the noodles among 6 large, deep soup bowls. Ladle about ¼ cup of the hot broth over the noodles, and evenly distribute the meat. Garnish with the bean sprouts, cilantro, mint, shiso, crispy garlic, shallots, and peanuts. Serve with daikon and papaya.

TOM YUM NOODLE SOUP

SERVES: 4 TO 6

BROTH

4 stalks lemongrass, prepared
(see page 28) and cleaned and bruised

1-inch piece of fresh galangal, bruised

⅓ cup cilantro root, bruised

2 quarts homemade Chicken Stock
(page 36) or low-sodium canned
chicken stock or broth

¼ cup Chili Jam (page 51)

2 medium shallots, cut into large dice,
plus 4 shallots, quartered

6 fresh kaffir lime leaves, left whole
and bruised

5 ounces unsweetened Chaokoh
coconut milk

¼ cup Red Boat fish sauce

Sugar, to taste

TO ASSEMBLE

1 pound ground pork 80/20

3 tablespoons Squid Brand fish sauce,
plus more to taste

1 pound fresh rice noodles

12 premade white fish balls (see Note)

16 cherry tomatoes, halved

2 shallots, thinly sliced lengthwise

½ cup fresh cilantro leaves

¼ cup Crispy Garlic (see page 43)

3 scallions (green parts only),
thinly sliced, for garnish

Freshly squeezed lime juice

When I lived in Bangkok, I would eat a bowl of noodle soup for breakfast 4 or 5 days a week. I would rotate between the stalls in my neighborhood, but my favorite noodle soup of all was a version of this hot and sour soup. There are many variations of this soup, but they all contain lemongrass, kaffir lime leaves, and galangal. I use chicken stock instead of shrimp stock, and I also add a touch of coconut milk for sweetness and richness. This soup can be made and on the table in 30 minutes.

1. Prepare the broth: Combine the lemongrass, galangal, and cilantro root in a large stockpot, add the stock, and bring to a boil. Add the chili jam, diced shallots, kaffir lime leaves, and coconut milk and bring to a boil over high heat. Remove from the heat, add the fish sauce, and sugar to taste, cover, and let steep for 15 minutes. Strain into a clean pot.

2. Finish the soup: Bring 1 cup of water to a boil in a large high-sided sauté pan over high heat. Add the pork, breaking it up into small pieces with a wooden spoon. Cook for 6 to 8 minutes, until completely cooked. Drain the pork into a colander and transfer to a bowl. Add the fish sauce and stir to combine. Let cool.

3. Bring a large pot of water to a boil, add the noodles, and cook for 20 seconds. Drain.

4. Bring the broth to a simmer over medium heat. Add the fish balls, tomatoes, and shallots. Cook for 3 minutes. Add the cooked pork and remove from the heat.

5. To serve: Divide the noodles among 4 to 6 large bowls. Ladle the broth and all of its components over the noodles. Garnish with the cilantro leaves, crispy garlic, and scallions. Add lime juice to taste and additional fish sauce, if needed.

Note:

Asian white fish balls can be found online and in the frozen section of the Asian markets. I use Best brand in my restaurants.

WONTON MEE

SERVES: 4

CHAR SUI (PORK)

2 tablespoons Kikkoman light soy sauce

1 tablespoon rice vinegar

1 tablespoon oyster sauce

½ teaspoon five-spice powder

1 drop red food coloring (optional)

2 garlic cloves, finely chopped

2-inch piece of fresh ginger, coarsely chopped

12 ounces skinless, boneless pork belly

1 tablespoon clover honey

SAUCE

2 cups homemade Chicken Stock (page 36)

2-inch piece of fresh ginger, smashed

3 tablespoons oyster sauce

⅓ cup Kikkoman light soy sauce

2 tablespoons dark soy sauce

2 tablespoons Garlic Oil (page 43)

2 tablespoons rendered pork belly fat

2 teaspoons toasted sesame oil

This noodle dish, which can be found in Malaysia and Singapore, consists of wonton noodles *and* delicate homemade wontons filled with pork and shrimp. The noodles are tossed in a salty, sweet black sauce and served with greens (choy sum) and lots of pickled chilies, which add heat. The first time I ever had this dish was at a hawker stall in Penang, and I immediately fell in love with the combination of flavors and textures. There are two versions of this dish: a wet version and a dry version. The wet version is a noodle soup with lots of broth. The dry one (which isn't technically dry) has just enough broth to coat the noodles, with additional broth being served on the side. My version is somewhere in between.

1. Make the pork: Stir together the soy sauce, vinegar, oyster sauce, five-spice powder, food coloring (if using), garlic, and ginger in a small baking dish. Add the pork and poke the entire surface with a fork. Turn to coat the entire piece of meat in the marinade. Cover and marinate in the refrigerator for at least 8 hours and up to 12 hours.

2. Preheat the oven to 325 degrees F. Remove the pork from the marinade and place on a baking rack set over a baking sheet. Combine 1 tablespoon of the marinade with 1 tablespoon of water and the honey and mix well until combined. Brush the top of the pork belly with half of the glaze and roast in the oven for 20 minutes. Turn the pork, brush with the remaining glaze, and roast for 20 minutes longer or until fork-tender.

3. Remove the pork from the oven and let it rest on a cutting board, loosely tenting it with foil. Reserve 2 tablespoons of the rendered fat for the sauce recipe below.

4. Make the sauce: Combine the chicken stock, ginger, oyster sauce, soy sauces, garlic oil, pork fat, and sesame oil in a medium saucepan. Bring to a boil over high heat, reduce to a simmer, and cook for 5 minutes. The sauce can be made 1 day in advance and stored, tightly covered, in the refrigerator.

5. Make the wonton filling: Combine the shrimp and pork in a medium bowl. Add the soy sauce, sugar, sesame oil, white pepper, salt, MSG, scallion, ginger, and garlic and gently mix to combine. Let sit for 15 minutes to allow the flavors to meld. The filling can be made up to 2 days in advance and stored, tightly covered, in the refrigerator or frozen for up to 1 month.

RECIPE AND INGREDIENTS CONTINUE

WONTON

2 large shrimp, peeled, deveined, and finely chopped

4 ounces ground pork 80/20

1½ teaspoons Kikkoman light soy sauce

½ teaspoon granulated sugar

¼ teaspoon toasted sesame oil

⅛ teaspoon ground white pepper

⅛ teaspoon kosher salt

⅛ teaspoon MSG

1 tablespoon finely chopped scallion

1 teaspoon finely chopped ginger

1 teaspoon finely chopped garlic

16 wonton wrappers

TO SERVE

12 ounces thin wonton noodles

8 ounces choy sum, cut into 1-inch pieces

4 tablespoons pickled chili liquid

Char Sui, thinly sliced across the grain

3 Pickled Chilies (page 57), thinly sliced

6. Make the wontons: Place a teaspoon of the mixture in the middle of each wonton wrapper, and then lightly moisten the edges of the wrapper with water. Seal the edges to form a triangle shape, then press the edges to thin out the dough. Bring the corners together and squeeze to form a "money bag." Repeat with the rest of the wrappers. Set aside on a plate until ready to cook.

7. Assemble: Put the sauce in a large high-sided sauté pan and bring to a simmer over low heat.

8. Bring a large pot of water to a boil. Add the wontons in batches and cook until they float to the top, then cook an additional 30 seconds longer, until tender. Stir occasionally to prevent them from sticking to the bottom of the pot. Remove the wontons with a spider or slotted spoon to a large bowl and set aside.

9. Bring the water back to a boil. Add the wonton noodles and cook until just tender, about 20 seconds. Drain well and add to the sauce.

10. Bring the water back to a boil. Add the choy sum to the water and cook for about 2 minutes, until just crisp tender. Drain well.

11. Divide the noodles and sauce among 4 bowls and add 1 tablespoon of the pickle brine to the sauce. Shingle some of the char sui pork over the top of each, and 4 wontons to one side and the choy sum to the other side. Garnish with the pickled chilies.

BEEF PHO

SERVES: 6 TO 8

BROTH

5 pounds beef bones (marrow and knuckle included)

¼ cup kosher salt

2 large Spanish onions, peeled and halved, plus 1 medium Spanish onion, halved and thinly sliced and soaked in a bowl of ice water for 30 minutes

1 heaping tablespoon rock sugar or granulated sugar

3-inch piece of fresh ginger, skin on and sliced into ½-inch-thick slices

3 whole star anise

2 cinnamon sticks

3 whole cloves

1 teaspoon coriander seeds

1 to 2 black cardamom pods (optional)

1 pound beef brisket, extra fat trimmed

TO ASSEMBLE

12 ounces banh pho ¹⁄₁₆-inch noodles (page 32)

½ pound bean sprouts

8 ounces raw sirloin, thinly sliced

1 cup packed fresh cilantro leaves

1 cup packed fresh Thai basil leaves

2 scallions, thinly sliced

Lime wedges (optional)

Sriracha or hoisin (optional)

Red Boat fish sauce to taste

This is the most famous and beloved soup of Vietnam. Its popularity has exploded in the US during the last few years. It's one of the easiest noodle soup dishes to make but one of the hardest to master because it is all about the broth. The broth is the star in this dish, and the goal is to have a clear broth that is deep, complex, and light. Depth of flavor and clear. Not oily. No one spice should take over. They should all work in harmony. When we make big batches of pho broth at the restaurant, we cook the bones for 6 to 8 hours. But when I make smaller batches at home, I don't cook the stock for as long. Everyone enjoys their pho differently, which is why I prefer to serve the lime, hoisin, and sriracha on the side.

1. Make the broth: If you have time, soak the bones overnight in cold water with 2 tablespoons of the salt (this may seem fussy, but this is how I make the broth, and it is worth the extra step). Drain and rinse well before making the broth. If not, put the bones in a very large stockpot, cover with cold water by 2 inches, bring to a boil over high heat, and cook for 10 minutes. Drain the bones in a colander and rinse well with cold water. Rinse the pot well and return it to the stove. (This is the start of making a clear broth.)

2. Return the bones to the pot and add 5 quarts of cold water. Add one of the peeled onions, the remaining 2 tablespoons salt, and the rock sugar and bring to a boil over high heat. Reduce the heat to medium-low and cook for 2 hours, skimming any of the scum that rises to the top.

3. While the stock is cooking, prepare the aromatics: Heat a grill pan or cast-iron pan over medium heat until it begins to smoke. Add the remaining peeled onion, cut-side down, and cook for about 5 minutes, until golden brown and charred. Transfer to a plate. Add the ginger and cook for about 3 minutes per side, until golden brown on both sides. Remove to the plate with the onion. If there is any char on the onion or the ginger, rinse it off before adding to the pot (a char will make the soup bitter and darken the color).

4. Add the star anise, cinnamon sticks, cloves, coriander, and cardamom (if using) to the pan and toast them for about 2 minutes, tossing a few times, until fragrant. Remove the spices, put them in a few pieces of cheesecloth, and create a bouquet garni by tying the top with string. Add the brisket,

RECIPE CONTINUES

sliced onion, ginger, and bouquet of spices to the pot. Cook for another 60 to 90 minutes, until the brisket is fork-tender. Remove the brisket to a plate and rest until cool enough to handle, about 15 minutes. Slice across the grain into ½-inch-thick slices.

5. At this point, the stock is ready to serve, or you can cook it longer to increase the flavor, if preferred. Strain the broth into a clean pot and adjust the seasoning, if needed, by adding a bit more salt.

6. Assemble the soup: Bring 8 cups of water to a boil in a large saucepan over high heat. If using fresh noodles, cook for 15 to 20 seconds, until just tender, drain and run under cold water to stop cooking if not using immediately. If using dried noodles, soak the noodles in warm water for 30 minutes. Once the noodles are tender, drain them and cook in boiling water until just tender but chewy, 1 to 2 minutes. Again, if not using immediately, run the noodles under cold water to stop the cooking.

7. To serve: Divide the onions, bean sprouts, and noodles (in that order) among 6 to 8 deep bowls. Add the meats, then ladle the hot broth over the top. Garnish with the cilantro, Thai basil, and scallions. Serve lime wedges, sriracha or hoisin, and fish sauce on the side, if desired.

8

CURRIES

Curry isn't just the yellow brown spice mix you see at the supermarket. It's something way more interesting, powerful, and diverse. In Southeast Asian cooking, it's a sauce really, a huge seasoning component. While each country has its own, I spent the most time studying Thai curries, so we'll start there.

To make curries, we start with the paste. A good base is what you need for a phenomenal curry, and the good news is that they stay good for at least a week in the fridge and a month in the freezer. Pastes are the key ingredient to have on hand to turn any dinner into something special.

There are three basic, commonly used pastes: red, yellow, and green. Red, as you can imagine, is the hottest. Its base is red chilies. While it is delicious solo, you can also easily doctor it into a Massaman curry paste by adding sweet spices such as cinnamon or cardamom or using it as a base for the broth that I've seen popping up like crazy across the States, the fiery Khao Soi (page 193).

Yellow and green pastes are a bit milder. Yellow curry paste has strong notes of turmeric and lemongrass, which keep it light and perfect for fish. My green curry paste is made with the addition of bright herbs like basil, which invigorate dishes, even plain vegetables.

In addition to red, yellow, and green curry pastes, I've also included another basic recipe for the Malaysian Rendang curry paste. Rendang curry forms the base of the king of all curries: Beef Rendang (see Beef Rendang with Potato Puree and Garlic Kale, page 242). Malaysian curries are different from other Southeast Asian curries because there are candlenuts in the paste, which act as a thickener.

Here's the trick to making perfectly cooked pastes for the base of your curries: fry them. I know that sounds weird, but it's what adds depth.

To make the perfect curry paste, I use a mix of coconut milk and oil because I am not using fresh coconut cream, which you traditionally use for frying. If using fresh coconut cream, the natural oil separates and you fry in that oil. This is an amazing one-two punch that toasts the spices, pulls out the flavors of the aromatics, and steeps the coconut milk with all of those in one. You'll cook it until it almost looks curdled and then begin to add in more liquid—water, stock, more coconut milk. Some curries are thicker than others, but typically once it coats the back of a spoon, you're all set. Realistically, you're going to have a hard time not just eating all of it off the spoon itself.

RENDANG PASTE

YIELDS: ABOUT 2 CUPS

24 dried Thai chilies, stems removed and seeded

7 medium shallots, chopped

15 garlic cloves, chopped

10 stalks trimmed lemongrass, chopped

½ cup peeled and diced galangal

¼ cup chopped candlenuts or macadamia nuts

1 teaspoon whole black peppercorns

1 teaspoon ground turmeric

1 tablespoon plus 1 teaspoon kosher salt

This is the only Malaysian curry paste in this book, and it is the base for one of the most popular Malaysian dishes in the country, Beef Rendang with Potato Puree and Garlic Kale (page 242). I learned how to make it a few years ago from the chef of the five-star Majestic Hotel. While Rendang in general is a bit dry, I like adding some of the beef braising liquid to make it saucier. One thing that differentiates Malaysian curries from Thai curries is the addition of candlenuts. Candlenuts grow in tropical areas and have a very high oil content, which makes them go rancid quickly. Fresh candlenuts can be found in Asian stores and online, but macadamia nuts can also be used as a substitute. In addition to beef, this curry paste works well with lamb and pork, but it's a bit overwhelming for seafood.

1. Grind the dry chilies, in batches if necessary, in a spice grinder (coffee grinder) to a fine powder.

2. Combine the shallots, garlic, lemongrass, and galangal in the bowl of a food processor and process until coarsely chopped, adding a few ice cubes if needed to get the mixture going. Add the chilies, nuts, peppercorns, turmeric, and salt and continue to process until a smooth paste forms, stopping and scraping the side and bottom of the bowl a few times and adding a few more ice cubes if needed. This process can take about 5 minutes to create a smooth paste. Scrape the paste into a bowl. The paste can be made up to this point and stored in the refrigerator, tightly covered, for 3 days and up to 3 months in the freezer.

RED CURRY PASTE

YIELDS: 1 QUART

32 dried Thai chilies, seeds and stems removed (about 1½ cups; see Tip)

4 medium shallots, chopped

30 garlic cloves, chopped

3 medium stalks lemongrass, trimmed and thinly sliced

3-inch piece of fresh galangal, peeled and chopped

20 fresh red Thai chilies, stems removed and chopped

20 fresh kaffir lime leaves, chopped

1½ tablespoons Thai shrimp paste

The most versatile of the curry pastes, red curry paste is found in a wide range of dishes throughout Thailand. My paste is the base for my version of the famous Northern Thai noodle soup, Khao Soi (page 193). It also serves as the base for Massaman Curry (page 227), and I also like using it to flavor things such as Thai Herbal Sausage (page 73).

1. Grind the dry chilies, in batches if necessary, in a spice grinder (coffee grinder) to a fine powder.

2. Combine the shallots, garlic, lemongrass, galangal, fresh chilies, and kaffir lime leaves in the bowl of a food processor. Add a few ice cubes (if needed) and process until finely chopped, stopping and scraping the bottom and sides of the machine several times. Add the dried chilies and shrimp paste and process until a smooth paste forms, adding a few more ice cubes if needed, stopping several times to scrape the bottom and sides of the machine. It can take about 5 minutes for the smooth paste to form.

3. Scrape into a container with a lid. The curry will last 5 days in the refrigerator and up to 3 months in the freezer.

TIP:
Snip the top off the chili and remove the stem. Give it a shake with the hole pointing down on a flat surface. Most of the seeds should fall out. If all do not fall out, cut farther up the side and use your finger (wearing plastic gloves is a good idea) to remove the rest.

SOUTHERN CURRY PASTE

YIELDS: ABOUT 1 QUART

8 whole guajillo chilies, seeded and soaked

1½ tablespoons Thai chili powder

1 large shallot, chopped

6 garlic cloves, chopped

2-inch piece of fresh ginger, peeled and chopped

2½ teaspoons kosher salt

2 teaspoons ground turmeric

1 teaspoon coriander seeds, toasted and ground

1 teaspoon ground cinnamon

2 tablespoons canola oil

¼ cup Squid Brand fish sauce

½ cup palm sugar

⅓ cup Tamarind Paste (page 42)

2 cans Chef's Choice coconut milk

This curry paste is the base for the Southern Curry Chicken Wings (page 226) at Pig and Khao. You must use Thai chili powder in this recipe—there is no substitution. This curry is even delicious served along grilled meats as a dipping sauce. The hefty amount of palm sugar used in the curry makes it sweeter than most.

1. Combine the guajillo, Thai chili, shallot, garlic, ginger, salt, turmeric, coriander, and cinnamon in the bowl of a food processor and process, scraping the sides and bottom of the bowl several times, until a smooth paste forms, adding a few ice cubes if needed to help it blend more evenly. Scrape the paste into a bowl, use immediately, or cover and refrigerate for up to 5 days or freeze for up to 3 months.

2. Heat the oil in a large saucepan over high heat until it begins to shimmer. Add the curry paste and cook, stirring constantly, for about 5 minutes, until the paste deepens in color and becomes fragrant and the rawness of the shallot and garlic cooks out. Add the fish sauce, sugar, and tamarind paste and cook until the sugar melts.

3. Whisk in the coconut milk, bring to a boil, and cook for 5 minutes. Reduce the heat to medium and cook for about 30 minutes, until the sauce is reduced by half and is slightly thickened. Transfer to a bowl and let cool before use. This will keep, tightly covered, in the refrigerator for up to 3 days.

GREEN CURRY PASTE

YIELDS: ABOUT 1 QUART

1 tablespoon coriander seeds

1 tablespoon cumin seeds

1 teaspoon whole white peppercorns

8 large stalks lemongrass, cleaned, outer stalk removed, and chopped

40 green Thai chilies

36 garlic cloves, chopped

4 shallots, chopped

¾ cup cilantro root or cilantro stems

30 fresh kaffir lime leaves

2 tablespoons Thai shrimp paste

1 tablespoon kosher salt

My green curry paste is a mash-up between two green curries that I learned to make at two different restaurants in Thailand. One is fine dining and the other is more mom-and-pop. Green curry sauce in Thailand is not typically a vibrant green; it is earthier, paler in color. Wanting to add more color to mine, naturally, I took a bit of my French training and applied it to this recipe by blending the basil into the coconut milk instead of adding both separately. This would not typically be done in Southeast Asia, but I love how it looks and it gives it more flavor. One of my favorite ways to use this paste is in the recipe Scallops with Green Curry, Corn, Shrimp, and Tomatoes (page 211).

This recipe calls for kaffir lime leaves, but they would never be used in Thailand—instead the actual peel of the kaffir lime is used and pounded into the paste. Unfortunately, kaffir limes are easier to get on the West Coast but virtually impossible to get on the East Coast, and when you can find them, they are prohibitively expensive and dry. I use the leaves and so should you.

1. Combine the coriander, cumin, and white peppercorns in a small sauté pan and toast over medium heat for about 2 minutes, stirring constantly until fragrant. Remove from the heat, let cool for 5 minutes, then grind to a fine powder in a spice grinder or coffee grinder. If you have time, toast the spices separately.

2. Combine the lemongrass, chilies, garlic, and shallots in the bowl of a food processor, add a few ice cubes if needed and process until finely ground, stopping the machine several times to scrape down the bottom and sides of the bowl. Add the cilantro and kaffir lime leaves and continue processing, stopping a few times again to scrape down the bottom and sides of the bowl until a smooth paste forms, adding another ice cube or two if moisture is needed. Add the shrimp paste and salt and process another minute to combine.

3. Scrape the mixture into a container with a tight-fitting lid. The curry paste can be refrigerated for up to 5 days and frozen for up to 3 months.

YELLOW CURRY PASTE

YIELDS: 2 CUPS

8 medium stalks lemongrass, trimmed and sliced (see page 28)

2-inch piece of fresh turmeric, sliced

3 medium shallots, diced

20 large garlic cloves, chopped

Ice cubes

30 large fresh red Thai chilies, stems removed

¼ cup shrimp paste

1 tablespoon kosher salt

Thai yellow curry has a mild, slightly sweet taste, and my favorite way to use it is in seafood dishes, as it does not overpower the mild, sweet taste of the seafood. I use it as a base for the sauce for my Pineapple Curry with Mussels (page 191), or to marinate my fish in my Grilled Cod in Banana Leaf with Yellow Curry and Coconut Cream (page 201). If you don't pound by hand in a mortar and pestle, as is classically done, adding ice cubes to the bowl of a food processor is a trick that I learned while working in Thailand. It helps lubricate the mixture, making it easier to blend and make smooth.

1. Combine the lemongrass, turmeric, shallots, and garlic in the bowl of a food processor. Add a few ice cubes if needed and process until finely chopped, stopping and scraping the bottom and sides of the bowl several times.

2. Add the chilies, shrimp paste, and salt and process until a smooth paste forms, adding a few more ice cubes if needed (however, the goal is to add as little water or ice as possible), stopping several times to scrape the bottom and sides of the machine to ensure a smooth paste. It can take about 5 minutes for the smooth paste to form. Scrape into a container with a lid. The curry will last 5 days in the refrigerator and up to 3 months in the freezer.

MASSAMAN CURRY PASTE

YIELDS: ABOUT 2 CUPS

1½ teaspoons whole cumin seeds, toasted

1 teaspoon coriander seeds, toasted

2 cardamom pods

Scant ½ teaspoon ground cinnamon

¼ cup roasted unsalted peanuts, chopped

1¾ cups Red Curry Paste (page 183) or Maesri brand (see page 20)

This curry is heavily influenced by Indian curries with the addition of sweeter spices such as cinnamon and cardamom. I use my Red Curry Paste (page 183) as the base, and my red curry is really spicy, so this Massaman may be more fiery than the ones that you have eaten in the past. One of my favorite ways to use it is in my recipe for Braised Lamb Shoulder with Massaman Curry (page 227).

1. Combine the cumin, coriander, cardamom, cinnamon, and peanuts in a spice grinder and grind into a powder.

2. Put the curry paste into the bowl of a food processor, add the spice mixture, and blend until combined. Scrape into a bowl. The paste can be stored, tightly covered, in the refrigerator for up to 3 days and in the freezer for up to 3 months.

CHU CHEE CURRY

YIELDS: 1¼ CUPS

1½ teaspoons whole coriander seeds

¼ teaspoon whole white peppercorns

5 dried Thai chilies

3 pulla chilies

2 medium stalks lemongrass, trimmed and thinly sliced

4 medium shallots, diced

12 garlic cloves, chopped

2-inch piece of fresh galangal, peeled and chopped

Ice cubes

¼ cup chopped cilantro root or cilantro stems

17 fresh kaffir lime leaves

3 tablespoons canola oil

¼ cup plus ½ cup Chaokoh coconut milk

2 tablespoons Squid Brand fish sauce

1 tablespoon palm sugar

¼ teaspoon Thai chili flakes

Fresh lime juice, to taste

This is the newest curry that I learned on my last trip to Thailand. It's drier than the saucier versions, and the name comes from the noise it makes when it's cooking in the pan. I learned this from Chef Hanuman Aspler (a.k.a. Thai Food Master) in Chiang Mai. Most recipes online will describe this as just a red curry, and I agree that it is a red curry, but the pulla chilies, with their licorice and berry undertones, give this paste a much different flavor. If you can't find pulla chilies, you can substitute guajillo. It is usually served with the fried fish of your choice, but any mild-flavored protein such as chicken or pork will work, too.

1. Put the coriander in a small sauté pan over medium heat and toast, stirring constantly, for about 2 minutes, until fragrant. Remove from the heat and let cool for 5 minutes. Transfer the coriander and the peppercorns to a spice grinder or coffee grinder and process until a fine powder.

2. Put the pan back over medium heat and toast the chilies, in batches, for about 2 minutes per side, until fragrant and the color deepens slightly. Remove from the heat and remove the seeds.

3. Combine the lemongrass, shallots, garlic, and galangal in the bowl of a food processor, add a few ice cubes for moisture, and process until coarsely ground, stopping the machine and scraping down the bottom and sides of the bowl several times.

4. Add the cilantro, 12 of the kaffir lime leaves, chilies, and spice blend and process for about 5 minutes, until a smooth paste forms, adding a few more ice cubes if needed and stopping the machine again a few times to scrape down the sides and bottom of the bowl.

5. Scrape the paste into a container with a tight-fitting lid and refrigerate for up to 3 days or freeze for up to 3 months.

6. Heat the oil and ¼ cup of the coconut milk in a medium pot over medium heat. Add the chu chee paste and cook, stirring constantly until the paste becomes aromatic and gets a deeper color, about 7 minutes. Add the fish sauce and palm sugar to season the curry and then cook for another 1 to 2 minutes.

7. Slowly add the remaining coconut milk, stirring constantly. Add the remaining 5 kaffir lime leaves and bring up to a boil

RECIPE AND INGREDIENTS CONTINUE

LEAH'S FAVORITE FRIED WHOLE FISH

1½ pounds whole dorade or red snapper, scaled and gutted

Kosher salt

1 quart canola oil

5 Thai basil leaves

2 tablespoons coconut cream

2 kaffir lime leaves, thinly sliced

and then down to a simmer and cook for 10 to 15 minutes on low heat. Add the chili flakes and season with lime juice to taste. Keep warm.

8. Prepare the fish: Make 3 diagonal slices into the flesh of one side of the snapper, cutting halfway to the bone and spacing the slices 2 inches apart. Repeat with the other side of the fish. Season both sides with salt.

9. Line a plate with paper towels. Heat the oil in a wok or high-sided sauté pan over medium heat until it reaches 350 degrees F on a deep-fry thermometer. Add the basil leaves and fry for 20 seconds, until crisp. Remove to the paper towel–lined plate. Carefully place the fish into the hot oil so it is almost completely submerged. Fry the fish until deep golden and very crispy, 8 to 10 minutes. As it cooks, use a large metal spoon or ladle to carefully pour hot oil over any exposed part of the fish to ensure it cooks evenly. Carefully remove the fish from the oil using a spider strainer and place on a wire rack to drain briefly. Season immediately with salt.

10. Ladle some of the chu chee curry sauce onto a dinner plate. Top with the fried fish, drizzle with the coconut cream, and garnish with the kaffir and basil.

PINEAPPLE CURRY WITH MUSSELS

SERVES: 4 TO 6

3 tablespoons canola oil

¾ cup Yellow Curry Paste
(page 186)

2 cans Chaokoh unsweetened
coconut milk

3 tablespoons Red Boat fish sauce,
plus more to taste

5 cups pineapple juice

10 fresh kaffir lime leaves

3 pounds mussels, scrubbed

¼ cup fresh Thai basil leaves

Lime juice, to taste

My Yellow Curry Paste (page 186) is the base of this sweet and fruity broth (courtesy of the pineapple). It is great for steaming fish and seafood such as shrimp, scallops, clams, snapper, and of course, mussels!

1. Heat the oil in a large saucepan over medium heat until the oil begins to shimmer. Add the curry paste and cook, stirring constantly to prevent it from burning, for about 5 minutes, until you can smell the spices toasting and the color deepens. Add the coconut milk and cook, stirring constantly, for 5 minutes. Deglaze with the fish sauce and cook for 2 minutes.

2. Add the pineapple juice and kaffir lime leaves, bring to a boil, reduce to a simmer, and cook, stirring occasionally, for about 30 minutes, until slightly thickened and reduced by about a third.

3. Stir in the mussels, bring to a simmer, cover, and cook for 3 to 4 minutes, until the mussels open. Discard any that do not open. Stir in the Thai basil leaves.

4. Remove from the heat, remove the kaffir leaves, and stir in the lime juice and more fish sauce to taste. Spoon into bowls.

KHAO SOI

SERVES: 4 TO 6

BROTH
Yields: About 3½ cups

2 tablespoons canola oil

½ cup Red Curry Paste (page 183) or store-bought

2 heaping tablespoons Thai Curry Powder (page 39)

2 cans Chef's Choice unsweetened coconut milk

¼ cup Red Boat fish sauce, plus more to taste

2 tablespoons palm sugar

1½ cups homemade Chicken Stock (page 36) or low-sodium canned chicken stock or broth

⅛ to ¼ teaspoon Thai chili flakes

1 quart canola oil

16 ounces uncooked thin wonton noodles

1 pound skinless, boneless chicken thighs, diced

Freshly squeezed lime juice, to taste

½ cup diced red onions

½ cup diced Fermented Mustard Greens (page 41), or 2 packed cups raw mustard greens, coarsely chopped

¼ cup fresh cilantro leaves

While I was traveling on my culinary journey, my brother came to Chiang Mai (a large city in Northern Thailand) to visit me. We had few things in mind for our little adventure together, but the one thing we had to do was find the perfect Khao Soi. We ate so much of it in those few days that I swear my skin smelled like curry. At that point, I realized I had to find out how to make it myself. I called up every cooking school in Chiang Mai to ask if anyone could teach me. Dozens of spots said no, but one, Asia Scenic Thai Cooking School—and, most important, the chef there, Gayray—said yes. Gayray taught me how to make her version from start to finish—homemade Red Curry Paste (page 183), curry powder, and Fermented Mustard Greens (page 41) included. To this day, it's her version you'll see on the menu at Pig and Khao. FYI, this is definitely one of the spiciest dishes in my repertoire. If you can handle the heat, then use ¼ teaspoon of the chili flakes. If you are not into really spicy food, then use ⅛ teaspoon or less of the flakes.

1. Make the broth: Heat the oil in a large saucepot over high heat until the oil begins to shimmer. Add the curry paste, curry powder, and 1 cup of the coconut milk and cook the paste for about 5 minutes, until it begins to look curdled. Deglaze with the fish sauce and cook for 1 minute. Add the palm sugar and cook a few minutes longer, until melted.

2. Add the remaining coconut milk, chicken stock, and chili flakes and bring to a boil, reduce the heat to low, and cook for about 30 minutes, stirring occasionally, until thickened to a sauce consistency.

3. Line a baking sheet with paper towels. Heat the oil in a large pot over medium heat until it registers 350 degrees F on a deep-fry thermometer. Remove a quarter of the noodles and fry them, in batches if necessary, in the oil for about 2 minutes, until golden brown and crispy. Drain on the baking sheet.

4. Bring the khao soi base to a simmer, add the chicken thighs, and cook for about 5 minutes, until the chicken is just cooked through. Season to taste with lime juice and fish sauce.

5. Put the cooked noodles in a bowl, ladle the broth on top, and add some of the cooked chicken. Garnish with the red onion, mustard greens, crispy noodles, and cilantro. Serve with a lime wedge. Traditionally, the mustard greens and red onion are served on the side.

9

SEAFOOD

You'll find seafood in just about every meal in Southeast Asia, whether it's the star of the dish or an essential accent ingredient like fish sauce for umami, shrimp paste for funk, or crispy anchovies for texture. Seafood is an integral part of the culture, the history, and even the economy. People have lived off the sea for centuries, and as a result, they've learned how to cook ingeniously and resourcefully with every part of the fish. We've seen how to cook with fish sauce and shrimp paste for maximum flavor, but in this chapter we'll make fresh seafood the center of the plate.

The seafood is so fresh in most Southeast Asian cities, and you will find it being cooked in the stalls in many different ways. There are stands that specialize in whole fried fish—like my Whole Fried Fish with Hot and Sour Broth (page 199). Others specialize in a simple preparation like steaming and grilling it in banana leaf to infuse those lovely herbal notes gently.

The number of ways to prepare seafood is astonishing. Beyond fried, grilled, and steamed, you'll find dishes like Kinilaw (page 209), the Filipino version of ceviche. It's raw fish or shrimp seasoned with ginger, chilies, coconut milk and citrus juices, and a splash of lemon-lime soda that sounds totally crazy but ends up totally great. It's even garnished with corn nuts which is not traditional but adds a delicious crunch.

The seafood recipes in this chapter range from raw dishes like Kinilaw to Sinigang (page 206), a Filipino soup I grew up eating when I was sick, to main dishes like a fried whole fish I love or my Singaporean White Pepper Lobster (page 217). There are hundreds more recipes to share, but these are a few of my favorite hits.

FRIED RED SNAPPER WITH GREEN MANGO, CASHEWS, AND CRISPY GARLIC

SERVES: 4

This is a light and refreshing salad found on many menus in Thailand. Even though you may see fried fish and think heavy, the mango keeps it light, and the lemongrass and kaffir lime leaves add flavor and brightness. The lemongrass grown in Thailand is much less fibrous than the lemongrass grown in other parts of Southeast Asia, so it's common to eat it raw. I recommend using the innermost stalks, which are the most tender, and slicing them very thinly with a very sharp chef's knife for this salad.

SAUCE

¼ cup Squid Brand fish sauce

¼ cup freshly squeezed lime juice

2 tablespoons palm sugar

1 tablespoon Chili Jam (page 51)

2 garlic cloves, finely chopped

1 fresh Thai chili, thinly sliced

1 teaspoon toasted rice powder (see page 26)

3 fresh kaffir lime leaves, julienned

SALAD

1 large green mango, peeled and shredded

2 medium stalks lemongrass, trimmed (see page 28), inner stalk used and sliced very thinly

2 medium shallots, thinly sliced

2 fresh culantro leaves, cut into ½-inch pieces

¼ cup fresh cilantro leaves

¼ cup roasted, unsalted cashews

1 tablespoon Crispy Garlic (see page 43), for serving

FRIED FISH

1 quart canola oil

1 cup potato starch

4 red snapper fillets, cut 1 inch thick (about 8 ounces each) and then cut into 2-inch cubes

Kosher salt

1. Make the sauce: Combine the fish sauce, lime juice, palm sugar, chili jam, garlic, and chili in a blender and blend until smooth. Transfer to a bowl and stir in the rice powder and kaffir lime leaves.

2. Let the sauce sit at room temperature for at least 30 minutes before serving. It can be made 3 days in advance and stored, tightly covered, in the refrigerator. Bring to room temperature before serving.

3. Make the salad: Combine half of the sauce, the mango, lemongrass, shallots, culantro, cilantro, and cashews in a large bowl.

4. Make the fried fish: Put the oil in a large wok or high-sided sauté pan and heat over medium heat until it reaches 350 degrees F. Line a baking sheet with several layers of paper towels and set aside.

5. While the oil is heating, prepare the fish: Put the potato starch into a shallow baking dish. Pat the fish dry with paper towels and season with salt.

6. Dredge the fish cubes, in batches, in the potato starch. Tap off the excess starch and put the fish cubes into the oil, in batches, and fry, turning a few times, for about 3 minutes, until golden brown and crispy. Transfer to the prepared baking sheet and sprinkle with a bit more salt. Repeat with the remaining fish.

7. To serve: Divide the salad and fish cubes among 4 plates. Pour the remaining sauce on top of the fish and salad and garnish with the crispy garlic.

WHOLE FRIED FISH WITH TURMERIC

SERVES: 2

This is a really popular dish throughout southern Thailand and Bangkok. I love the simplicity of the dish and I still remember the first time that I ate it at my favorite restaurant in Bangkok called Soei. Their version was prepared with small fried mackerel.

It is all about the freshness of the fish and the bright flavor of the marinade. The longer you let it marinate (a minimum of 5 hours and up to 2 days), the better the flavor.

This dish calls for fresh turmeric, which coats the skin, and you actually eat once it is fried. But if you can't find it, just add a teaspoon of dried turmeric to the marinade.

DIPPING SAUCE

¼ cup freshly squeezed lime juice (about 3 limes)

1½ tablespoons Squid Brand fish sauce

1 small garlic clove, finely chopped

1 red Thai chili, stem removed and thinly sliced

FRIED FISH

6 garlic cloves, chopped

2 medium stalks lemongrass, trimmed and thinly sliced

2-inch piece of fresh turmeric, thinly sliced

½ teaspoon kosher salt, plus more for frying the fish

1½- to 2-pound dorade or red snapper, cleaned and scored with diamonds on both sides

4 cups canola oil

Kosher salt

¼ cup fresh cilantro leaves, coarsely chopped

1 scallion (white parts only), thinly sliced

1. Make the sauce: Whisk together the lime juice, fish sauce, garlic, and chili in a small bowl. The sauce can be made 48 hours in advance and stored, covered, in the refrigerator. Bring to room temperature before using.

2. Make the fish: Combine the garlic, lemongrass, turmeric, and salt in a mortar and pestle (or a mini prep food processor) and pound or process to a coarse paste. Rub the paste over both sides of the fish, being sure to get into the flesh. Transfer to a plate, cover with foil, and let marinate in the refrigerator for at least 5 hours but preferably 24 hours.

3. Remove the fish from the refrigerator, scrape all of the paste off the fish, and transfer the paste to a piece of cheesecloth. Squeeze out all of the liquid from the paste, then put it on paper towels to dry out even more. You will be frying this paste and serving it on top of the fish after you have fried the fish.

4. Line a baking sheet with paper towels. Heat the oil in a wok or high-sided sauté pan until it reaches 350 degrees F on a deep-fry thermometer. Season the fish on both sides with salt and fry for 8 to 10 minutes, until golden brown and just cooked through, turning a few times. Remove with a spider or tongs to the prepared baking sheet to drain.

5. Add the dried paste to the oil and cook, stirring constantly, until golden brown and crispy, about 4 minutes. Transfer to a small bowl and mix in the cilantro. Put the fish on a small platter and top with the fried paste and cilantro. Garnish with the scallion whites and serve the dipping sauce on the side.

WHOLE FRIED FISH WITH HOT AND SOUR BROTH

SERVES: 4

HOT AND SOUR BROTH

1 quart homemade Chicken Stock (page 36) or low-sodium chicken broth

¼ cup cilantro roots, bruised, or 8 cilantro stems, bruised

1-inch piece of fresh galangal, smashed

2 small stalks lemongrass, trimmed and bruised

3 tablespoons plus 1 teaspoon oyster sauce

2 tablespoons Chili Jam (page 51)

2 tablespoons Squid Brand fish sauce

2 tablespoons Tamarind Paste (page 42)

6 fresh kaffir lime leaves, torn

3 shallots, cut in medium dice

½ cup cherry tomatoes, cut in half

1 cup torn oyster mushrooms

½ cup picked fresh Thai basil leaves

Freshly squeezed juice of 1 lime

FRIED FISH

Canola oil

One 2-pound whole branzino

Kosher salt

½ cup rice flour

¼ cup fresh cilantro leaves

One of my favorite ways to eat fish is served whole on the bone and fried. This dish is a version of something I had while I was living in Thailand. The broth is the star of the dish and pairs really well with the fried fish. Homemade chicken broth really lends more flavor, so if you have time, try to make it.

1. Make the broth: Combine the stock, cilantro roots, galangal, lemongrass, oyster sauce, chili jam, fish sauce, tamarind paste, and kaffir lime leaves in a large pot, bring to a boil over high heat, cover, turn off the heat, and let steep for 1 hour.

2. Strain the liquid and transfer to a bowl. The broth can be made up to 3 days in advance and stored, tightly covered, in the refrigerator, or in the freezer for up to 1 month.

3. Combine the broth, shallots, cherry tomatoes, and oyster mushrooms in a large saucepan. Bring to a boil over high heat, reduce the heat, and let simmer for 10 minutes.

4. While the broth is heating, make the fish: Heat 3 inches of oil in a large high-sided sauté pan over medium heat until the oil reaches 350 degrees F.

5. Scale, gut, and rinse the fish well with cold water and pat dry with paper towels. Score each side of the fish with 3 slits, each 2 inches long. Line a baking sheet with paper towels.

6. Season the fish liberally on both sides with salt. Put the rice flour in a shallow baking dish, dredge the fish, and tap off any excess flour. Carefully put the fish into the oil away from you and fry for about 8 minutes, turning once, until golden brown on both sides and just cooked through. Remove the fish to the prepared baking sheet and season with a bit more salt.

7. Just before serving, stir the basil and lime juice into the broth. Pour the broth into a large shallow bowl, top with the fish, and garnish with the cilantro leaves.

GRILLED COD IN BANANA LEAF WITH YELLOW CURRY AND COCONUT CREAM

SERVES: 4

½ cup fresh coconut milk (can use canned Chaokoh, but fresh is preferred)

1½ teaspoons rice flour

Pinch of kosher salt

Pinch of granulated sugar

2 large eggs

1½ tablespoons oyster sauce

1½ tablespoons Squid Brand fish sauce

⅓ cup plus 1 tablespoon Yellow Curry Paste (page 186)

¼ cup fresh cilantro leaves

2 scallions, thinly sliced

1¼ pounds fresh cod, cut into 1½-inch dice

4 large fresh or thawed frozen banana leaves

Freshly squeezed juice of 2 limes

¼ cup Crispy Garlic (see page 43)

There is something about taking fish, eggs, and curry paste; stuffing it into a banana leaf; and then grilling it that you don't see in everyday Western cooking. It is one of the many reasons that I love this dish. Banana leaves are a great way to cook fish because they impart a lovely mild flavor, but if you can't find them, just wrap the fish in parchment paper and then foil and grill it. I add herbs, coconut cream, and a squeeze of lime to give the dish a bright but fattier mouthfeel than other versions.

1. Whisk together the coconut milk, rice flour, salt, and sugar and cook over medium heat until thickened, about 5 minutes. Set aside and keep warm.

2. Whisk together the eggs, oyster sauce, fish sauce, and curry paste in a large bowl until combined. Add half of the cilantro. Then add the scallions and the fish and gently fold to combine.

3. Lay one banana leaf out on a flat surface. Put a quarter of the fish mixture into the center of the leaf. Fold the bottom edge of the leaf over the fish, fold in the sides over the fish, and then fold the package away from you to enclose the fish in the leaf. Use toothpicks to keep the packages sealed. Repeat with the remaining fish and banana leaves.

4. Preheat a grill to high or a grill pan over high heat. Arrange the packets on the grill and grill, about 4 minutes per side, turning once, until the fish has cooked through (the fish will become opaque and firm to the touch). Remove the packets from the grill and let sit 5 minutes.

5. To serve: Transfer the packets to 4 plates and gently cut them down the middle, lengthwise, using a paring knife to open the banana leaf. Squeeze lime juice over each packet, top each with a heaping tablespoon each of the coconut cream and crispy garlic, and garnish with the remaining cilantro.

SAMBAL SKATE

YIELDS: 1½ CUPS

SAMBAL PASTE

⅓ cup canola oil

2 shallots, chopped

8 garlic cloves, smashed

1-inch piece of fresh ginger, chopped

1 large stalk lemongrass, trimmed and chopped

20 fresh long red Thai chilies, chopped

4 dried Thai chilies, seeded and soaked in warm water for 15 minutes

2 teaspoons Malaysian plain shrimp paste, toasted in foil in the oven, on the grill, or over medium heat on top of the burner for 2 to 3 minutes

¼ cup Chaokoh coconut milk

3 tablespoons palm sugar

2½ tablespoons Tamarind Paste (page 42)

2 tablespoons Squid Brand fish sauce

This is one of the must-eat dishes while visiting both Malaysia and Singapore, though when you have it there, it will be made with stingray and not skate. You will find the locals grilling it on the street open-faced on a banana leaf, but I prefer to enclose the fish in the banana leaf so it steams more evenly and doesn't burn. Sambal is one of the most important condiments or sauces in the region and there are many different versions. This version uses lemongrass and coconut milk.

1. Make the sambal paste: Combine the oil, shallots, garlic, ginger, lemongrass, chilies, and shrimp paste in a blender and blend until smooth.

2. Scrape the paste into a small saucepan and cook over low heat, stirring occasionally, for about 8 minutes, until fragrant and the color deepens. Add the coconut milk, palm sugar, tamarind, and fish sauce and cook for about 7 minutes, until the mixture thickens. Remove from the heat and let cool. The paste can be stored tightly covered and refrigerated for up to 3 days.

3. Prepare the dipping sauce: Whisk together the lime juice, calamansi juice, fish sauces, shallots, sugar, salt, and chili in a bowl and set aside. The sauce can be made 2 days in advance and stored, tightly covered, in the refrigerator for up to 5 days.

4. Prepare the fish: Season skate fillets on both sides with salt. Spread the paste in an even layer on both sides of the fish.

5. Assemble: Unfold the banana leaves. Use kitchen shears to cut off (and reserve) the tough center rib that runs along the bottom edge of each leaf. Cut the ribs into 12- to 14-inch strips for tying the packets, or you can use wooden skewers to secure the packets. Gently cut the leaves into four 12-inch squares, being careful not to split them.

6. Slowly run a banana-leaf square across the flame of a gas burner, just enough to "melt" the outer coating on the leaf (it will become quite shiny; if you have an electric stove, hold the leaf slightly above the burner on moderately high).

SAMBAL SKATE DIPPING SAUCE

¾ cup freshly squeezed lime juice

½ cup plus 1 tablespoon calamansi juice

⅓ cup Squid Brand fish sauce

¼ cup Red Boat fish sauce

¼ cup plus 2 tablespoons finely diced shallot

2 tablespoons granulated sugar

1 teaspoon kosher salt

1 fresh red Thai chili, thinly sliced

FISH

6 skin-off, bone-in skate wings, about 6 ounces each

Kosher salt

8 banana leaves, rinsed and patted dry (about 1 foot each)

TO SERVE

6 lime wedges

1 large shallot, finely diced

1 cup chopped cilantro leaves

7. Place a piece of skate in the center of the banana leaf. Fold the bottom edge of the leaf over the fish, fold in the sides over the fish, and then fold the package away from you to enclose the fish in the leaf. Tie the packet closed with the strips of banana leaves. Repeat with the remaining skate and banana leaves.

8. Preheat a grill to high or a grill pan over high heat. Arrange the packets on the grill and grill for about 5 minutes per side, turning once, until the fish has cooked through (the fish will become opaque and firm to the touch). Transfer to a serving plate and let rest 5 minutes.

9. To serve: Open the fish packets to expose the fish. Squeeze lime over the fish and garnish with the shallot and cilantro.

CHA CA LONG VONG

SERVES: 6

6 medium stalks lemongrass, trimmed and chopped

¼ cup Tamarind Paste (page 42)

¼ cup palm sugar

2-inch piece of fresh turmeric, sliced

2 fresh red Thai chilies, sliced

5 tablespoons Squid Brand fish sauce

1½ pounds fresh cod or grouper, cut into 6-ounce fillets

1 cup rice flour

¼ cup canola oil

½ cup (1 stick) unsalted butter, cut into tablespoons

¼ cup chopped fresh dill fronds

¼ cup fresh lime juice (3 to 4 limes)

1 pound cooked vermicelli rice noodles, drained

1 cup Nuoc Cham (page 49), plus more for serving

GARNISH

¼ cup whole dill fronds

¼ cup torn fresh mint leaves

¼ cup torn fresh cilantro leaves

¼ cup roasted unsalted peanuts

This dish originated in Hanoi and is another example of a recipe that doesn't make sense but totally works and is one of my very favorites. You will not find a lot of dishes in Vietnam that use dill and you will also rarely see butter used as an ingredient, even with the French influence in the country. There are restaurants in Vietnam that make this to order right in front of you, and the smell of the curry-like paste, butter, and dill is intoxicating. Bun rice noodles and a side of Nuoc Cham (page 49) are served with this dish.

1. Combine the lemongrass, tamarind, palm sugar, turmeric, and chilies in the bowl of a food processor and process for about 5 minutes, until a smooth paste forms, stopping the machine and scraping down the bottom and sides of the bowl several times. Add a few ice cubes if needed to add moisture.

2. Scrape into a bowl and stir in 3 tablespoons of the fish sauce. The paste will keep, tightly covered, in the refrigerator for up to 3 days and in the freezer for up to 1 month.

3. Put the fish fillets into a 9 x 13-inch baking dish and spread the paste on both sides of each fillet. Cover and refrigerate the fish for at least 12 hours and up to 24 hours.

4. Scrape the marinade off of the fish. Put the flour into a large shallow bowl. Dredge each fillet in the flour and tap off any excess.

5. Heat the oil in a large cast-iron or nonstick pan over high heat until the oil begins to shimmer. Add the fish and cook for about 3 minutes per side, until golden brown on each side. Add the butter and the remaining 2 tablespoons fish sauce and baste the fish with the butter constantly until just cooked through, about 2 minutes longer. Stir in the dill and lime juice.

6. While the fish is cooking, combine the noodles and nuoc cham in a large bowl and toss to coat. Garnish with the dill, mint, cilantro, and peanuts. Serve the fish on top of the noodles, drizzled with some of the butter sauce. Serve with nuoc cham on the side.

SINIGANG

SERVES: 4 TO 6

1 tablespoon canola oil

1 medium Spanish onion, diced

3 garlic cloves, smashed

1 large plum tomato, diced

6 cups Lobster Stock
(see page 37)

¼ cup Tamarind Paste (page 42)

3 tablespoons Squid Brand
fish sauce

3 Thai chilies, bruised

1 heaping teaspoon granulated
sugar

¼ cup Mama Sita's Sinigang powder
(optional)

1 red snapper fish head (optional)

2 pounds red snapper, cut into
2-inch pieces

12 cherry tomatoes, halved

2 small shallots, quartered

¼ pound long beans, cut into
1-inch pieces and blanched
(see page 31)

8 okra, sliced into ¼-inch-thick
slices on the bias

½ cup thinly sliced daikon

½ bunch morning glory, trimmed,
or 2 ounces spinach leaves

Steamed Jasmine Rice
(see page 150)

Comfort in a bowl, Sinigang is one of the most famous soups in the Philippines and *the* soup that my mom made for me when I was sick as a child. It can include pork, chicken, or seafood, but my mom always used seafood, and to this day it's the only variation that I will make or eat. It is also the only time that I ever use soup starter pack. I use Mama Sita's brand—a very popular seasoned soup starter pack—because it gives that authentic flavor that reminds me of childhood. Of course, instead of water, I use homemade Lobster Stock (page 37) and add a good dose of fish sauce and tamarind paste. The more sour, the better.

1. In a large saucepan, heat the oil over high heat until it begins to shimmer. Add the onion and cook for about 4 minutes, until soft. Add the garlic and cook 1 minute longer. Add the plum tomato and cook for about 3 minutes, until most of the liquid has evaporated.

2. Add the lobster stock, tamarind paste, fish sauce, chilies, sugar, and Sinigang powder and bring to a boil. Reduce the heat to low and simmer for 30 minutes to allow the flavors to meld. Taste for seasoning and add more tamarind if you like your broth more sour or more fish sauce if you like it saltier. Strain the broth into a large bowl. The broth can be used immediately, or cooled to room temperature and stored, tightly covered, in the refrigerator for up to 3 days and the freezer for up to 1 month.

3. Bring the broth to a boil in a large high-sided sauté pan over high heat, reduce the heat, and bring to a simmer. Add the fish head (if using) and the fish and cook, without stirring, for 4 minutes.

4. Add the cherry tomatoes, shallots, long beans, okra, and daikon and continue cooking for about 3 minutes longer, until the fish is just cooked through and the veggies are tender. Remove from the heat and stir in the morning glory and let wilt.

5. Divide the fish among 4 to 6 bowls and serve with rice.

TOM YUM GOONG THAI HOT AND SOUR SOUP

SERVES: 4

1 pound large head-on shrimp (21–25), shells removed and set aside, deveined

2 tablespoons canola oil

2 quarts Lobster Stock (page 37), Shrimp Stock (page 37), Chicken Stock (page 36), or cold water

2½ tablespoons Chili Jam (page 51)

1 tablespoon chopped fresh cilantro root, bruised

1 medium shallot, thinly sliced lengthwise

4 red Thai chilies, stems removed and smashed

3 medium stalks fresh lemongrass, trimmed and bruised (see page 28)

One 1-inch piece of fresh galangal, smashed

4 fresh kaffir lime leaves

8 large oyster mushrooms, torn into quarters

1 cup halved cherry tomatoes

¼ cup Squid Brand fish sauce or to taste

2 to 4 tablespoons freshly squeezed lime juice, depending on your taste

⅛ teaspoon granulated sugar or more to taste

½ cup fresh cilantro leaves

This is probably the very first Thai dish that I ever had. When I was growing up, my parents were always working, and so we'd often order in from the pizza places and Italian restaurants that were down the hill from our house. There was also a Thai restaurant a few blocks away, and one night, instead of my usual pepperoni pizza order, I ordered this soup and Pad Thai instead and my love affair with Thai food began. This soup is known for its perfect balance of sweet, spicy, and sour.

1. Squeeze the juice (a.k.a. the brains) out of each shrimp head into a small bowl and set aside.

2. Heat the oil over high heat in a large high-sided sauté pan, add the shrimp shells, and cook, stirring occasionally, for about 2 minutes, until the color becomes a deep red and the aroma is toasty. Add the stock, chili jam, cilantro root, and the shrimp liquid, bring to a boil, reduce to a simmer, and let cook for 20 minutes. Strain the stock into a clean large saucepan.

3. Add the shallot, chilies, lemongrass, galangal, kaffir lime leaves, mushrooms, tomatoes, and fish sauce and cook for about 15 minutes, until the flavors have melded. At this point, you can remove the lemongrass, galangal, and kaffir and discard or leave them in the soup for a more rustic, traditional feel.

4. Add the shrimp and cook for about 2 minutes, until just cooked through. Remove from the heat and stir in the lime juice and sugar and garnish with the cilantro.

KINILAW

SERVES: 4 TO 6

A Filipino ceviche that uses vinegar and lime juice to "cook" the fish. The addition of coconut milk gives this dish a richer flavor, and the addition of Sprite to the marinade gives it a little sweetness, which helps balance out the acid. This is a great appetizer and it goes well with beer.

KINILAW SAUCE

32 ounces fresh or canned unsweetened coconut milk

3 tablespoons lemon-lime soda, such as Sprite

2 tablespoons fresh ginger juice (see note below)

1 tablespoon freshly squeezed lime juice

1 tablespoon freshly squeezed lemon juice

1½ teaspoons Red Boat fish sauce

2 fresh red Thai chilies, thinly sliced

1 garlic clove, finely chopped

¾ teaspoon kosher salt

½ teaspoon granulated sugar

¼ teaspoon MSG

FISH

1 pound very fresh white flaky fish, such as red snapper or fluke, cut into ½-inch dice

2 tablespoons finely diced red onion

¼ cup chopped cilantro leaves

Salt to taste

Freshly squeezed lime juice to taste

TO SERVE

¼ cup corn nuts, plus more for garnish

Micro cilantro or cilantro leaves, for garnish

1. Make the Kinilaw sauce: Whisk together the coconut milk, soda, ginger juice, lime juice, lemon juice, fish sauce, chilies, garlic, salt, sugar, and MSG in a large bowl until the sugar and salt have dissolved. Cover and refrigerate for at least 1 hour and up to 12 hours to allow the flavors to meld.

2. Combine the fish, onion, cilantro, and 1 cup of the Kinilaw sauce in a large bowl. Add the salt and lime juice to taste and let sit for 10 minutes and up to 1 hour maximum before serving.

3. Serve in bowls, using a slotted spoon. Top with a few corn nuts and garnish with cilantro. Spoon some of the remaining sauce on top of the bowl.

SCALLOPS WITH GREEN CURRY, CORN, SHRIMP, AND TOMATOES

SERVES: 4

While there are times of the year where certain fruits and vegetables are in season, seasonal cooking is really not a thing in Thailand like it is in the United States because the climate and the growing season are pretty much the same year-round. But if it were, this dish would scream SUMMER. That's the season I love to make it in—when the corn and tomatoes are at their peak. I use a little French technique to make this dish by blending the cream and basil together. It's not the authentic way to make the dish, but it keeps the sauce greener.

GREEN CURRY SAUCE

2 cans plus ½ cup Chef's Choice unsweetened coconut milk

½ cup packed Thai basil leaves

2 tablespoons canola oil

½ cup plus 1 tablespoon Green Curry Paste (page 185)

2 tablespoons Red Boat fish sauce, or to taste

2 tablespoons palm sugar, or more to taste

8 fresh kaffir lime leaves

Freshly squeezed lime juice to taste

SCALLOPS

16 U-10 sea scallops, patted dry

Kosher salt

5 tablespoons canola oil

2 cups fresh corn kernels

8 large shrimp (21–25), peeled and deveined

½ cup quartered grape tomatoes (about 12)

1 cup blanched sugar snap peas, cut on the bias into ½-inch slices

Freshly squeezed lime juice to taste

¼ cup coconut cream

¼ cup fresh cilantro leaves

2 fresh kaffir lime leaves, very thinly sliced

TO SERVE

Steamed Jasmine Rice (page 150)

---

1. Prepare the green curry sauce: Combine 2 cans of the coconut milk and the basil in a blender and blend until smooth.

2. Heat the oil and remaining ½ cup coconut milk in a medium saucepan over high heat until the mixture begins to shimmer. Add the curry paste and cook, stirring constantly, for about 5 minutes, until it begins to deepen in color and becomes fragrant, stirring constantly so that it does not burn, about 5 minutes longer, until it begins to look curdled. Deglaze with the fish sauce and palm sugar, and cook for 1 minute, stirring constantly.

RECIPE CONTINUES

3. Add the basil–and–coconut milk mixture, bring to a boil, reduce the heat to medium-low. Add the kaffir lime leaves and cook, stirring occasionally, for about 20 minutes, until the flavors have melded and the sauce has reduced slightly. Season with lime juice to taste. Remove from the heat, cover, and keep warm while you prepare the rest of the dish.

4. Prepare the scallops: Season the scallops on both sides with salt. Heat ¼ cup of the oil in a large nonstick pan over high heat until the oil begins to shimmer. Add the scallops and cook for about 2 minutes, until the bottoms are golden brown and the scallops are cooked about three-quarters of the way. Turn the scallops over and cook for 30 seconds longer. Remove the scallops to a plate.

5. Add 1 tablespoon of the oil to the pan and heat until it begins to shimmer. Add the corn and press into a single layer and cook for about 2 minutes, until the bottom is golden brown and slightly charred. Turn over and cook until the other side is golden brown and charred, 2 minutes longer.

6. Stir in the shrimp and cook for 2 minutes. Add the tomatoes and snap peas and cook, stirring a few times until just warmed through, about 3 minutes longer. Add lime juice to taste and season with salt.

7. To serve: Ladle some of the green curry sauce onto a plate, top with some of the vegetable mixture, then top that mixture with 4 scallops. Drizzle some of the coconut cream over and garnish with cilantro leaves and the remaining 2 kaffir lime leaves. Serve with rice.

MALAYSIAN BUTTER PRAWNS

SERVES: 4

SAUCE

3 tablespoons Lee Kum Kee Premium Soy Sauce

1½ tablespoons Shaoxing wine

1 teaspoon granulated sugar

PRAWNS

2 cups plus 2 tablespoons canola oil

16 shell-on, deveined (U15) shrimp

4 garlic cloves, chopped

3 green Thai chilies, thinly sliced

20 curry leaves

6 tablespoons unsalted butter, cut into pieces

4 large egg yolks, whisked until smooth

2 tablespoons freshly squeezed lime juice (about 2 limes)

1 large scallion (white parts only), thinly sliced on the bias

¼ cup cilantro leaves

Steamed Jasmine Rice (page 150)

I first ate this unique dish while staying at a hotel in Kuala Lumpur, and my mind was blown away. To this day, I have never seen it served anywhere outside of Malaysia. It is not a pretty dish to look at, so forget about that whole eating-with-your-eyes thing, but my LORD it is delicious. However, you must forget everything that you have ever learned about thickening a sauce because this dish tosses all French technique out the window. I call for a specific soy sauce for this dish because that is what I learned to make it with and it is what I prefer, but any good-quality soy sauce will do.

1. Make the sauce: Whisk together the soy sauce, wine, and sugar in a small bowl until the sugar has dissolved. Let rest while you prepare the dish.

2. Make the prawns: Heat 2 cups of the canola oil in a large saucepan over medium heat until it reaches 350 degrees F. Line a baking sheet with a few layers of paper towels.

3. Fry the shrimp in batches, for about 2 to 3 minutes, until lightly golden brown and almost cooked through. Transfer with a slotted spoon or spider to the prepared baking sheet.

4. Heat the remaining 2 tablespoons oil in a large sauté pan or wok over high heat until it begins to shimmer. Add the garlic, chilies, and curry leaves and cook for about 45 seconds, until the garlic is just lightly toasted. Add the soy sauce mixture and butter and stir for about 1 minute, until the butter is melted.

5. Add the egg yolks and cook, stirring constantly, 4 to 6 minutes, until the eggs become curds and start to get crispy and the butter browns. Stir in the shrimp and continue to cook for another 30 seconds. Season with the lime juice, remove from the heat, and stir in the scallion and cilantro. Serve with rice.

STIR-FRIED COCKLES WITH CHILI JAM AND THAI BASIL

SERVES: 4

2 tablespoons canola oil

5 garlic cloves, finely chopped

2 pounds cockles, cleaned

3 tablespoons Chili Jam (page 51)

1 or 2 red Thai chilies, thinly sliced (depending on how spicy you like it)

¼ cup freshly squeezed orange juice

Freshly squeezed juice of 1 lime

¾ cup torn fresh Thai basil leaves

Kosher salt

Steamed Jasmine Rice (page 150)

This is a perfect example of a quick and easy stir-fry full of flavor and a great way to use Chili Jam (page 51). There are many different types and sizes of clams in Thailand. For this dish, I recommend just buying the smallest and freshest ones that you can find. I like eating these clams with a bowl of Steamed Jasmine Rice (see page 150) to soak up all the goodness of the broth.

1. Heat the oil in a wok or a large sauté pan over high heat until the oil begins to shimmer. Add the garlic and cook for about 30 seconds, until lightly golden brown (do not let it burn).

2. Add the cockles and cook, stirring constantly, for 30 seconds. Add the chili jam, chilies, and ½ cup of water. Cover the pan and cook until the cockles just open. (Cockles open quickly, so begin checking after 1 minute.) Once all of the cockles have opened, stir in the orange juice, lime juice, and Thai basil. Taste for seasoning and add more orange juice, lime juice, and salt to taste. Discard any cockles that do not open. Serve with steamed jasmine rice.

SINGAPOREAN WHITE PEPPER LOBSTER

SERVES: 2

SAUCE

½ cup Lobster Stock (page 37)

2 tablespoons oyster sauce

1 tablespoon low-sodium soy sauce

½ teaspoon white pepper

Pinch of granulated sugar

Pinch of MSG

LOBSTER

Two 1¼-pound lobsters

Kosher salt

TO ASSEMBLE

6 garlic cloves, pounded

1 long red fresh Thai chili, stem removed, pounded

3 tablespoons canola oil

2-inch piece of fresh ginger, peeled and thinly sliced

3 tablespoons unsalted butter, cut into pieces

3 Tokyo scallions or leeks, white and pale green parts cut into ½-inch-thick slices and dark green parts cut into 1-inch pieces

Steamed Jasmine Rice (see page 150)

This dish is usually served with crab in Singapore, but crab is *so much work*. Lobster is easier and it is actually cheaper, so use it as a substitute. I recommend using a wok for the best results.

1. Prepare the sauce: Whisk together the lobster stock, oyster sauce, soy sauce, pepper, sugar, and MSG in a small bowl.

2. Prepare the lobster: Bring a large pot of water to a boil over high heat and season with 2 tablespoons of salt. Prepare an ice bath by filling a large bowl with ice cubes and a few cups of water.

3. Separate the tail and claws from the lobster (or ask your fishmonger to do this for you). Cook the claws for 5 minutes, remove with a spider, and put directly into the ice bath. Bring the water back to a boil, add the tails, and cook for 1½ minutes. Remove with a spider to the ice bath. Let the claws and tails sit in the ice bath for about 5 minutes, until chilled.

4. Split each in tail half lengthwise in the shell. Remove the intestinal track and discard. Cut each tail crosswise into thirds.

5. Separate the knuckles from the claws and crack them so that some of the meat is exposed. Dry the lobster on paper towels before cooking.

6. Assemble the dish: Combine the garlic and chili in a mortar and pestle (or mini food processor) and pound or process until coarsely chopped.

7. Heat a wok over high heat for 1 minute. Add the oil and heat it until it just begins to shimmer. Add the garlic-chili paste and ginger and cook for 20 seconds. Add the lobster and cook, stirring constantly, for 2 minutes. Add the sauce and cook for 1 minute. Add the butter and scallions and cook 1 minute longer, or until the lobster is fully cooked, then season with a pinch more salt.

8. To serve: Divide between 2 shallow bowls and garnish with a bit more ground white pepper. Serve with steamed jasmine rice.

10

MEATS

While meat is often the centerpiece of most meals in the United States, it tends to play a smaller part in the cuisine of Southeast Asia. Most meals are centered around rice, noodles, and vegetables, with meat as an added component. That said, there are some pretty amazing meat dishes I've come across in my travels that I want to share.

Beef, believe it or not, is the least common meat. It's harder to come by and fairly expensive—especially for the quality you can find. Because of that, I love cooking it in flavorful stir-fries with Thai basil. The basil, garlic, and chilies create a beautiful flavor palate that you can toss ground or even finely chopped beef into. I top it with a crispy fried egg and serve it over rice.

Poultry is widely available and not super expensive. I love grilling it with lemongrass and cilantro and serving it with Isaan Sauce (page 46). You'll get a few of my favorite tricks for crispy skin in my Thai Grilled Chicken (page 221). If you want to get a little fancy, try my Vietnamese Butter Quail with Salt and Pepper Dipping Sauce (page 225). It's a dish that never fails to impress company because of its mix of French technique and Southeast Asian flavor.

Pork is a very popular meat in Southeast Asia (except in Muslim parts of the countries, where beef, lamb, and goat are eaten). If you own a pig, you're considered wealthy. Pigs are fed kitchen scraps, keeping the cost of maintaining the animal relatively low. Additionally, once slaughtered, the large animal can feed many mouths for many meals. Pig fat is rendered and used as inexpensive cooking oil to stir-fry vegetables, meat, and seafood. Additionally, every part of the animal is used in cooking, from head to tail, the skin, offal, blood, meat, and bones.

Of all of the Southeast Asian countries, the most meat-heavy, by far, is the Philippines. When I say meat, I really mean pork. Filipinos were tail to snout before it was popular in the United States. I grew up snacking on pig ears and cooking lumpia in leftover pork fat, my family ensuring that each bite was infused with just a little bit of pork. Because of that, I have to share with you my Crispy Pata (Braised Pork Shank, page 235). It's full of vinegar and soy, the acid and salt balanced by the richness of the pork itself. It's something you'll find yourself making for company over and over, as my relatives often do.

THAI GRILLED CHICKEN (GAI YANG)

SERVES: 4 TO 6

8 large garlic cloves, smashed

¼ cup palm sugar

1½ tablespoons whole white peppercorns

½ cup chopped fresh cilantro roots or cilantro stems

2 tablespoons Squid Brand fish sauce

2 tablespoons oyster sauce

1½ teaspoons ground turmeric

1 teaspoon kosher salt

2 whole chickens (about 1½ pounds to 2 pounds each), spatchcocked and skin pricked with a fork

2 medium stalks lemongrass, trimmed and bruised

¼ cup Garlic Oil (page 43)

This is one of the most popular street foods in Thailand. In fact, you can't walk a few blocks without smelling it and seeing it. The flavorful marinade yields tender meat and layers of flavors and really crispy skin, thanks in part to the palm sugar. The key to really crispy chicken skin is to let the skin render slowly on the grill—low and slow always is the way to go with skin-on chicken. A gas grill or grill pan will work fine, but this chicken is really best when grilled over charcoal. I serve it the way it is served in Thailand, with Sticky Rice (page 151), sweet chili sauce, Isaan Sauce (page 46), and papaya salad.

1. In a mortar and pestle or the bowl of a food processor, combine the garlic, palm sugar, peppercorns, cilantro roots, fish sauce, oyster sauce, turmeric, and salt and pound or process to a paste.

2. Line a baking sheet with parchment paper or foil. Put the chickens on the baking sheet and rub the marinade all over them, including under the skin, too. Cover with foil and marinate in the refrigerator for at least 8 hours and up to 24 hours.

3. Remove the chicken from the refrigerator 30 minutes before grilling. Preheat the grill to medium or a grill pan over medium heat. Dip the lemongrass stalks into the garlic oil and brush both sides of the chicken with some of the oil. Grill the chicken skin-side down for about 20 minutes, until the fat has rendered and the skin becomes crispy, basting with some of the oil every 5 minutes. Turn the chicken over and continue cooking and basting for about 15 minutes longer, until the chicken reaches an internal temperature of 155 degrees F on an instant-read thermometer. Remove the chicken from the grill, loosely tent with foil, and let rest for 10 minutes before cutting.

CHICKEN ADOBO

SERVES: 6

¼ cup canola oil

6 chicken thighs

6 chicken drumsticks

1 large Spanish onion, halved and thinly sliced

6 garlic cloves, smashed

1 cup Kikkoman light soy sauce

½ cup Chaokoh coconut milk

½ cup coconut vinegar (can substitute apple cider vinegar)

3 tablespoons granulated sugar

1 teaspoon freshly ground black pepper

½ teaspoon ground bay leaf powder

Steamed Jasmine Rice (page 150)

2 tablespoons Crispy Garlic (see page 43)

2 scallions (green and pale green part), thinly sliced

While Lumpia Shanghai may have been the first Filipino food that my mother served me, this dish was the first Filipino dish that she taught me how to cook. Chicken Adobo is a simple one-pot dish with five staples that all Filipinos have on hand—soy sauce, vinegar, black pepper, garlic, and bay leaves. I add in a few more ingredients to really amplify the flavor. While working in other kitchens over the years, this has always been my go-to staff meal. It is easy to make, and while it braises away in the oven, I can get my prep done. Most important, the staff always loves it.

1. Heat 2 tablespoons of the oil in a large Dutch oven over high heat until the oil begins to shimmer. Add the chicken thighs and cook for about 3 minutes per side, until golden brown on both sides. Transfer to a large plate.

2. Add the remaining 2 tablespoons oil to the pan and heat until the oil shimmers. Add the chicken legs and cook for about 3 minutes per side, until golden brown on both sides. Transfer to the plate with the thighs.

3. Remove all but 2 tablespoons of the fat from the pan; add the onion and cook, stirring occasionally, for about 5 minutes, until soft.

4. Add the garlic, soy sauce, coconut milk, vinegar, 1 cup of water, the sugar, pepper, and bay leaf powder and stir until combined. Return the chicken to the pot and bring to a boil. Reduce the heat to low, cover, and cook for about 1 hour, until the chicken is tender. If the liquid reduces too quickly or becomes too salty, add a bit of water. Serve with steamed jasmine rice and garnished with the crispy garlic and scallions.

CHICKEN INASAL WITH ATCHARA AND PATIS SAUCE

SERVES: 4

2 cups lemon-lime soda

¾ cup coconut vinegar

3 tablespoons freshly squeezed lemon juice

3 tablespoons freshly squeezed lime juice

One 4-inch piece of fresh ginger, coarsely chopped

3-ounce piece of fresh lemongrass, bruised and chopped (see page 28)

8 garlic cloves, chopped

¼ cup palm sugar

1 tablespoon kosher salt

1½ teaspoons freshly ground black pepper

Two 3-pound chickens, halved and rib cage removed

¼ cup Annatto Oil (page 43) or canola oil

Patis Sauce (page 46), for serving

Atchara (page 57), for serving

This is one of the most popular grilled chicken dishes that you will find in the Philippines. So popular that there is a chain restaurant called Mang Inasal that would be equivalent to Kentucky Fried Chicken in our country. If you ever get there, order the Chicken-Rice Combo. Using soda may seem strange, but the acid breaks down the chicken, adds flavor and a bit of tang, and all that sugar helps to caramelize the skin. Cooking in parchment paper before grilling keeps it moist and tender and renders some of the fat before hitting the grill for a bit of char.

1. Combine the soda, vinegar, lemon juice, lime juice, ginger, lemongrass, garlic, palm sugar, salt, and pepper in a blender and blend until smooth.

2. Put each split chicken in a large resealable plastic bag and divide the marinade evenly between the bags. Seal the bags, removing as much air as possible, and massage the marinade around the chicken to coat evenly. Refrigerate overnight.

3. Preheat the oven to 325 degrees F.

4. Remove the chicken from the refrigerator 30 minutes before cooking and pat dry with paper towels. Cut four 12 x 17-inch pieces of parchment paper. Put 1 chicken half in the center of each piece of paper.

5. Fold the parchment over, then make small overlapping pleats to seal and create half moon–shaped packets. Bake on two rimmed baking sheets for 20 minutes. The chicken will not be cooked through at this point. Carefully, remove the chicken from the paper and keep on the baking sheets. Brush each half with annatto oil.

6. Preheat a grill to medium or a grill pan over medium heat. Grill the halves, in batches if needed, skin-side down, for about 10 minutes, until the skin is golden brown and crispy. Turn the chicken over and continue cooking for about 7 minutes longer, until golden brown and just cooked through. Transfer to a cutting board and let rest for 5 minutes before serving.

7. Serve each person 1 half chicken with patis sauce and atchara on the side.

VIETNAMESE BUTTER QUAIL WITH SALT AND PEPPER DIPPING SAUCE

SERVES: 4

QUAIL

¼ cup plus 2 tablespoons Kikkoman light soy sauce

¼ cup plus 1 tablespoon oyster sauce

3 tablespoons honey

1 tablespoon mushroom powder (see page 79)

2½ teaspoons baking soda

1½ teaspoons kosher salt

1 teaspoon five-spice powder

¾ teaspoon freshly ground black pepper

8 garlic cloves, chopped

½ small shallot, chopped

8 quail, rib cage removed, butterflied, rinsed, and patted dry with paper towels

1 quart canola oil

½ cup (1 stick) unsalted butter

DIPPING SAUCE

1 cup freshly squeezed lime juice

¼ teaspoon kosher salt

¼ teaspoon freshly ground black pepper

¼ teaspoon granulated sugar

The French influence in this dish is evident thanks to all the butter, which you would not normally see in authentic Vietnamese cooking. It is traditionally grilled, but I like the texture that frying gives.

When I first had this quail in Ho Chi Minh City, it was simply served with a ramekin of salt on one side and pepper on the other and two lime wedges in the center. The limes in Southeast Asia are smaller and sweeter, so if you can find key limes, use those; otherwise, add a pinch of sugar to the sauce. It is best to let this dish marinate for at least 8 hours before cooking. Serve with Steamed Jasmine Rice (see page 150) and pickled vegetables.

1. Make the quail: Whisk together the soy sauce, oyster sauce, honey, mushroom powder, baking soda, salt, five-spice powder, black pepper, half of the garlic, and shallot in a large bowl. Add the quail and gently toss to coat in the marinade. Cover and refrigerate for at least 8 hours and up to 24 hours.

2. Make the sauce: Whisk together the lime juice, salt, pepper, and sugar and let sit while you prepare the quail.

3. Line a baking sheet with paper towels. Heat the oil to 350 degrees F in a wok or high-sided sauté pan. Remove the quail from the marinade and pat dry. Fry the quail in batches (do not overcrowd the pot) for about 5 minutes, until golden brown and crispy. Transfer the quail to the prepared baking sheet.

4. Melt the butter in a large sauté pan over medium heat. Add the remaining 4 cloves of garlic and the quail and sauté until the garlic begins to turn lightly golden brown. Transfer the quail to a large platter and serve with black pepper–lime sauce to dip.

SOUTHERN CURRY CHICKEN WINGS

SERVES: 4

MARINADE

1 quart buttermilk

1 batch (1 quart) Southern Curry Paste (page 184)

2 teaspoons sriracha

2 tablespoons Squid Brand fish sauce

1½ teaspoons kosher salt

ASSEMBLE

4 pounds chicken wings, trimmed, rinsed well, and patted dry

4 cups all-purpose flour

6 cups canola oil

½ cup chopped fresh cilantro leaves

I never really thought that Pig and Khao would be a hit for Super Bowl catering, but these wings made us something of a football darling this year. Traditionally, we marinate these wings in curry and brush them with the same sauce as they grill. We decided to turn it up a bit. We still use the same marinade—a perfect combination of the sweet, salty, tangy, spicy combination I crave, but then we fry them. We coat them twice, as they do over most of Southeast Asia, getting them super crispy and ensuring that they can stand up to those bold flavors they soak up in their overnight marinade and then tossed into the curry.

1. Make the marinade: Whisk together the buttermilk, ⅓ cup of the curry, the sriracha, fish sauce, and salt in a large bowl.

2. Assemble: Add the chicken wings and toss to coat in the marinade. Cover and marinate in the refrigerator for at least 8 hours and up to 24 hours.

3. Remove the wings from the marinade. Set a baking rack over a half sheet pan.

4. Place 2 cups of the flour in a large baking dish, dredge the wings in the flour in batches, and tap off any excess. Place the wings on the rack and place in the refrigerator for 30 minutes.

5. Heat the oil in a wok or high-sided sauté pan over medium heat until it reaches 300 degrees F on a deep-fry thermometer. Line a baking sheet with paper towels.

6. Dredge the wings once more, in batches, in the flour and tap off any excess. Fry the wings, in batches, for about 5 minutes, until light golden brown. Remove with a slotted spoon to the baking sheet. (This part can be done several hours ahead and up to 1 day ahead, and stored, covered, in the refrigerator.)

7. Raise the heat of the oil to 350 degrees F. Fry the wings again, in batches, until deep golden brown and crispy, 5 to 7 minutes longer. The internal temperature should reach 165 degrees F on an instant-read thermometer.

8. Place the remaining curry in a bowl, add the chicken wings, and toss to coat. Remove with a slotted spoon to a large platter and garnish with chopped cilantro leaves.

BRAISED LAMB SHOULDER WITH MASSAMAN CURRY

SERVES: 8 TO 10

½ cup plus ¼ cup canola oil

5 pounds cleaned lamb shoulder, cut into 2-inch cubes

Kosher salt

2 quarts homemade Chicken Stock (page 36) or low-sodium canned chicken broth or stock

4 cans Chef's Choice unsweetened coconut milk

⅓ cup Squid Brand fish sauce

2 tablespoons palm sugar

5 medium shallots, peeled and halved

½ cup garlic cloves, smashed

3 stalks lemongrass, trimmed and bruised (see page 28)

5 fresh cilantro roots, cleaned and bruised

8 fresh kaffir lime leaves

1 cinnamon stick

2 star anise

2 cardamom pods

2 whole cloves

I use my Massaman Curry Paste (page 186) and the braising liquid from the lamb shoulder as the base of this very creamy Massaman sauce. It is packed full of flavor and a touch of sweetness by the addition of palm sugar and sweet spices such as cinnamon, cardamom, and star anise. The addition of potatoes most likely comes from the Indian and Malay influences of this curry, but it is still served over rice so carb lovers rejoice. If lamb is not your thing, feel free to use beef chuck, round, or short ribs.

1. Preheat the oven to 325 degrees F.

2. Heat half of the oil in a large wok or high-sided sauté pan over high heat until it begins to shimmer. Add the lamb pieces, in batches, and season with salt. Cook for about 8 minutes, until golden brown on all sides. Remove the lamb to a baking sheet with a slotted spoon. Repeat with the remaining oil and lamb. Discard the oil and return the pot to the stove over high heat.

3. Add the stock, 1 can of the coconut milk, fish sauce, sugar, 1½ teaspoons salt, shallots, garlic, lemongrass, cilantro roots, and kaffir lime leaves and bring the mixture to a boil. As the mixture comes to a boil, combine the cinnamon stick, star anise, cardamom, and cloves in a piece of cheesecloth and tie with butcher's twine to make a sachet. Add the sachet to the pot. As soon as the braising liquid comes to a boil, return the lamb to the pot, cover, and transfer to the oven.

4. Cook the lamb for 2 to 2½ hours, until fork-tender. Start checking the meat at 2 hours. Once the lamb is finished cooking, remove it with a slotted spoon to a large bowl and cover with foil to keep it warm. Strain the braising liquid into a large bowl. Wipe out the pan and return it to the stove over high heat.

5. Heat the remaining 6 tablespoons of oil and 1 can of the coconut milk in the Dutch oven over high heat until it begins to shimmer. Add the Massaman curry and tamarind paste and cook for 5 to 7 minutes, until fragrant and the color deepens and the mixture thickens.

6. Add 4 cups of the braising liquid and the 2 remaining cans of coconut milk and bring to a boil over high heat. Cook until

RECIPE AND INGREDIENTS CONTINUE

1 cup Massaman Curry Paste
(page 186)

1 cup Tamarind Paste (page 42)

2 large Yukon Gold potatoes,
peeled and cut into ½-inch dice

Steamed Jasmine Rice
(see page 150)

Fresh cilantro leaves

Roasted, unsalted peanuts

Lime wedges

reduced by half. Reduce the heat to medium, add the potatoes, and cook for about 10 minutes, until almost cooked through (a skewer inserted meets with some resistance). Return the lamb to the pot and cook until heated through and the potatoes are tender, about 5 minutes longer.

7. Serve with rice on the side and garnish with cilantro leaves, peanuts, and lime wedges.

BBQ BABY BACK RIBS

SERVES: 4 TO 6

RIBS

5 tablespoons freshly ground black pepper

¼ cup kosher salt

3 tablespoons five-spice powder

4 racks baby back ribs, trimmed

BBQ SAUCE

3 cups hoisin sauce

¾ cup rice vinegar

½ cup Squid Brand fish sauce

¼ cup plus 2 tablespoons low-sodium soy sauce

1½ cups granulated sugar

4 shallots, finely diced

4 garlic cloves, finely chopped

3-inch piece of fresh ginger, peeled and finely grated

1 tablespoon five-spice powder

FOR SERVING

Crispy Garlic (see page 43)

3 scallions (green and pale green parts), thinly sliced

½ cup chopped fresh cilantro leaves

These ribs aren't something I learned while traveling so much as something I was able to put together because I had traveled. A friend had invited me to a Fourth of July barbecue, and I knew I needed to come up with something bold, something all-American combined with something that represented the melting pot that is America. Hoisin and soy sauce replace the typical ketchup and Worcestershire found in most Western barbecue sauce, and ginger and five-spice pair beautifully with the smoke to create these sweet and tangy sticky ribs that just might become a tradition at your next summer holiday.

1. Preheat the oven to 300 degrees F.

2. Combine the pepper, salt, and five-spice powder in a small bowl. Generously rub each rack of ribs on both sides with the mixture and wrap each rack in heavy-duty foil.

3. Place the racks on a large baking sheet and cook in the oven for about 2½ hours, until tender. Remove the ribs from the oven and let cool completely, about 30 minutes.

4. Prepare the BBQ sauce: Whisk together the hoisin, vinegar, fish sauce, and soy sauce in a medium bowl. Set aside.

5. In a medium, heavy-bottomed saucepan, add the sugar in an even layer over the bottom and cook over medium-high heat, stirring until the sugar just begins to melt. Cook for about 8 minutes, without stirring, until it turns a deep amber color.

6. Slowly (the mixture will bubble) add the hoisin mixture to the caramel and continue whisking until smooth. Whisk in the shallots, garlic, ginger, and five-spice powder and bring to a boil. Reduce the heat to medium-low and continue cooking, whisking occasionally, for 20 minutes. Remove from the heat and let cool for 10 minutes. The BBQ sauce can be made up to 5 days in advance and stored in a container with a lid in the refrigerator.

7. Once the ribs are cool, cut them into individual ribs, transfer to a large baking sheet, and toss them with 1 cup of the BBQ sauce.

8. Preheat a grill to high or a grill pan over high heat. Grill the ribs on each side until slightly charred, about 2 minutes per side, brushing with more of the glaze.

9. Transfer the ribs to a large platter and garnish with crispy garlic, scallions, and cilantro. Serve with additional sauce on the side.

BRAISED PORK BELLY ADOBO

SERVES: 4 TO 6

1⅔ cups Kikkoman light soy sauce

⅔ cup Chaokoh coconut milk

⅓ cup coconut vinegar

2 tablespoons canola oil

¼ cup granulated sugar

6 garlic cloves, peeled and smashed

2½ teaspoons freshly ground black pepper

6 bay leaves

½ cup kosher salt

¼ cup apple cider vinegar

2 whole star anise

1 teaspoon ground black peppercorns

3 pounds pork belly

6 cups canola oil

6 Poached Eggs (see page 106)

2 scallions (green parts only), thinly sliced

1 tablespoon Crispy Garlic (see page 43)

¼ cup fresh cilantro leaves

Pinch of ground Szechuan peppercorns (optional)

Steamed Jasmine Rice (see page 150), for serving

This is a modern take on what is typically a very simple one-pot meal from the Philippines. I begin by braising the pork belly in a milder (watered-down) version of adobo. I do this because the liquid really is only used to braise the dish. If you were to reduce my adobo sauce, it would be way too salty. I also like adding a poached egg, not because it seems like the hip thing to do these days, but because I love the richness it adds to the dish, and the egg, in addition to the rice, also helps to soak up some of the saltiness of the sauce.

1. Preheat the oven to 325 degrees F.

2. Combine 1 cup of the soy sauce, the coconut milk, coconut vinegar, ⅓ cup of water, the oil, 2 tablespoons of the sugar, 3 garlic cloves, 1½ teaspoons black pepper, and 1 bay leaf in a medium saucepan and bring to a boil over high heat. Reduce the heat to low and simmer for 20 minutes. Remove and discard the garlic and bay leaf before serving the sauce with the pork belly.

3. Combine the remaining ⅔ cup soy sauce, 12 cups of water, the salt, apple cider vinegar, the remaining 2 tablespoons sugar, the remaining 3 cloves garlic, the remaining 5 bay leaves, the star anise, black peppercorns, and the remaining 1 teaspoon pepper in a large Dutch oven and bring to a boil over high heat. Add the pork and bring back to a boil, then cover and transfer to the oven.

4. Cook the pork until tender, but not falling apart, about 2 hours. Start checking at 1 hour and 45 minutes. Remove the pork from the braising liquid and put on a baking sheet. Let cool to room temperature, then refrigerate, uncovered, for at least 8 hours and up to 12 hours. Cut the pork into 6 equal portions.

5. Heat the oil in a wok or high-sided sauté pan over medium heat until it reaches 375 degrees F on a deep-fry thermometer. Fry the pork, two pieces at a time, until golden brown. Remove and drain on a baking sheet lined with paper towels.

6. To serve: Ladle ¼ cup of the adobo sauce into six shallow bowls. Slice each piece of fried pork belly thinly and place on top of the sauce. Top with an egg, scallions, crispy garlic, cilantro leaves, and the Szechuan peppercorns. Serve with steamed jasmine rice on the side.

CRISPY PATA (BRAISED PORK SHANK)

SERVES: 4

4 whole fresh pork shanks, skin on, bone in (each 1¼ to 1½ pounds)

⅓ cup light soy sauce

¼ cup apple cider vinegar

2 tablespoons kosher salt

1½ tablespoons granulated sugar

8 garlic cloves, crushed

4 whole bay leaves

2 whole star anise

2 teaspoons whole black peppercorns

4 cups canola oil

¼ cup Crispy Garlic (page 43)

¼ cup cilantro leaves

Soy Dipping Sauce (page 48)

Liver Sauce (also referred to as Lechon Sauce; page 47)

Pickled Green Mango (page 55)

I have noticed that Filipinos eat a lot of pork, more than other Southeast Asian countries and this is one of the most popular pork dishes in the Phillipines. Classically made with pork trotter or knuckles, I prefer using bone-in pork shank, which is easier to find and gives the dish a lot more flavor. Be sure to remove the bone before you chill the meat overnight and while it is still warm, for easier removal. Leaving the meat uncovered in the refrigerator overnight allows the skin to dry out and makes it extra crispy when you fry it. This dish is traditionally served with Liver Sauce (page 47) and a pickled side.

1. Preheat the oven to 325 degrees F.

2. Put the pork shanks in a large pot and add enough cold water just to cover. Add the soy sauce, vinegar, salt, sugar, garlic, bay leaves, star anise, and peppercorns and cook in the oven until just tender but not falling off the bone. Begin testing after 1½ hours; it should take close to 2 hours.

3. Once the shanks are cooked, take them out of the liquid and put them on a baking sheet with a rack. Let cool at room temperature until cool enough to handle, about 10 minutes then remove the bones. Place in the refrigerator, uncovered, to air-dry overnight.

4. Heat the oil in a wok or high-sided sauté pan until it registers 350 degrees F on a deep-fry thermometer. Fry the shanks, in batches if needed, for about 7 to 10 minutes, until golden brown and crispy. Slice and serve on a platter garnished with crispy garlic and cilantro leaves. Serve with soy dipping sauce, liver sauce, and pickled green mango on the side.

HUMBA (DEEP-FRIED PORK BELLY WITH SQUASH PUREE)

SERVES: 4 TO 6

One of my line cooks taught me how to make this Filipino dish a few years ago and, truth be told, I had never heard of it before. It is very similar to adobo and it hails from the Visayas Island in the Philippines. According to him, it is a cousin of adobo, and he grew up eating it in the Philippines. The original typically contains fermented black beans and banana leaves, which his does not, but it is still delicious and I love it. Occasionally this delicious recipe appears on my menu where I serve it like this, with Kabocha squash puree, or sweet potatoes would go well, too.

HUMBA

⅓ cup Kikkoman light soy sauce

¼ cup apple cider vinegar

3 tablespoons kosher salt

1 tablespoon granulated sugar

5 whole garlic cloves, smashed

2 bay leaves

1 whole star anise

1 teaspoon coarsely ground black pepper

3 pounds skin-on, boneless pork belly

HUMBA SAUCE

1 tablespoon canola oil

2 garlic cloves, chopped

1-inch piece of fresh ginger, chopped

¼ teaspoon Thai chili flakes

2 cups homemade Chicken Stock (page 36) or low-sodium chicken stock or broth

1 cup dark soy sauce

⅔ cup distilled white vinegar

¾ cup unsweetened coconut milk

½ cup (packed) light brown sugar

2 whole star anise

1. Make the humba: Preheat the oven to 325 degrees F.

2. Combine 8 cups of water, the soy sauce, vinegar, salt, sugar, garlic, bay leaves, star anise, and pepper in a stockpot. Add the pork and make sure there is enough liquid to cover; if not, add enough water to cover. Wrap the top with foil and then put the cover on the pot and cook until the pork is tender but not falling apart, about 2 hours.

3. Remove the pork from the pot and transfer to a cutting board. Let sit for about 15 minutes, until cool enough to handle. Divide the pork into 4 to 6 equal portions and put on a baking sheet and let cool, uncovered, in the refrigerator for at least 8 hours and up to 24 hours. Discard the braising liquid.

4. Make the humba sauce: About 30 minutes before frying the pork, heat the oil in a medium saucepan over medium heat. Add the garlic and ginger and cook for about 2 minutes, until soft. Add the chili flakes and cook for 30 seconds.

5. Add the stock, soy sauce, vinegar, coconut milk, brown sugar, star anise, and black pepper and bring to a boil over high heat. Reduce the heat to low and cook until slightly reduced, stirring constantly, about 20 minutes.

6. Whisk together the cornstarch and 2 teaspoons of water in a small ramekin until smooth. Bring the sauce to a boil, add the slurry mixture, and cook, whisking constantly until slightly thickened to a sauce consistency; if too thick, add a few tablespoons more of the stock or water to thin out. Strain the sauce and keep warm while you fry the pork.

7. Make the squash puree: Bring a large pot of water to a boil. Add 1 tablespoon of kosher salt and the squash and cook for about 20 minutes, until tender. Drain well and transfer to the bowl of a food processor.

¼ teaspoon freshly ground
black pepper

1 teaspoon cornstarch

KABOCHA SQUASH PUREE

1 tablespoon kosher salt

2 pounds Kabocha squash, peeled,
seeded, and cut into large dice

One 14-ounce can unsweetened
coconut milk

6 tablespoons unsalted butter

1 tablespoon granulated sugar

1 garlic clove, finely chopped

Freshly squeezed juice of 1 lime

Canola oil

8. Add the coconut milk, butter, granulated sugar, and garlic and process until smooth. Add the lime juice, pulse a few times to combine, and transfer to a bowl. Cover and keep warm while you fry the pork.

9. Line a baking sheet with paper towels. Heat 3 inches of oil in a wok or high-sided sauté pan until it reaches 350 degrees F on a deep-fry thermometer. Fry the pork in batches for about 5 minutes, until golden brown and crispy. Transfer to the baking sheet lined with paper towels.

10. To serve: Place the squash on the plate, top with a piece of pork, and ladle sauce over.

KARE-KARE

BRAISED OXTAIL

6 pounds bone-in oxtail, meatiest part cut into pieces

Kosher salt

¼ cup canola oil

1 large Spanish onion, halved and thinly sliced

1 head garlic, cloves removed and smashed

3½ quarts water or light beef stock or low-sodium canned beef broth

5 bay leaves

1 tablespoon whole black peppercorns

4-inch piece of fresh ginger, thinly sliced

½ pound long beans, cut into ½-inch pieces, blanched in salted water, and drained

EGGPLANT

3 Japanese eggplants, cut into 1-inch dice

3 tablespoons canola oil

Kosher salt and pepper

SAUCE

2 tablespoons Annatto Oil (page 43) (or 2 more tablespoons of canola oil and 1 teaspoon annatto powder)

1 medium Spanish onion, finely diced

5 garlic cloves, finely chopped

4 fresh Thai chilies, thinly sliced

This hearty Filipino stew of braised oxtail is unique for many reasons. First of all, oxtail is not used in a lot of Filipino cooking. Second, the sauce is made with annatto, shrimp paste, and peanut butter—three very different ingredients that I would just never imagine combining in one dish. I serve it the traditional way, with rice, long beans, eggplant, bok choy, and peanuts.

1. Make the oxtail: Preheat the oven to 325 degrees F. Season the oxtail on both sides with salt. Heat the oil in a large pot over high heat until shimmering and sear the oxtail, in batches if needed, about 4 minutes per side, until golden brown on both sides. Remove the oxtail to a large plate.

2. Reduce the heat to medium, add the onion and garlic to the pan, and cook, stirring occasionally, about 5 minutes, until soft.

3. Return the oxtail to the pot; add the water or stock, bay leaves, peppercorns, and ginger; and bring to a boil. Cover and transfer the pot to the oven and cook until the oxtail is fall-off-the-bone tender, about 2½ hours (begin testing it at 2 hours).

4. Remove the oxtail to a large bowl and tent with foil to keep warm. Strain the braising liquid into a large clean bowl, wipe the pot out, and return it to the stove top. Raise the heat of the oven to 400 degrees F.

5. Roast the eggplant: Toss the eggplant in a bowl with 2 tablespoons of the oil and season with salt. Transfer to a rimmed baking sheet in an even layer and roast for about 15 minutes, until lightly golden brown but still holds its shape, stirring once. Remove and reserve.

6. Make the sauce: While the eggplant is roasting, heat the remaining 1 tablespoon canola oil and the annatto oil (or 3 tablespoons of canola oil and 1 teaspoon of annatto powder) in the Dutch oven over high heat until the oil begins to shimmer. Add the onion and garlic and cook until soft, about 4 minutes.

7. Add the chilies and shrimp paste and cook, stirring constantly, for 3 minutes. Stir in the vinegar.

RECIPE AND INGREDIENTS CONTINUE

¼ cup Filipino brand shrimp paste
(see page 20)

1½ tablespoons apple cider vinegar

1½ cups smooth peanut butter
(I prefer Skippy)

1½ teaspoons granulated sugar

½ cup roasted, unsalted peanuts,
chopped

1 teaspoon annatto powder

GARNISH

2 scallions, thinly sliced on the bias

¼ cup fresh cilantro leaves

Crispy Garlic (see page 43)
(optional to taste)

Crispy Fried Shallots (page 52)
(optional to taste)

¼ cup chopped peanuts

8. Add the braising liquid and bring to a boil. Whisk in the peanut butter and sugar until smooth. Add the peanuts, bring to a boil, reduce the heat to a simmer, and cook, stirring occasionally, for about 30 minutes, until slightly thickened and the peanuts soften. Remove from the heat and let cool slightly. (Putting really hot liquid into a blender can be dangerous, so always let it cool and only fill the blender halfway.)

9. Blend the sauce, in batches, until smooth and transfer to a large bowl. Clean the pot once again and return to the stove over medium heat. While blending the last batch, add the annatto powder and blend until smooth. Transfer to the Dutch oven.

10. Return the oxtail to the pot, fold in the eggplant and the long beans, and cook for about 5 minutes, until heated through. Season with salt and lime juice. Serve in the Dutch oven or transfer to a large shallow bowl. Garnish with scallions, cilantro, crispy garlic, crispy shallots, and peanuts.

GRILLED BEEF IN BETEL LEAF

YIELDS: 20

12 ounces ground chuck 80/20

1 large stalk lemongrass, trimmed and finely minced

1 tablespoon oyster sauce

1 tablespoon canola oil, plus more for brushing on the leaves

2 teaspoons Red Boat fish sauce

2 teaspoons Thai Curry Powder (page 39) or store-bought

¾ teaspoon granulated sugar

¼ teaspoon Thai chili flakes

¼ teaspoon kosher salt

¼ teaspoon MSG

⅛ teaspoon freshly ground black pepper

Freshly squeezed juice of 1 lime

20 (about ½ pound) betel leaves, cleaned and stems removed (see Note)

½ cup roasted, unsalted peanuts, chopped

Nuoc Cham (page 49)

The betel leaves are what makes this very popular Vietnamese appetizer so interesting. Betel leaves have an intoxicating smell, and the flavor is somewhat earthy and almost medicinal. It is a unique flavor unlike anything you have tasted. If you can't find betel leaves, then don't make this dish—there is no substitute and nothing comparable.

You can eat it as an appetizer with Nuoc Cham (page 49) or eat it on top of rice noodles with chopped peanuts, herbs, and Crispy Fried Shallots (page 52), and nuoc cham to pour on top.

1. Put the beef in a large bowl. Add the lemongrass, oyster sauce, oil, fish sauce, curry powder, sugar, chili flakes, salt, MSG, pepper, and lime juice and gently mix to combine. Cover and refrigerate for 1 hour.

2. Line a baking sheet with parchment paper. Lay the leaf shiny-side down. Add 2 to 3 tablespoons of the filling (depending on the size of the leaf) to the leaf, starting on the fat-end side and roll toward the tip. Place seam-side down on the baking sheet.

3. Heat the grill to high or a grill pan over high heat. Lightly brush the leaves with oil and grill them seam-side down. They will cook for approximately 2 minutes per side. Garnish with peanuts and serve with a side of nuoc cham.

4. Alternatively, you can also serve these on top of room-temperature vermicelli rice noodles, crispy shallots, mint, cilantro, chopped peanuts, and nuoc cham.

Note:

To clean betel leaves, put them in a bowl, cover with cold water, swish them around in the water and then lift the leaves out of the water, put on a flat surface, and pat dry with paper towels. Remove the stem the same way you would remove the stems on spinach. You can also wipe the leaves with a wet cloth.

BEEF RENDANG WITH POTATO PUREE AND GARLIC KALE

SERVES: 6 TO 8

SHORT RIB BRAISE

¼ cup plus 2 tablespoons canola oil

5 pounds boneless beef short ribs, excess fat trimmed, patted dry

Kosher salt

2 quarts homemade Chicken Stock (page 36) or low-sodium canned chicken broth or stock

2 cans Chaokoh unsweetened coconut milk

½ cup lightly toasted coconut flakes (see Note), 1 tablespoon reserved for garnish

2 cinnamon sticks

3 whole star anise

2 whole cloves

½ cup Squid Brand fish sauce

½ cup palm sugar

¼ cup Tamarind Paste (page 42)

1 batch (2 cups) Rendang Paste (page 182)

This slow-braised Malaysian curry fuses sweet, sour, and savory elements to create a dish layered with complex flavors, with the curry picking up a creamy richness from two forms of coconut (milk and flakes). In Malaysia, this would come to you in a bowl with meat and sauce and rice on the side, but this preparation is an all-American way to put a new spin on meat and potatoes.

1. Preheat the oven to 300 degrees F. Heat ¼ cup of the oil in a large pot over high heat until the oil begins to shimmer. Add half of the short ribs, season with salt, and sear on both sides for about 2 minutes per side, until golden brown. Transfer to a baking sheet and repeat with the remaining oil and beef. Drain the oil from the pot and discard.

2. Add the stock, coconut milk, and coconut flakes to the pot and bring to a boil. While the mixture is coming to a boil, put the cinnamon, star anise, and cloves in a small piece of cheesecloth and tie it to create a sachet and add it to the liquid. Once the liquid has come to a boil, return the beef to the pot, cover, and transfer to the oven. Cook the beef for about 2½ hours, until fork-tender (begin checking at about 2 hours).

3. Once the beef is tender, transfer it to a large bowl and cover with foil to keep warm. Remove the sachet. Transfer broth to a large bowl. Wipe out the pot for use in the next step.

4. Whisk together the fish sauce, palm sugar, and tamarind paste in a bowl until the sugar begins to dissolve. Heat 2 tablespoons of the oil in a large pot over high heat until it begins to shimmer. Add the Rendang paste and cook, stirring constantly, for about 10 minutes, until the color deepens and the rawness of the shallot and garlic has been cooked out. Add the fish sauce mixture and cook, stirring constantly, for about 5 minutes, until the pan is deglazed and the paste has thickened slightly.

5. Whisk in the braising liquid until smooth. Bring the sauce to a boil over high heat and continue cooking, whisking often, for about 40 minutes, until the sauce is reduced by half.

POTATO PUREE

3 pounds Yukon Gold potatoes, peeled and diced

2 tablespoons kosher salt

¾ cup (1½ sticks) unsalted butter, cut into pieces

1 cup heavy cream

GARLIC KALE

3 tablespoons canola oil

2 garlic cloves, chopped

1 large bunch kale, washed and still slightly damp, ribs removed and coarsely chopped

Kosher salt

TO SERVE

Cilantro leaves, for garnish

Crispy Fried Shallots (page 52), for garnish

Lime wedges

Roti Dough (page 252)

6. Make the potato puree: Put the potatoes into a large saucepan and cover by 2 inches with cold water. Add the salt. Bring to a boil over high heat and cook for about 25 minutes, until the potatoes are fork-tender. Drain the potatoes well, return to the pot, and cook over high heat for a minute to dry out the potatoes. Transfer the potatoes, in batches to a ricer and rice into a large bowl.

7. While the potatoes are cooking, combine the butter and cream in a small saucepan and bring to a simmer over low heat. Cook until the butter is completely melted. Add the mixture to the potatoes and mix until combined. Taste for seasoning. Keep warm.

8. Return the beef to the pot and cook until the beef is warmed through, about 5 minutes longer.

9. Sauté the kale: Heat the oil in a large sauté pan over low heat, add the garlic, and cook for about 2 minutes, until soft. Raise the heat to high and add the kale in bunches until it begins to wilt. Then add more and continue cooking until the kale is soft and wilted but still green. Season with salt.

10. Put the potato puree in the center of each plate and top with some of the kale. Put the beef on top of the kale and spoon the curry sauce over and around the beef. Garnish with cilantro, crispy shallots, and the reserved coconut flakes. Serve with lime wedges and roti on the side.

Note:

To toast the coconut: Preheat the oven to 325 degrees F. Spread the coconut on a sheet pan in an even layer and bake, stirring a few times, until lightly golden brown, about 8 minutes.

GRILLED SIRLOIN WITH ISAAN SAUCE

SERVES: 6 TO 8

⅔ cup oyster sauce

⅓ cup palm sugar

⅓ cup Squid Brand fish sauce

⅓ cup granulated sugar

Two 16-ounce sirloin steaks

Napa Cabbage leaves, quartered

1 English cucumber, cut into spears

Isaan Sauce (page 46)

Crispy Garlic (see page 43)

¼ cup fresh cilantro leaves

The star of this dish is the Isaan sauce also known as Jaew. Isaan is *the* sauce for meat. The marinade helps the steak caramelize as it cooks. This dish has been on the menu since day one at Pig and Khao. I usually use sirloin, but skirt steak and flank would work well, too. Traditionally, you wouldn't wrap the meat in the cabbage—it would be served alongside to help cool down the mouth after you eat the spicy sauce.

1. Whisk together the oyster sauce, palm sugar, fish sauce, and granulated sugar in a large baking dish. Add the steaks and turn to coat. Cover and refrigerate for at least 8 hours and up to 24 hours (the longer, the better).

2. Remove the steaks from the marinade 30 minutes before grilling and let sit at room temperature. Heat the grill to high or a grill pan over high heat. Grill the steak on both sides until golden brown and charred and cooked to desired doneness. I recommend medium-rare doneness, which is about 5 minutes per side. Remove the meat from the grill and let rest for 10 minutes. Slice crosswise into ¼-inch-thick slices.

3. Serve the slices with cabbage, cucumbers, and Isaan sauce on the side. Garnish the steak with the crispy garlic and cilantro.

STIR-FRIED MINCED BEEF WITH THAI BASIL

SERVES: 3 TO 4

2 tablespoons Kikkoman light soy sauce

1 tablespoon plus 1 teaspoon oyster sauce

½ teaspoon white pepper

½ teaspoon kosher salt

½ cup water or homemade Chicken Stock (page 36) or low-sodium canned chicken broth

2 tablespoons canola oil

2 Thai green chilies, coarsely chopped (see Note)

2 Thai red chilies, coarsely chopped

5 garlic cloves, coarsely chopped

12 ounces ground beef

2 teaspoons dark soy sauce

2 long beans, trimmed and sliced or 4 green beans, trimmed and sliced

1 packed cup holy basil or Thai basil leaves

6 kaffir lime leaves, thinly sliced

2 Fried Eggs (see page 106)

Steamed Jasmine Rice (page 150)

Lime wedges, for garnish

This is just one of those quick-and-easy Thai stir-fries that is full of flavor and served everywhere in Thailand, both at street vendors and at restaurants. People eat it for breakfast, lunch, and dinner. Ground meat (pork, beef, or chicken) is pretty typical, but you can also slice or dice the meat, too. Traditionally, this dish is made with holy basil, which is a variation of Thai basil that doesn't have as strong a licorice flavor—it is more peppery. It can be tough to find. Thai basil works as a substitute.

1. Make the sauce: Whisk together the soy sauce, oyster sauce, pepper, salt, and water or stock in a small bowl. Set aside.

2. Heat the oil in a wok or large sauté pan over high heat. Add the chilies and garlic and cook for about 20 seconds. Be careful not to burn the garlic.

3. Add the beef and cook, making sure to break up any lumps. Cook this for about 4 minutes, until the liquid evaporates and the meat starts to brown. Add the dark soy sauce and cook until completely evaporated, about 20 seconds.

4. Add the sauce and the long beans and cook until thickened and the beans are crisp-tender, about 2 minutes longer. Remove from the heat and stir in the basil and kaffir. Transfer to a large shallow bowl, top with the fried eggs, and serve with rice and lime wedges on the side.

Note:

Typically, the chilies and garlic would be smashed to a paste in a mortar and pestle before adding to the oil. If you don't have a mortar and pestle or don't feel like using one, you can just finely chop the chilies and garlic with a chef's knife.

11

DESSERTS

Desserts in Southeast Asia are not what you would typically find in Europe or America. Chocolate isn't big and the dairy you'll find is either condensed milk or evaporated milk. Because refrigeration wasn't always available, margarine also plays a bigger role than butter. Rice, legumes, and fruit are actually very common ingredients in desserts because they're abundant. You will also see root vegetables like purple yam, taro, and sweet potatoes in a sweet stew.

In addition to the different ingredient bases, you'll also notice different textures in Southeast Asian desserts. There are lots of gelatinous dishes—grass jelly, nato de coco, tapioca. There are also lots of frozen dishes due to the extreme heat—shaved ice is a huge one, with all kinds of awesome additions like sweetened condensed milk, flan, and even pinipig (which is similar to American Rice Krispies).

I have always had an interest in desserts and even thought about becoming a pastry chef a few moons ago. That said, I was always way more into baking than actually eating dessert and, if given the option, would pick an extra savory course any day.

When I turned thirty, though, something clicked, and now I swear I have a full-on sugar addiction. I still blame one of my line cooks, too, because he used to bring me a pastry every morning. Now it's a tradition, and I can't have coffee without something sweet.

That and the fact that none of the other cooks in my kitchen want to bake means I'm in charge of pastry at Pig and Khao.

I've taken a combination of classic dishes like Halo-Halo (page 250) and Coconut Sticky Rice with Mango (page 259) as well as Thai Tea Ice Cream (page 253), applied some of the French technique and recipes that I learned in culinary schools, and played with all of these elements to make desserts that are all mine. You won't find them on a dessert menu in Southeast Asia, and they are definitely geared toward the Western palate, but they are inspired by desserts from my travels. I hope you enjoy these sweets the way that I do and learn to explore the diverse world of desserts.

HALO-HALO

SERVES: 4

FLAN

1 cup granulated sugar

10 large egg yolks

One 12-ounce can evaporated milk

One 14-ounce can sweetened condensed milk

1 tablespoon pure vanilla extract

CARAMELIZED PLANTAINS

½ cup canola oil

4 ripe (blackened skins) plantains cut in half lengthwise

¼ cup (½ stick) unsalted butter

1 cup (packed) light brown sugar

HALO-HALO MILK

One 14-ounce can condensed milk

Three 12-ounce cans evaporated milk

Shaved ice (super fine; see Note)

Shredded macapuno

1 quart ube ice cream

Toasted pinipig or Rice Krispies, for garnish

A bowl of cereal on crack! You love it or you hate it. There is no in-between. I love it, and my husband, Ben, hates it. It is the famous dessert in all of the Philippines. *Halo-halo* means "mix-mix," and traditionally, it is made with sweet corn, garbanzo beans, red beans, and shaved ice, followed by milk, ice cream, or flan. There are no rules, and the whole thing is served in a milk-shake glass with a long spoon so you can mix everything up. As a child, I loved it but I would always spit out the beans. In my late teens, my parents took me to Razon's, a famous chain restaurant in the Philippines that is known for its halo-halo. Razon's is a family-friendly restaurant that I would compare to a Denny's in the United States. I fell in love with their halo-halo because they don't use beans or chickpeas. Their version is on my menu today at Pig and Khao, and now you can make it, too. Macapuno is a mutant coconut that is candied in a heavy sugar syrup and sold in jars. Pinipig is pounded sweet rice that is toasted in a pan—think of it as the Philippines version of Rice Krispies. Note: This recipe requires some advance preparation.

1. At least 8 hours before you intend to eat or serve the halo-halo: Pour the sugar into a medium saucepan and cook over high heat, stirring just until it begins to melt. Stop stirring and continue cooking for about 8 minutes, until it turns a deep amber color. Immediately pour the caramel into a 9-inch round ceramic or glass baking dish or a metal cake pan that's at least 2 inches deep. Tilt the dish to coat the bottom (use caution—the dish will be hot). Cool until hardened, 10 to 15 minutes.

2. Make the flan: Fill a large saucepan with 3 inches water and bring to a simmer over medium heat. Whisk together the yolks in a large bowl until smooth. Add the evaporated milk, condensed milk, and vanilla and whisk until smooth. Pour the custard through a fine mesh sieve over the caramel in the dish, tightly cover with foil, put the pan in a steamer basket and then put the steamer basket over the simmering water and put the top on. Steam the flan until the custard is set but still wobbly in the center when gently shaken, 45 minutes to 1 hour. Begin testing for doneness at 45 minutes by removing the foil and jiggling the dish. If not done, cover tightly and continue cooking. Transfer the dish to a rack to cool completely, about 40 minutes. Chill the flan, covered, until cold, at least 8 hours and up to 48 hours.

3. Caramelize the plantains: Heat the oil in a large high-sided sauté pan over medium heat until the oil begins to shimmer. Cook the plantains, in batches, if needed, until golden brown on both sides. Carefully remove and transfer to a plate lined with paper towels.

4. In a large nonstick sauté pan, add the butter and cook over high heat until melted. Add the brown sugar and ½ cup of water and cook for about 5 minutes, until the sugar has melted and the sauce has thickened. Add the plantains to the sauce and cook until tender (a skewer inserted meets with no resistance) but still holding their shape, about 5 minutes.

5. Transfer to a cutting board, let cool, and cut into 1-inch dice.

6. Make the halo-halo milk: Whisk together the condensed milk and evaporated milk in a large bowl until combined.

7. Unmold the flan: Run a thin knife around the edge of the dish to loosen the custard. Invert a large platter with a lip over the baking dish. Holding the dish and platter securely together, quickly invert and turn out the flan onto the platter. Caramel will pour out over and around the flan. Cut the flan into 1-inch dice.

8. For individual servings: Place a heaping cup of shaved ice in a large bowl, top with 6 pieces of the flan, 3 spoonfuls of the macapuno, ¼ cup caramelized plantains, 1 scoop of ube ice cream, and ½ cup of halo-halo milk. Garnish with a few tablespoons of pinipig. Serve immediately.

Note:

This recipe is easy to make with a shaved ice maker. Shaved ice makers are easy to assemble and to clean! But if you do not have one, put a few cups of ice cubes at a time into a high-powered blender and blend until crushed. Transfer to a bowl and freeze until ready to use.

ROTI DOUGH

YIELDS: 12

5 cups all-purpose flour

2 tablespoons kosher salt

1 tablespoon granulated sugar

¾ cup melted ghee (can use clarified butter), kept warm

1 large egg

¾ cup whole milk

Thai roti can be sweet or savory. There are many different types of roti. This Thai version can be used as a base for savory or sweet dough. I love smearing roti with Nutella and sliced bananas for a sweet treat with coffee in the morning, and I also love eating it with Beef Rendang with Potato Puree and Garlic Kale (page 242) to help sop up the spicy curry sauce.

1. Combine the flour, salt, and sugar in the bowl of a stand mixer fitted with the dough hook. Mix at low speed for 20 seconds to combine. Slowly add ¼ cup of the ghee and mix for 2 to 3 minutes, until the dough just starts to come together and the flour is coated in the butter.

2. Whisk together the egg, milk, and ½ cup of water and add to the flour mixture. Mix until the dough begins to form a ball. Keep mixing until smooth, about 5 minutes longer.

3. Transfer the dough to a clean surface and continue kneading for 5 minutes longer. Divide the dough into 12 equal portions. Place on a baking sheet and coat each ball with ½ teaspoon of ghee and cover in plastic wrap. Make immediately, or refrigerate for up to 2 days until ready to use.

4. To roll out the dough: Remove the dough from the refrigerator and let it come to room temperature (it will not stretch out if it's too cold). Spread 1 tablespoon of ghee on the countertop. Grease your hands with ghee to help pull the dough.

5. Grab one piece of dough and flatten it out with your palm, Make sure to flatten it out evenly. Slowly work your way around the outside of the dough, pulling outward to stretch the dough. The first couple of times pull 3 to 4 inches each time. Make sure to go slowly and pull all around the circle. The dough should reach approximately 2 feet in diameter.

6. Drizzle 1 teaspoon of ghee all around the circle and then, using both hands, fold the top quarter of the dough over itself almost to the middle of the circle.

7. Fold the top of the dough over again on top of itself. Then take one side of the dough and coil into a pinwheel shape (it should resemble a turban). At this point let the dough rest for 10 minutes and then flatten and stretch the dough out until it's 8 inches in diameter.

8. Heat up a griddle, large nonstick sauté pan, or cast-iron pan over medium heat and cook one roti at a time until golden brown on both sides, about 2 minutes per side.

THAI TEA ICE CREAM

YIELDS: 1 QUART

3 cups half-and-half

One 14-ounce can sweetened condensed milk

½ cup powdered Thai tea leaves

4 large egg yolks

½ cup granulated sugar

1 tablespoon kosher salt

Thai tea is really just strongly brewed Ceylon tea mixed with lots of sugar and condensed milk, and I love it so much that I wanted to turn it into an ice cream, so I did. This is the recipe. Enjoy!

1. Combine the half-and-half and condensed milk in a large saucepan and bring to a simmer over low heat. Stir in the tea leaves, turn off the heat, and let steep for 5 minutes. Strain the mixture into a bowl. Rinse out the pot and return it to the stove.

2. Whisk together the egg yolks, sugar, and salt in a large bowl until pale and fluffy. Slowly temper in the hot cream mixture and return to the pot on the stove. Cook the custard, stirring constantly with a wooden spoon, over medium heat for about 5 minutes, until it thickens and coats the back of the spoon (or reaches 170 degrees F on an instant-read thermometer).

3. Strain the custard through a fine mesh sieve into a bowl set into a larger bowl of ice. Stir until the custard is room temperature. Cover and refrigerate until very cold, at least 4 hours.

4. Churn in an ice cream machine according to the manufacturer's instructions. Serve directly from the machine for soft serve, or store in the freezer until needed.

FRIED ENSAYMADA ICE CREAM SANDWICHES

YIELDS: 12 SANDWICHES

2 envelopes active dry yeast

¾ cup warm milk (105 degrees F to 110 degrees F)

5 tablespoons granulated sugar, plus ¼ cup more for sprinkling on the dough

3 cups all-purpose flour, plus more for rolling

2 cups bread flour

4 teaspoons kosher salt

3 large eggs

9 large egg yolks

¾ pound (3 sticks) unsalted butter, at room temperature and cut into pieces

1 cup shredded macapuno (see page 250)

6 cups canola oil

Ensaymada is a baked good people in the Philippines eat in the morning or as a snack. Though you wouldn't see ensaymada used in an ice cream sandwich, and truth be told, you wouldn't see it fried, either, I just love the contrast of sweet fried pastry and cold creamy ice cream. I also use the vividly vibrant violet-hued ube ice cream (made from purple yams) at Pig and Khao, but vanilla, coffee, strawberry, or any flavor, for that matter, would be delicious.

1. Combine the yeast, warm milk, and 1 tablespoon of the sugar in the bowl of a stand mixer fitted with the paddle attachment. Stir with a spoon and let sit until the mixture is foamy and the yeast is activated, about 5 minutes.

2. Sift the flours, the remaining ¼ cup sugar, and salt into a large bowl. Add the flour mixture to the yeast mixture and beat for about 3 minutes, until it forms a smooth mixture.

3. While the dough is mixing, whisk together the eggs and egg yolks until smooth. Add the eggs to the dough and mix on medium speed until the eggs are incorporated and the dough comes together, about 5 minutes longer.

4. Transfer the dough to a lightly floured surface and roll out to a ¼-inch thickness. Place half of the butter in the middle of the dough, then fold over one side of the dough onto the butter. Place the other half of the butter in the middle of the dough, then fold over the other side of the dough onto the butter.

5. Fold the dough into a little package or ball shape, and place back in the work bowl of the stand mixer. Switch to the dough hook attachment and knead the dough and butter for 10 to 15 minutes on medium speed, until the butter is well incorporated and the dough becomes glossy and elastic.

6. Remove the dough from the mixer and place in a lightly greased large bowl. Loosely cover with plastic wrap and let it rise in a warm place until doubled in volume, about 1 hour. After the dough has doubled in size, punch it down, roll it into a ball again, then place it back in the greased bowl and cover with plastic wrap. Place the covered bowl in the refrigerator overnight to rise again.

7. The next day, divide the dough into 24 equal balls and place on a lightly floured surface. Loosely cover with clean tea towels and let rise until doubled in volume, about 1 hour.

8. Roll out a ball of dough on a lightly floured surface until the dough is about 12 x 4 inches. Sprinkle sugar and macapuno in the center of the rolled-out dough. Roll the dough over the filling lengthwise into a rope shape about 14 inches long. Repeat with the rest of the dough balls until you have 24 ropes.

9. Take two of the ropes and twist them around each other to braid them. Repeat with the other ropes until you have 12 sets of braids. Then form each of the braids into a spiral shape, making sure to tuck in each of the ends—they should look like a turban.

10. Put the oil into a deep fryer or a large wok or high-sided sauté pan and heat to 375 degrees F on a deep-fry thermometer. Line a baking sheet with paper towels. Fry the dough in batches of 2 for about 5 minutes, until golden brown on both sides. Transfer to the prepared baking sheet and sprinkle with some of the remaining sugar. Let cool, then slice in half lengthwise. Fill with your favorite ice cream. I love ube flavor, but salted caramel (page 261) or vanilla would work fine, too!

RICOTTA DOUGHNUTS WITH CALAMANSI POSSET

SERVES: 4 TO 6

CALAMANSI POSSET

2 cups heavy cream

½ cup plus 3 tablespoons granulated sugar

¼ cup calamansi juice

DOUGHNUTS

1 quart canola oil

1½ cups all-purpose flour

1 tablespoon baking powder

¼ teaspoon fine sea salt

1¾ cups ricotta cheese

1½ cups granulated sugar

6 large eggs

Finely grated zest and juice of 2 limes

1 teaspoon pure vanilla extract

Since I do not have a pastry chef in my restaurants, I like to keep desserts easy, delicious, and idiot proof, while incorporating some of my favorite things.

Warm, just-out-of-the-fryer-tender little ricotta doughnuts served alongside cold, creamy, citrusy thickened cream is a match made in dessert heaven and both couldn't be easier. No yeast needed for the doughnuts and no water bath needed for the custard. Calamansi is to Southeast Asian cooking what yuzu is to Japanese cuisine. Calamansi is a cross between citrus and kumquat, and its flavor can't be substituted for anything else. There is a really good frozen brand that you can get online from a company called Boiron, or you can substitute a combination of lemon and lime or Meyer lemon. It won't taste the same, but it will still be delicious.

1. Make the posset: Combine the cream and sugar in a medium nonreactive saucepan over high heat, bring to a boil, and cook for about 5 minutes, until reduced and the sugar has melted.

2. Remove from the heat, stir in the juice, and let sit, untouched, for 15 minutes. Pour through a strainer into a bowl with a lip or a pitcher. Divide the custard among six 4-ounce ramekins or four 6-ounce ramekins. Refrigerate, uncovered, for 1 hour, then wrap in plastic wrap and refrigerate until firm, about 4 hours.

3. Make the doughnuts: Put the oil in a large wok or high-sided sauté pan over medium heat and heat until it reaches a temperature of 360 degree F on a deep-fry thermometer.

4. While the oil heats, whisk together the flour, baking powder, and salt in a small bowl.

5. In a large bowl, whisk together the ricotta and sugar until smooth. Add the eggs, lime zest, lime juice, and vanilla and whisk until smooth. Add the flour mixture and gently mix until just combined. Don't overmix.

6. Put ½ cup of the sugar in a shallow bowl. Working in batches, using either a tablespoon or a small ice cream scoop, gently drop level spoonfuls of the batter into the hot oil and fry, turning occasionally, until golden, about 5 minutes. Using a slotted spoon, transfer to paper towels to drain. Let cool for a minute then roll in the remaining 1 cup sugar. Allow the oil to return to 360 degrees F between batches. Eat alone or dip into the posset.

COCONUT STICKY RICE WITH MANGO

SERVES: 4

¾ cup granulated sugar

1 cup full-fat unsweetened coconut milk

1 teaspoon kosher salt

1 cup Thai sticky rice (I prefer Cock brand for this), prepared according to the recipe on page 151

2 ripe mangoes (preferably yellow variety), peeled, pitted, and cut into thick slices lengthwise

½ teaspoon white sesame seeds, lightly toasted, or crispy split mung bean, optional

This is pretty much as good as it gets with dessert in Thailand. "Rice Pudding" in Thailand is typically just made with leftover sticky rice from last night's meal, cooked together with coconut milk and yellow Thai mangoes. Yellow mangoes, unlike the red-colored Mexican version, have a hint of tartness that complements the sweetness of this dessert. If you can't find the yellow mangoes, just use a slightly underripe red and add a squeeze of lime juice. I love garnishing with crispy yellow split mung beans, which add a nice crunch to this otherwise creamy dessert. If you can't find mung beans, toasted sesame seeds are a delicious substitute.

1. Combine the sugar, coconut milk, and salt in a medium saucepan over high heat and cook, whisking a few times, until the sugar has completely melted.

2. Put the cooked rice into a large bowl. Pour the warm milk over the rice and cover the top of the bowl tightly with plastic wrap. Let sit at room temperature, without touching, until the rice has absorbed all the milk, about 20 minutes.

3. Serve warm or at room temperature in bowls with a few slices of the mango and garnish with a sprinkling of sesame seeds, if desired.

TURON (CRISP BANANA FRITTERS) WITH CHOCOLATE-HAZELNUT SAUCE AND SALTED CARAMEL ICE CREAM

SERVES: 4

¾ cup (packed) light brown sugar

1½ teaspoons ground cinnamon

4 small ripe bananas, peeled, halved crosswise, then each half cut in half lengthwise

16 spring roll wrappers, thawed and separated

1 large egg beaten with 3 tablespoons of cold water

2 cups canola oil

Chocolate Hazelnut Sauce, for serving (recipe follows)

Salted Caramel Ice Cream (recipe follows)

Turon and Halo-Halo (page 250) are the most popular desserts in the Philippines. In some ways, Turon is the dessert version of Lumpia (page 67)—it's a kind of sweet spring roll filled with banana, jackfruit, and brown sugar and fried to perfection, sold on the streets, and eaten out of hand. On its own, it is delicious. But not one to leave well enough alone when it comes to desserts, I have added two of my favorites: ice cream and chocolate sauce for dipping. I like Turon without jackfruit, and that's how I serve it at my restaurant.

1. Line a large plate or baking sheet with paper towels.

2. Mix together the brown sugar and cinnamon in a shallow dish. Evenly coat each banana quarter in the mixture.

3. Place a spring roll wrapper in front of you in a diamond shape and sprinkle surface with a bit of the mixture. Place a banana two-thirds of the way down from the top. Fold the sides and then roll up tightly from the bottom to the top to form a long cylinder. Brush the turon with egg wash to seal.

4. Heat the oil over medium heat in a medium high-sided sauté pan or wok until the oil begins to shimmer or reaches 350 degrees F on an instant-read thermometer. Fry the turon, in batches, until golden brown, turning once. Let drain on paper towels. Serve with chocolate-hazelnut sauce and salted caramel ice cream.

SALTED CARAMEL ICE CREAM

Yields: About 1 quart

1 cup whole milk

1 cup granulated sugar

2 tablespoons unsalted butter

2 cups heavy cream

2 teaspoons kosher salt

2 teaspoons pure vanilla extract

6 large egg yolks

1. Put the milk in a bowl set over a larger bowl filled with ice and water. Set aside.

2. In a medium pot over medium heat, melt the sugar, swirling the skillet frequently until the sugar turns mahogany brown in color, about 8 minutes.

RECIPE CONTINUES

3. Slowly whisk in the butter, heavy cream, salt, and vanilla. Simmer until the caramel melts and the mixture is completely smooth. Remove the pot from the heat. In a separate bowl, whisk the yolks. Whisking constantly, slowly whisk about one-third of the hot cream into the yolks, then whisk the yolk mixture back into the pot with the cream.

4. Return the pot to medium-low heat and gently cook, whisking constantly, until the mixture is thick enough to coat the back of a spoon. Strain through a fine-mesh sieve into the bowl with the milk. Stir until the mixture becomes cool. Cover and chill at least 4 hours or overnight.

5. Churn in an ice cream machine according to manufacturer's instructions. Serve directly from the machine for soft serve, or store in the freezer until needed.

CHOCOLATE-HAZELNUT SAUCE

1 heaping cup chocolate-hazelnut spread, such as Nutella

½ cup whole milk

¼ cup heavy cream

¼ teaspoon kosher salt

1. Combine the chocolate spread, milk, cream, and salt in a medium bowl.

2. Fill a medium saucepan one-quarter of the way with water and bring to a boil over high heat. Reduce the heat to low, place the bowl on top of the pot, and cook, whisking constantly, until the sauce is smooth and just heated through, about 5 minutes.

BURMESE SEMOLINA CAKE WITH MANGO SAUCE AND TOASTED COCONUT CHIPS

YIELDS: 1 8-INCH CAKE

2 cups semolina flour

6 tablespoons unsalted butter, melted

21 ounces unsweetened coconut milk (1½ cans), well-stirred (use the other half for the whipped cream)

¾ cup whole milk

½ cup heavy cream

2 large eggs

1 cup granulated sugar

1½ teaspoons kosher salt

2 teaspoons pure vanilla extract

3 tablespoons demerara sugar (optional)

Mango Sauce (recipe follows)

Coconut Whipped Cream (recipe follows)

Dang brand toasted coconut chips, for garnish

I first had this twice-cooked pudding/cake while staying in Yangon, which is the capital of Burma (now Myanmar). I remembered thinking, why are they using semolina in Burma? Then I remember thinking, *Who cares, this is amazing!* Similar to mochi or cassava cake, it has a chewy texture that you do not expect and a nuttiness thanks to the toasting of the flour. You will definitely taste the coconut milk, and because I love coconut so much, I also add it to the whipped cream and garnish with it, too. The mango sauce adds a touch of tartness and color but is totally optional.

1. Preheat the oven to 350 degrees F.

2. Spread the flour onto a baking sheet into an even layer and bake in the oven until lightly toasted, stirring a few times, about 10 minutes. Transfer the flour to a bowl and let cool slightly. Raise the heat of the oven to 400 degrees F.

3. Brush the bottom and sides of an 8 x 8-inch baking dish with 2 tablespoons of the melted butter.

4. Combine the coconut milk, milk, cream, eggs, sugar, salt, and 2 more tablespoons of the butter in a large saucepan and whisk until smooth. Bring to a simmer over medium heat, whisking constantly. Slowly add the flour in a steady stream, continuing to whisk, and cook until thickened, about 5 minutes. Remove from the heat and stir in the vanilla.

5. Scrape the mixture into the prepared pan and bake until a toothpick inserted comes out clean, about 30 minutes, rotating the cake once during baking after 15 minutes. Transfer to a baking rack, brush the top with the remaining butter, and let cool. This cake is delicious as written, but at the restaurant, where it is served as a plated dessert, I like to take it one step further by brûléeing the top with demerara sugar and a torch (or you can use the broiler). To brûlée the cake, follow the step below once the cake has cooled.

6. Broiler: Put the rack in the upper third of the oven and preheat the broiler. Carefully transfer the cake to baking sheet and evenly sprinkle the sugar in a thin layer over the top of the cake. Put the pan under the broiler and broil until golden brown and bubbly, about 1 to 3 minutes depending on your broiler.

RECIPE CONTINUES

7. Torch: Carefully transfer the cake to baking sheet and evenly sprinkle the sugar in a thin layer over the top of the cake. Take the safety off the torch, press the ignition to turn it on and lock it in the "on" position. Hold the flame approximately 2 inches (5 centimeters) away from the sugar, and move it back and forth or in circles across the surface until golden brown and caramelized.

8. Ladle some of the mango sauce onto a plate, top with a slice of the cake, and garnish with coconut whipped cream and coconut chips.

MANGO SAUCE

3 ripe mangoes (about 2½ pounds), peeled and pitted

Finely grated zest of 1 lime

Freshly squeezed juice of 2 limes

2 to 4 tablespoons granulated sugar (depending on the ripeness of mangoes)

1. Coarsely chop 2½ of the mangoes and transfer to a blender. Finely dice the remaining mango half, add to a medium bowl, and set aside.

2. Add ¼ cup of water, the lime zest, and the lime juice to the blender and blend until smooth. Taste the sauce and begin adding sugar, 1 tablespoons at a time, until the desired sweetness. Transfer the sauce to the bowl with the diced mango and stir to combine. Cover and refrigerate until ready to use. The sauce can be made 1 day in advance and stored tightly covered in the refrigerator.

COCONUT WHIPPED CREAM

1½ cups very cold heavy cream

½ can unsweetened coconut milk

3 tablespoons confectioners' sugar

½ teaspoon pure vanilla extract

Combine the cream, coconut milk, confectioners' sugar, and vanilla in a bowl and whisk until soft peaks form. Cover and refrigerate until ready to use. Can be made 4 hours in advance.

ACKNOWLEDGMENTS

To my mom and dad, thank you for always believing in me and giving me the opportunity to follow my dreams. You have always supported my decisions and taught me the value of hard work. Dad, you are the nicest person I have ever met and you always find a way to stay positive even during the worst of times. I am amazed by your selflessness and how much you genuinely like to make people happy. When we decided to open Pig and Khao you gave me the opportunity to show homage to Mom's culture (and my culture) and for that I am forever thankful. Mom, you have taught me how to be tough, strong woman, which is necessary in this difficult industry. You had a tough childhood being the eldest of eight and losing your parents so young. You have always been there to hold your family together and I am in awe of your strength. Thank you both for bringing me to the Philippines at such a young age, opening my eyes to the world. It has undoubtedly shaped who I am as a person and as a chef.

To my husband, Ben, thank you for always being my ride-or-die. I love what we have created from Pig and Khao to Piggyback and, most important, our family with Carter G and Kimchi. I could not ask for a better partner in life and in business. You always push me to be a better chef, a better businesswoman, and a better person. Since the beginning when we started working together, you have always tried to make my life better, easier, and way more fun. I am always amazed with everything you know how to do or make up on the fly. I know you never get the credit you deserve for everything you do behind the scenes, whether it's the food styling in this book or the vibe and service at the restaurants, but please know I never take it for granted and think you are amazing. "We all we got we all we need."

To my brother, Josh, thank you for being there for me my whole life and especially during the infancy and creation phase of Pig and Khao. You helped me during my pre Pig and Khao popups, you helped me come up with the name Pig and Khao and you were my part-time travel partner in Thailand during my year abroad. I still remember when you came to visit me in Thailand and we went to Chiang Mai for Songkran and we ate endless bowls of khao soi . . . those were the days!

To my staff at Pig and Khao and Piggyback, past and present. Thank you for believing in what we do. If it weren't for all of you, my restaurants wouldn't exist. I appreciate all of the hard work and dedication you have given. There has been a lot of staff that has been with me for a long time, but no one has been more down for the cause than Fay Kelly.

To all of the customers who have supported my restaurants over the years I would like to say thank you. There are a million dining options in New York City and the fact that we have so many regulars makes me love what I do. Thank you for choosing to eat with us over and over again and allowing me to cook the food that I love.

INDEX

Note: Page numbers in *italics* indicate photos separate from recipes.